Brother Men

Brother Men

THE CORRESPONDENCE

OF EDGAR RICE BURROUGHS

AND HERBERT T. WESTON

Edited and with an Introduction by

Matt Cohen

Duke University Press Durham and London 2005

Designed by C. H. Westmoreland

Typeset in Scala with Golden Cockerel display

by Tseng Information Systems, Inc.

Library of Congress Cataloging-in-Publication

Data appear on the last printed page of this book.

frontispiece:

Edgar Rice Burroughs and Herbert T. Weston,

photographer and location unknown, circa 1927.

Courtesy Edgar Rice Burroughs, Inc.

FOR MY GRANDPARENTS

Contents

ACKNOWLEDGMENTS ix

INTRODUCTION 1

NOTE ON THE TEXT 49

CORRESPONDENCE 51

NOTES 287

INDEX 301

Acknowledgments

Reproducing a correspondence as historically and visually rich as this one takes much work, and work of many different kinds. But without Danton Burroughs—his enthusiasm for the project, his help in filling out the collection, his willingness to allow the letters to be published—there would have been no work to do. Danton's reflections on his family, and the expert assistance of the staff at Edgar Rice Burroughs, Inc., came at a crucial time in the development of this project.

There are familial debts on my side of the correspondence as well. First, I must thank Marian Weston and Sue O'Neill for letting me use the Weston letters and for sharing their memories. My mother, Katharine Weston, collected secondary material and challenged me in valuable discussions about the history of gender, family, and the West. Socorro Finn performed the initial transcriptions and consulted on the project as it evolved. Michael Cohen guided me with his knowledge of scholarly publishing, and Bridget Finn offered support and constructive criticism on drafts of the introduction. Other brave readers included Christopher Labarthe, Timothy Barnard, Robert Nelson, and Richard S. Lowry; their discussions of theories of early-twentieth-century masculinity and their enactments of more recent forms of male friendship were invaluable.

A host of people at a range of institutions made this book possible. George McWhorter of the Edgar Rice Burroughs Collection at the University of Louisville gave me productive leads and time-saving caveats, as he has done for virtually everyone who has written on Burroughs in the past few decades. Rick Paben of Paben Photography in Beatrice, Nebraska, provided excellent images from a pile of glass plate negatives. Bob Hartman at Culver Educational Foundation provided information on the Weston children who attended there. My colleagues Rob Mitchell, Priscilla Wald, and Marianna Torgovnick were incisive but encouraging critics of the project. The staff at Duke University Press; my editor, J. Reynolds Smith; and the anonymous readers of the manuscript made *Brother Men* better by leaps and bounds. Finally, thanks to the Arts and Sciences Research Council at Duke University for financial assistance toward the preparation of the manuscript and to the Rare Books and Special Collections librarians at Duke University, whose warmth, expertise, and professionalism make archival work a joy.

Brother Men

We historians are proverbially truthful, except when we are chronicling the lives of our national heroes, or living rulers within whose grasp we may be, or of enemy peoples with whom our country has been at war, and upon other occasions.

—EDGAR RICE BURROUGHS

Introduction

[N]ewer formations of manhood . . . affectively and ideologically
isolated men in a newer form of individualist competitiveness.
— DANA NELSON, *National Manhood*

I always knew that [Theodore] Roosevelt had me in the palm of his
hand, but until his death I never suspected that I also had a personal feeling for the man. His going has put a real crimp in me. It is
said that no man is necessary — but to my way of thinking, we could
much better spare the next ten greatest men in the USA. Honestly
I dont know whatinhell we are going to do without THE Colonel!
— HERBERT T. WESTON TO EDGAR RICE BURROUGHS,

15 January 1919

As I may have intimated once or twice, people mean a lot more to
me than things or places. I get more that way the older I get, and
I just could not have a better time than to just jimmy around with
you Burroughses. I think your children are peaches. I wish I could
have seen more of them. [. . .] What I would like to do would be to
hang around the Burroughs Wyoming ranch house for a few days
(I could sleep in the 4d truck) and have you pay no attention to me,
and watch you come and go, read your books, play with the rats,
be bitten by Lobo and Jet, ride a horse and shoot a little golf. Not
strenuous perhaps, but joy enough for me!
— WESTON TO BURROUGHS, 13 April 1927

I WAS IN GRADUATE SCHOOL in Virginia, working on the last stages of a dissertation about bachelors in America and deeply interested in the complicated relationships among emotion, economics, and identity in men's lives of the nineteenth century. Needing a break, feeling the isolation of sustained writing, I headed to Beatrice, Nebraska, to spend a few days with my mother and my grandmother. While I knew that they would ask me how my work was coming along (the unsettling litany of graduate school: "Is your dissertation finished yet?"), I also knew that they would not press me about my interpretations of the residual culture of ascetic masculinity or the connections between postcolonial anxiety and imperialist manhood in American fiction. I could relax; or so I thought.

After I had finished describing some of the more entertaining parts of my research—on men's lives in the bachelor hotels that began to proliferate during the Gilded Age—my grandmother wondered out loud if, considering my focus on men's friendships, I might be interested in "the Burroughs letters." My mother immediately agreed that I would, and they began talking about people and places from our family's past that were completely unfamiliar to me. Becoming aware of my confusion, they explained that my great-grandfather, Herbert Weston, and the author of the Tarzan books, Edgar Rice Burroughs, went to military school together and afterward sustained a lifelong correspondence, much of which was currently right there in our house. My mind swam with questions: How many letters were there? What period did they cover? Did we only have half of the correspondence, as is usually the case with such collections? Their answers astonished me: There were hundreds of items, including letters, photographs, telegrams, postcards, and drawings; they dated from the early years of the twentieth century to after the Second World War; and most important of all, my great-grandfather kept carbon copies of his letters. As I delved into the collection, my vacation ended and I did not even notice.

The letters would be worth publishing if they were only rich and lively documents illuminating Edgar Rice Burroughs's daily life and career, but they are much more than that. They are uncharacteristic as a collection, not least because they survived the stock market crash of 1929 and the Great Depression. The forms of labor (agriculture and popular literature) and capital (land investments) that these men engaged in buffered them from the worst effects of the crash. Burroughs bought an airplane during this time; and both men took up home movie making, with all the expensive equipment that entails, as a hobby (they did use cheaper paper for their letters during the Depression). But the letters have further value. Until now, only fragments of a few letters from Burroughs's vast correspondence have been published. This collection of documents will enable cultural historians to examine an important American author and his most famous product in great depth.

Some have already done so; in fact, Tarzan, if not Burroughs himself, has emerged at the center of recent debates among cultural studies scholars and theorists interested in the development of mass media, imperialism, and gender and sexuality. With these letters we can begin to bring this symbolic analysis into dialogue with Burroughs's social and intimate lives. The letters and images offer a fascinating, detailed look at masculine self-generation during a time of tremendous change. Because these two men were products of the 1870s and 1880s, their correspondence traces their encounters with modernity and America's rise onto the world stage. They were friends and old school buddies, but they were also in business with each other. Both struggled with masculine self-definition—Burroughs early, Weston late—and discussed their problems with a circle of male friends. A near-constant ironic banter shapes the letters, but there are many moments of powerful emotional self-exposure as well. Within these pages readers will find a panorama of the difficulties, advantages, and possibilities of middle-class white manhood in the early twentieth century.[1]

The quotations that begin this introduction trace my own rethinking of some critical assumptions about manhood. Dana Nelson's work on masculinity illuminates our understanding of both the means and the costs of the generation of white masculine subjectivity. As her comment shows, however, there remains a pervasive sense that, in Bryan Garman's words, "most bourgeois men sought to shun close emotional attachments" at the dawn of the twentieth century.[2] Weston's response to the news of the death of Theodore Roosevelt is an example of the kind of national emotion that Nelson has taught students of American cultural history to perceive: Weston's "personal feeling" for a man he had never (as far as we know) seen forms a romance of citizenship with the dead president as ideal partner. The final image, which collapses Roosevelt's kaleidoscopic career into his military identity, signals Weston's participation in a national imaginary that posits individuality in the service of ideals—in this case, of Roosevelt's famous "strenuous life." But the final quotation complicates this reading. Here Weston imagines the dissolution of his identity into the Burroughses' in a perpetual visit to Tarzana, Burroughs's California ranch. A national subservience becomes an intensely personal one ("I think your children are peaches") and an idyll of leisure ("shoot a little golf"). Weston's final pronouncement, "Not strenuous perhaps, but joy enough for me," replaces Roosevelt's strenuousness with the ecstasy of intimate proximity.

This introduction will first trace the biographical and historical backgrounds of Burroughs and Weston. Some areas—politics, sports, and travel—are discussed at length and with considerable coherence in the body of the correspondence and need little further discussion here. Burroughs's life has been written about extensively by other scholars. Because the letters offer an unprecedented sense of the ways the two men's lives related to each other, I have chosen to integrate the story of their lives rather than treating each man separately. This story lays the groundwork for the claims of the final section of the introduction, which brings the evidence of the letters into the larger current debate among cultural historians about the nature of male subjectivity and the uses of homosocial intimacy.

Beginnings: Lifelong Side-Partners

"Remember my Father and my Mother's family settled
this town, and I am the ole Original Sin if there are any"
—WESTON TO BURROUGHS, 13 April 1927

Ed Burroughs and Bert Weston were born less than a year apart, in September 1875 and April 1876, Burroughs in Chicago and Weston in Lincoln, Nebraska. Burroughs grew up in the rapidly expanding gateway to the West, while Weston spent most of his childhood in his small hometown, Beatrice.[3] But despite this apparent disparity in their early environments, the men shared quite similar socioeconomic situations. Both boys grew up in well-off families and were established white males in communities that were financially and ethnically diverse.

Burroughs was the youngest son of Mary Evaline and George Tyler

Burroughs of Chicago. George Burroughs had been a major in the Union Army during the Civil War, and in his civilian life became one of the owners of the American Battery Company.[4] Edgar Rice grew up in a large brick home on Washington Boulevard in the West Side with his brothers George, Harry, and Frank, and came of age in a family whose position as owners of production meant that children had much expected of them. Carlo Rotella writes of turn-of-the-century Chicago:

> Chicago was the right place at the right time, a city visibly produced at near-miraculous speed by the industrial transformations, population movements, and rapid urbanization shaping the terrain of America in the late nineteenth and early twentieth centuries. The central place of a vast region stretching from the Rockies to the Cumberland Gap and from the Mississippi Delta to the north woods, commanding the rail and water routes along which passed extracted resources and manufactured goods, a center of heavy industry as well as a center of commercial and financial activity, Chicago was early twentieth century America's "national economic city"—the prototypical modern industrial metropolis.[5]

Burroughs's brothers George and Harry drew energy from the development of industry in Chicago and its concomitant culture of professionalization. In 1889 they graduated from the Sheffield Scientific School, Yale's renowned engineering program. After working for their father at the American Battery Company they moved on to ventures of their own in western mining. From the standpoint of nineteenth-century male gender politics, they set a high mark for Edgar, who had already shown signs of restlessness in school and a sickly constitution.

By a strange symmetry, living next door to the Burroughses and their four sons was a family with four daughters (and a young son), the Hulberts. Emma Centennia Hulbert—born, as her middle name suggests, in 1876—and Ed Burroughs formed a friendship when they were quite young that blossomed into romance and marriage in 1900 (in the face of resistance from the Hulberts). Like most residents of Burroughs's neighborhood, the Hulberts were solidly upper middle class. Alvin, Emma's father, operated expensive hotels in Chicago and St. Louis. He was elected alderman of the Twelfth Ward in 1880, a post he filled during the years in which his daughter and Burroughs became friends.

Burroughs had few steady friends other than Emma, in part because sickness, listlessness, and hooky led him to attend at least three different schools in Chicago. After working as a ranch hand for his brothers in Idaho, he was sent to Phillips Academy in Andover, Massachusetts, where he lasted almost two semesters. In his brief time there, Burroughs managed to get himself elected class president, evidence of both his popularity and his preference for extracurricular activity over schoolwork. Having proven his intransigence in the classroom, and approaching what his parents thought of as the age of responsibility, Burroughs was sent to the institution that had taken the place of the seminary for the youngest sons of the bourgeois: military school. He enrolled at Michigan Military Academy (MMA) in Orchard Lake, near Detroit, in 1892.

While Ed Burroughs's father was fighting the Civil War, Bert Weston's parents, Jefferson Burns "J. B." Weston and Helen Towle Weston, were building the town of Beatrice in what would soon become Nebraska.[6] The Beatrice settlers may have been somewhat unwilling founders: the town's history claims that the decision to stop in Beatrice was made while the founding families were stuck on a Missouri River sandbar; J. B. was one of the party that surveyed the site ultimately chosen for incorporation. Originally from Maine, J. B. left for the territories in 1857 after graduating from Union College. He and Helen, daughter of Beatrice's first postmaster, were married in 1860. By the time Bert was born, the Weston family was one of the most powerful in Nebraska. J. B. was a lawyer; president of the Beatrice National Bank; and, from 1872 to 1878, auditor of the state of Nebraska, a crucial position during the time of Nebraska's development. Bert was born during his father's tenure in this post. Bert was the youngest of four children, and his letters show a sustained and at times melancholy engagement with what he felt was a responsibility to live up to his family's legacy in the community.[7] His family's position, ties with the Westons who remained behind on the east coast, and an investment in national culture evidenced by the family's large collection of literary books and national periodicals made Bert subject to a set of class expectations similar to those felt by Burroughs.[8]

Though Weston was in some ways a better student than Burroughs, the education system in Nebraska did little to prepare youngsters to attend college at competitive east coast schools. The Westons heard about the relatively new military academy at Orchard Lake and sent Bert there in 1893 after some preparation at the University of Nebraska. During the summer before he left for school, Weston met the woman he would eventually marry: Margaret Butler Collins. Weston's early romance did not come from next door, but as with Burroughs, local connections were important. As he put it in a 1929 letter to Burroughs, "It is a matter of history that Maggie Collins and Bertie Weston officially met-up at the Evans Hotel, in Hot Springs, SoDak, in July 1893." Margaret was from Brooklyn, New York. Her father, Chester, had been involved in a set of railroad contracting ventures in the region, one of which was a partnership with the Kilpatrick Brothers of Beatrice. Much of the couple's early relationship was necessarily epistolary, and a few of their letters survive from his days at Michigan Military Academy.

When Weston and Burroughs first met, then, perhaps in the autumn of 1893, they had much in common. But other obsessions complemented their shared middle-class backgrounds, investment in the culture of masculine character, and romantic involvements. Perhaps the most significant, from the standpoint of joining the social sphere of a military academy, was their interest in football. Their first encounter was, at least rhetorically, love at first sight—mediated by sports: "I have a recollection of the day I arrived," Weston wrote to Burroughs many years later, "and you hard-boiled up to me and asked if I had ever played football. I blushingly replied that I had played two games as end on the Nebraska 'Varsity, and you almost kissed me!!"[9] Both men, but especially Weston, would retain a lifelong interest in football (fig. 1). All the Weston sons spent time at the University of Nebraska, whose nationally competitive team was (and is) a powerful locus of entertainment for the state.

Weston and Burroughs shared another characteristic significant in their historical moment—lack of interest in religion. When filling out his application to Phillips Academy in 1891, Burroughs had put "none" in the blank for "Church Denomination." Weston's family, although officially Episcopalian, had not been particularly religious; he would write to Burroughs, suggestively, "I am no preacher, as well you

1. Michigan Military Academy football team portrait, Orchard Lake, Michigan, photographer unknown. Burroughs is in the bottom row, holding the football; Weston is in the middle row, second from the left. *Weston Family Collection.*

know."[10] Neither man seems to have objected to organized religion in any political way; in fact, the contents of both men's libraries indicate a long-term interest in learning about a range of theologies (though in Burroughs's case, this could well have been for professional reasons). Certainly, however, their shared resistance to organized religion was one of the things that gave them a common space within which to become friends.

Michigan Military Academy had opened in 1877 and was thus a relatively new institution when Burroughs and then Weston arrived. It proved to be a short-lived one as well; it was closed by bankruptcy in 1908. Weston and Burroughs attended at the peak of the institution's popularity; there were around 150 students resident during each year they were there.[11] With tuition and incidentals costing about five hundred dollars per year, MMA was designed to keep children of the relatively well-to-do out of trouble. As a school catalog advertised in 1878–79, "Although within easy access of all parts of the county, cadets, by its location, are removed from every evil influence that surrounds the town." The school stressed the civil and moral sense a military preparation would instill in its graduates, all future Christian gentlemen, but Burroughs knew why he had been sent there. As he wrote many years later, MMA had "a sub rosa reputation as a polite reform school."[12]

Significantly, the school was neither intended nor expected to produce actual soldiers. Only one-fourth of those who enrolled in MMA ever graduated, and only about 5 percent of the graduates went on to military careers. More a disciplinary institution than an educational one, MMA prepared its students to enter eastern professional schools or military academies like West Point. In a well-known address to the school on 19 June 1879, William T. Sherman reminded cadets that they were being trained for, at most, militia or volunteer service: "Though but few of you are likely ever to be called on to carry a musket or sword in earnest, yet 'tis well that every young man should, at least once in life, feel that glorious impulse which leads to deeds of heroic action, if not of self-sacrifice to a noble patriotism."[13] That Weston and Burroughs bought into this effort to mold sacrifice into self-sacrifice, which requires a pseudomilitary "self," is evident in their letters written during World War I, when they and other white men of their generation grappled with aging and with nostalgia for the moment when the baton of national manhood had been passed to them.

Certainly the environment at MMA was conducive to close male friendships. Burroughs's roommate, Bob Lay, would remain his occasional employer, friend, and supporter for life (fig. 2). In the early 1930s, when an MMA reunion was held by schoolmates from their time, Weston and Burroughs received warm and nostalgic letters from several of their fellow cadets. But the geographic isolation, shared male ideology, and disciplinary subjugation were inseparable from the particular use made of these conditions by Burroughs and, to an extent, Weston. While football team photos and school pictures show the official side of the two men's friendship and a sense of unity among the cadets, a range of other photographs and documents from the time indicate that Burroughs had a theatrical bent that attracted a crowd of admirers and co-conspirators.

In fact, Burroughs was a troublemaker and a prankster, and these qualities are evident in the letters presented here. He could not stand being required to be orderly. Charles Bird King, a novelist and for a time the commandant of the academy, described Burroughs as "reck-

2. Robert Lay, Michigan Military Academy, Orchard Lake, Michigan, 1893, photographer unknown. *Courtesy Edgar Rice Burroughs, Inc.*

less, not vicious," but in his boarding school and military school antics Burroughs constantly pushed the envelope, often earning demotions and being threatened with expulsion.[14] Two things kept him at MMA. First, he became friends with the school's leaders, both faculty and students—a relationship promoted both by his personality and by his skills at riding and football. Second, he found that his talent for irony and tricksterism made him extremely popular at school; he published poems and cartoons in the school paper; he even performed a little theater. In an unpublished draft autobiography, Burroughs recounts staging a duel with another cadet as a hoax. Though school authorities intervened before the fake duel could proceed, the incident is emblematic of Burroughs's tendency to be a sort of "drama queen." The episode is also exemplary of his pranks, which went beyond the customary hazing or plebe mockery of disciplinary institutions, generally inverting or subverting authority structures by design.[15]

3. "The Windemere Eating Club." Probably Orchard Lake, Michigan, 1894, photographer unknown. Burroughs is second from the left on the bottom row; Weston is immediately above him. The ranks listed in the margins are exaggerated. *Courtesy Edgar Rice Burroughs, Inc.*

Much less is known about Weston's time at MMA. He rose quickly through the ranks, becoming a captain; he did well in classes and seems never to have been caught taking part in any of Burroughs's pranks. That he *did* participate is suggested, however, by a staged photograph from around 1894 which shows "The Windemere Eating Club," as it is described in Burroughs's hand (fig. 3). Empty bottles cover the table behind which eight cadets, whose names are indicated in the margins, strike a range of poses representing masculine stereotypes of epicurean excess.[16] Other prints and negatives from the Weston and Burroughs collections show cadets smoking (in flagrant violation of school policy) or holding up pictures and magazines while on guard duty. The very fact that Burroughs and Weston took or had taken so many photographs like these suggests that they imagined this as a time they would want to remember, but also that theatricalization of male friendship was a common idiom among these young men, a way of constituting friendship itself.

The appearance, in a later photo from Weston's time at Yale, of a framed image of the White Palace from the 1893 Columbian Exposition at Chicago suggests that he was present at a powerfully symbolic moment for the cadets (see fig. 6). It is possible, in fact, that the MMA cadets' role there as official escort to the princess of Spain, the Infanta Eulalie, persuaded Weston to attend MMA. The 140 cadets marched into the exposition on 2 June, spent two weeks there—in Burroughs's hometown—and held commencement exercises in the Music Hall (John Philip Sousa's band played for them).[17] They were a part of the exposition, performing maneuvers every day and demonstrating an ideal of American white democratic manhood: individuality suppressed for a greater cause. But in the specific context of escorting the Infanta, the cadets were also upholding an international gentility. The act was a kind of gender role-playing that infantilized Spanish power— containing it in a visually literal and politically figurative sense—at an event that ostensibly reminded attendees of the originary power of Spain in the New World. (It is less an irony than a fulfillment of the imperial logic of this event that some of these cadets would find themselves fighting in the Spanish-American War four years later.) MMA, then, offered more than just an environment in which to develop intimate homosociality. During Burroughs's and Weston's time there, it provided a way to connect that intimacy to a larger world—to imagine friendship as a way of achieving white male citizenship.

When Weston and Burroughs graduated from MMA in 1895, they set out on very different trajectories that would shape the dynamics of their friendship for the rest of their lives. Weston was admitted to Yale's Sheffield Scientific School (the same engineering school from which Burroughs's brothers had graduated) while Burroughs, failing the West Point admission exam, returned to MMA to serve as assistant commandant. He taught geology, cavalry, and Gatling gun technique and managed the football team.

Though he was attending school in New Haven with men who would become powerful figures in national and international business and science, Weston was a small-town boy who would never cut his ties with home. The entry in the Sheffield class book shows that Weston was reminded of his regional origins almost as a ritual of being folded into the "blood" of the eastern bourgeois:

> Young Lochinvar came in from the west, / With fringe on his trowsers and fur on his vest. The "Cowboy," "Ruffian," "Bandit," or, as he is commonly called, "McKuck," entered Lincoln, Neb., by a series of long leaps on April 15, 1876, with a gun in each hand and a yell in his mouth. Jefferson Burns Weston, a banker, is his father. Michigan Military Academy prepared him, and "Rudolph" came to Yale because he "knew several Harvard men." He fails to mention that he has blood, but no one can doubt its presence having once seen his hair.[18]

Yale became for Weston a shared experiment in white bourgeois identity-formation, in learning what fraternity and democracy meant in practice. A set of photos from 1897—examined in more depth below—suggests that Weston's experience at Yale was an extension or elaboration of the masculine world of the military academy. There he learned how masculinity, domesticity, and companionship worked hand in hand (see figs. 6–8).[19]

Weston made a number of friends at Yale who would remain, in his words, "life-long side-partners."[20] A friend from Beatrice, Lin Sherwood, matriculated at Sheffield in the same class; many years later Sherwood's daughter Marian would marry Weston's son Herbert Jr. Charles Lloyd is mentioned several times in the correspondence reproduced here. Weston corresponded with and frequently visited Seth Thomas, the clock manufacturer, and discussed those interactions with Burroughs. Soon after he returned to Beatrice, it would become clear that these connections, more than his training as an engineer, were the ones that would be essential for Weston's career in business and investing.

Though the correspondence between Burroughs and Weston from the post-school period has not survived, it is evident that they did maintain close contact. In part this was because both men were involved in romantic pursuits that were being frustrated by the young women's parents. In a letter to Margaret Collins, dated 2 March 1896, Weston

tells his beloved how much she will like his friend Burroughs. The remark comes as Weston is waxing poetic about his love and his great
happiness at having attained Margaret's true affection:

> I have told no one except my family and Burroughs about our relations.
> I wrote Ed about it because he loves me and will be glad to hear how suc-
> cessful I have been after having been through so much disappointment.
> He is a very nice boy, my friend and you dear will like him as well as I
> do. He has had an affair of his own, and was unfortunate and perhaps
> the likeness of our situations while we were at OLake rather tended to
> bind us more closely together.[21]

Margaret's parents, in fact, soon took their only child to Europe to im-
pose a cooling-off period. But Weston's interests found another focus.
In April 1898 the Spanish-American War was declared, and Weston
busied himself trying to find a place in combat. With his friend Lin
Sherwood, he joined the First Connecticut Light Artillery, Battery A.
His unit never saw action—a deep blow for Weston and a source of
much angst that is evident in the letters collected here.

Weston returned to Beatrice when the war ended, and he and Margaret were married (having passed the Collinses' "test") in 1903. The
couple spent their honeymoon in Idaho. A series from 1904—titled
"The Bertie and Maggie Series" in Burroughs's hand—from Burroughs's photograph album shows them making camp in mining territory (fig. 4). After the honeymooners returned to Nebraska, Weston
took a floating place in the family business, the Beatrice National Bank,
but also began to develop his own venture, Nebraska Corn Mills. By
this time the Collins family had amassed a large fortune and had considerable leverage in railroad contracting and bonds. When Chester
Collins withdrew in 1902 from the set of concerns he held with the Kilpatrick brothers in Nebraska, the company had contracted with Union
Pacific and the federal government for 3,339 miles of rail and 34 miles
of water pipe, reservoirs, and tunnels. The company also owned more
than eighty thousand acres of farm and livestock land in the West and a
huge Wyoming coal field. Given her wealth and New York background,
Margaret's insistence on maintaining a home in Beatrice is a source of
some mystery, and of considerable discussion in the Burroughs-Weston
correspondence. The Westons did make frequent long visits to Mar-

Sawing Wood

4. "Sawing Wood." Margaret Weston and Herbert T. Weston, Idaho, 1904,
photographer unknown. *Courtesy Edgar Rice Burroughs, Inc.*

garet's relatives in New York City, even after the births of their sons,
Collins (1906), Jefferson (1911), and Herbert (1914). Weston's correspondence indicates that he often stopped to visit the Burroughses,
while they were still in Chicago, on his way east.[22]

Burroughs, by contrast, never stayed in one place for very long. After
returning to MMA he enlisted in the army, and was eventually assigned
to Fort Grant, Arizona, where he spent 1896. Though he would ideal-
ize military service for most of his life, there was nothing ideal about
serving at Fort Grant, even by Burroughs's own account. Expressing
bitter irony at the political motives for the army's presence in the Southwest, Burroughs noted: "As I look at it now, we were just bait. A live
trooper did not amount to much, but a dead one would certainly have
demonstrated the fact that there were hostile Indians in the neighborhood."[23] At the onset of the Spanish-American War, Burroughs sent a
letter to Theodore Roosevelt asking to serve with his Rough Riders,
whose version of military life presumably more closely fit Burroughs's
imagination of ideal service.[24] (Roosevelt rejected his plea in May 1898.)
His numerous drawings and cartoons from Fort Grant, exhibiting the

15

mix of self-deprecation and insight that characterizes much of his informal writing, show Burroughs deeply engaged in both the aesthetics and the politics of daily life in the army.[25]

After leaving the service, Burroughs began a peripatetic employment history during which he served as, among other things, railroad policeman, miner, salesman, and "Office Boy."[26] Burroughs and Emma Hulbert were married in 1900, and after living in Idaho and Utah returned to the Chicago area and settled in Oak Park. Burroughs worked through a series of middle management and clerical positions, including time at Sears, Roebuck and Company and a stint as part owner of the ill-fated Stace-Burroughs Company, which (briefly) sold advice on "scientific salesmanship." During these years the Burroughses had their three children, Joan (born 1908), Hulbert (1909), and John Coleman (1913). It was also at this time that Burroughs began his publishing career, first writing short pieces for a range of small and short-lived periodicals, then drafting longer works for national mass-market magazines.

This period of Burroughs's life has been the subject of intense speculation and a certain degree of romanticization. Because it was during the first decade of the new century that Burroughs moved toward a career that became one of the most influential in U.S. literary history, the stakes in interpreting his turn to fiction writing would seem to be quite high. As John Kasson reminds us, Burroughs was writing *two* kinds of fiction when he began his career as a writer of fantasy stories. He was also employed to write for a business advice magazine called *System*, a position for which, given his history of commercial failures, he claims in his autobiography to have felt particularly underqualified.[27] But Burroughs's autobiography ends just after he tells about the appearance of *Tarzan of the Apes* in book form (1914). If we think of the autobiography as complete, instead of as incomplete, as it is usually considered to be, the work is a typical romance of authorial enterprise, with the well-off boy struggling against his own lack of discipline and — the modern opponent — poor health. Falling into destitution thanks to having fulfilled the heteronormative imperative of marriage and reproduction, he then triumphs by harnessing his unique talents and struggling against a publishing world unwilling to accept (and described as almost unworthy of) his productions. The world, in need of a lesson, foolishly prefers the fictions of his employment with *System* to the more fantastic, yet more honest, irrationalities of his novels.

Some critics have questioned this emphasis on the role of poverty in stimulating Burroughs's writing career. A 1908 poem full of self-loathing that Burroughs wrote about poverty seems to contradict that view; and his draft autobiography claims that poverty "is an indication of inefficiency, and nothing more."[28] Other evidence indicates that the Burroughses were never in dire straits. Burroughs's list of household expenses from this period shows that he and Emma kept a "girl" at five dollars per month (one-sixth of his own monthly salary).[29] Irwin Porges's biography of Burroughs recounts a number of episodes in which the Burroughs family sent money or helped him find work.[30] In his autobiography, Burroughs writes about Mexicans, Indians, and the poor as his inferiors; he might pal around with them, but he does not identify with their struggles. At Fort Grant, he was a member of a small group called the "May Have Seen Better Days Club," made up of soldiers from well-off urban families. Finally, and most important, Emma's family was quite capable of sustaining the young Burroughs family in its low moments. This helps explain why Burroughs manages to maintain an air of middle-classness even as he writes about hard times. The most likely explanation is that Burroughs chose deliberately to live as much on his own means as possible, and that Emma partnered with him in this project of reproducing class through gender roles and self-discipline (within limits—after all, they apparently did not give up the maid). For Burroughs, making a "man" of himself was a crucial part of establishing his character and his virtue, and that meant making his own way *even though it was not an economic necessity*. It did not, however, mean that the Burroughses were at any real risk of starving in the years leading up to his fiction-writing career.[31]

When he did begin to succeed at selling his stories, Burroughs took a methodical, empirical approach. Above his desk he kept a graph that tracked the word count of his fictional works; in 1913, for example, he wrote 413,000 words.[32] (He would continue to document how hard he worked at writing; the exchange with Weston from September to November 1940 reproduced here shows him still taking a Taylorized approach to literary labor.) He was a ruthless haggler with his publishers and doggedly circulated manuscripts until they were accepted. As World War I loomed, Burroughs had, in John Carter and Tarzan, established characters that were popular with the public and were even beginning to be drawn into the new and exciting world of motion picture production.

World War I, Raising Children

"What a miserable rotten age 'past forty' is!"
—WESTON TO SETH THOMAS, 17 July 1918

The entry of the United States into World War I placed white men of Weston's and Burroughs's generation in a powerful dilemma. Things had changed since Weston had waited in vain to see action in the Spanish-American War and Burroughs had been rejected by the Rough Riders. The fact that they had failed to participate in the first imperialistic man-making military experience the United States had to offer them was certainly one reason why they were devastated to find themselves too old to be deployed in the second. Weston, forty-one years old, managed only to be classified G-1; Burroughs, at forty-two, was made a captain in the Illinois Reserve Militia (Company A, 2nd Infantry).

On the one hand, the men addressed what they saw as their misfortune with the kind of irony that characterizes almost all of their correspondence (and can make it a challenge to read). "I notice in the new draft law," Burroughs wrote to Weston in 1918, "that bald headed men with three children are to be put into A-1 class so I suppose you and I will soon be in the front line trenches."[33] But on the other hand, even humorous comments like these often show a hint of longing, and the men's correspondence with their other friends shows a wide-ranging expression of helplessness among their cohort. Seth Thomas, for example, wrote to Weston in 1918 expressing his despair at his inability to join up; in a long letter in return, Weston first empathized with Thomas's frustration and then posited his emotional response as in itself a reason to leave the fighting to others:

Your mental attitude is not normal—it is warped by an intense fury toward the damned Hun, and a desire to get personally to him and at him. You want the Prussian wiped from the face of the earth, and you will never never feel right not [to] have added one man power to the direct act of wiping. . . . If I were fulfilling a useful civil service, and really helping things along as you are doing, I think I should be contented. Such duties arouse no enthusiasm it is true, but you ARE doing your six just the same, and that after all is the main thing.

"One man power," Weston reminds Thomas in this passage, does not fit the more constitutional model of collective service. But the conclusion of the letter revives the frustration of being unable to serve and excites it to another level by linking desire and history in a remarkable, sweeping vision of what was at stake for these men: "And the worst of this all is, that it is for all time. It is the biggest thing that has ever happened. . . . Things, and everything from now on are going to date forward and backward from right now. And the line is going to be drawn between those that DID and those that DID NOT. And it is not only going to classify us, but it classifies our children and their children."[34] For Burroughs and Weston and many other men "past forty," the Great War defined populations, not merely selves.

Once the war was over, Weston found himself occupied with three children, a floundering business (the Nebraska Corn Mills), and the declining health of his wife's parents (which increased the amount of time he spent managing the Collinses' financial affairs). The Westons, as the correspondence with Burroughs details, were frequently on the move in the interwar years; on vacations alone they traveled to California, Minnesota, New York, South Dakota, and Cuba. Burroughs often chided Weston about the family's frequent travels, saying in 1928 that they were "the travelingest family I ever saw. I suggest that you put a miniature railroad track in your backyard with an engine and private car, so that whenever Margaret has the urge to travel she can do so with the least effort."[35] Weston also shared Burroughs's fascination with new consumer technologies such as cars and photography, and the two sent films, photographs, and advice back and forth throughout the period.

Like their father, the Weston boys were sent to military school. With Michigan Military Academy undone by bankruptcy, the family turned to Culver Military Academy in Indiana, sending first Collins and then Jeff and Herb, whose time there overlapped.[36] Weston kept close tabs on his sons while they were away; the Weston Family Collection holds a sizable correspondence between Weston and the commanders under whom his sons studied. The letters contain detailed questions about the boys' social and academic progress. He consulted closely with the school about the future prospects for his sons and about what preparation might best suit their temperaments and abilities. The early twentieth century saw rapid changes in educational demographics. The percentage of Americans between fourteen and seventeen who attended high school doubled between 1900 and 1915 to about 14 percent.[37] As more people insisted on educating their children and encouraged them to get professional training, families like Weston's began to feel a new pressure to prepare their children to compete for admission to institutions of higher education.

Weston and his sons corresponded with each other as well, in long letters that ranged over a wide variety of topics. The boys even corresponded with Burroughs once or twice—including an occasion on which the latter asked Jeff and Herb to get a sense of their fellow cadets' reactions to the latest Tarzan serial. Though the boys were away at school, then, all the evidence suggests a continuing closeness among family members.

But try as he might, Bert Weston found himself unable to instill the "spark," as he called it, for enterprise that he hoped for in his children. None of the boys managed to get into Yale, and as far as their parents were concerned, they all spent too much money. Certainly they did not find their way into stable careers until the late 1930s. In 1933, as the Depression hit with a vengeance, Weston wrote to Burroughs, "I am trying desperately to make my three sons KNOW that nothing is an asset, till Same is hard-cashed in! I am trying hard to make them realize that a liability NEVER gets any less, and, as recently, a liability may increase amazingly."[38] Later that same year Bert wrote an astonishing, frank letter addressed to all three boys, upbraiding them for their lassitude and imposing sanctions on them agreed upon by both parents.

Weston had learned the vicissitudes of fortune for himself a decade before as he struggled to build Nebraska Corn Mills. Though not entirely independent of the Beatrice National Bank (his father's business) and the Collins interests in Beatrice, Nebraska Corn Mills was for the most part Weston's project. The business was successful early on and managed to fend off a federal audit of the company's 1918 returns. The Corn Mills and Bert and Maggie Weston even show up in Burroughs's fiction, most substantially in *The Mad King*, which appeared in serial form in 1914 and 1915.[39] But a host of factors, including drought years in the plains and foreign competition, made corn milling unprofitable, and the shareholders voted in 1923 to dissolve the corporation. Weston seems sanguine about the collapse in his letters to Burroughs that mention it, but the enthusiasm he expresses in the early letters responding to Burroughs's questions about milling hints at the disappointment he must have felt.

To make matters worse both emotionally and from the standpoint of Weston's expectations of himself, Chester Collins died in 1925, leaving Maggie and Bert in control of his interests. Margaret Collins, Maggie's mother, was in declining health and lived in Beatrice with the Westons. Maggie held controlling interest in the Collins group, and Bert worked as her negotiator, secretary, banker, and manager. All of the Weston boys did stints working for one of the family businesses during their struggles to identify careers. By the time Maggie's mother died in 1931 — which removed the Westons' last immediate familial tie to Beatrice — the Depression had left them one of the few stable economic entities in town. There was little chance that Weston would suggest that the family move away under the circumstances (as Burroughs repeatedly asks him to do in the letters); he was fifty-five years old, he was occupied with Maggie's investments, and he lacked financial backers for another venture.[40]

However disappointed he may have been with his inability to fight in the First World War, Burroughs found himself compensated by fame and financial latitude. Tarzan and John Carter had become household names, as had Burroughs's own. Even Theodore Roosevelt, who had dismissed Burroughs's petition to join the Rough Riders, enjoyed Burroughs's "breezy pages."[41] The family moved to California for good in January 1919. Burroughs purchased a 540-acre ranch in the San Fernando Valley, near the Santa Monica Mountains, within easy reach of Los Angeles. He called it Tarzana, a name the town there still bears.

Ed and Emma Burroughs worried as much about their children's education as the Westons did, especially now that they were relatively isolated. Like the Weston boys, none of the Burroughs children was interested in an elite college or extended professional training. Joan was virtually raised to a performing career, working on stage and in film and radio; in 1928 she married Jim Pierce, a former football star also working on a Hollywood career. Jack and Hulbert, however, vacillated: in 1933 Burroughs wrote to Weston a paragraph that exhibits Hulbert's indecision: "Hulbert is home fussing around with photography, which this week, he thinks, will be his life's work. I certainly feel sorry for him because he doesn't know what he wants to do, though he feels that he ought to be doing something. I am encouraging him to take up seriously still and motion picture photography, as this will work well with archaeology in which he is interested."[42]

The generation of parents to which Burroughs and Weston belonged laid the groundwork for the development of a middle-class ethos based on education, literacy, and the cultivation of taste, designed to appropriate and regulate the use of resources outside the domain of real property or industrial capital. But ironically, as Barbara Ehrenreich points out, the "barriers that the middle class erected to protect itself make it painfully difficult to reproduce itself. It is one thing to have children, and another . . . to have children who will be disciplined enough to devote the first twenty or thirty years of their lives to scaling the educational obstacles to a middle-class career."[43] Burroughs's struggles in school—and his children's after him—show just how difficult it could be to satisfy the demands of the middle class. Like Weston, Burroughs found himself employing his children in the family business—but Burroughs accomplished this in a novel way.

Burroughs had discovered that copyright was insufficient protection for his rights in his stories and characters in the multimedia circulation of popular fantasy literature. As Jane Gaines has pointed out, copyright is effectively a monopoly grant, but in Burroughs's time this monopoly was a shaky one at best and, by constitutional decree, not perpetual. Burroughs's solution was to employ another legal concept that more closely matched the needs of an author creating in one medium and selling in a multiplicity of them: on 26 March 1923 Burroughs created "Edgar Rice Burroughs, Inc., a California Corporation." Burroughs granted rights, title, and interest in all of his work to the corporation. The Burroughses were the shareholders and employees of the new entity; Ed and Emma held most of the shares. He also gave the corporation a body of real estate—tracts from the original Tarzana ranch that he was in the process of selling off in parcels. Burroughs, then, is in a sense still alive—he was an employee of his own corporation until his death, and the organization still controls licensing and reproduction rights to Burroughs's fictional characters, works, and worlds.[44] A letter from Burroughs to his editor Robert Davis at Munsey gives a wry warning that "you are doing business with a soulless corporation."[45]

On the one hand, Burroughs's decision to incorporate was a radical departure from the usual relations between authors and publishers of mass media entertainment. Mark Twain (whose work influenced Burroughs profoundly) had tried a similar experiment in the nineteenth century; Upton Sinclair likewise incorporated without success.[46] But seen in the context of his history of penny-by-penny grappling with editors for leverage, Burroughs's incorporation was merely the most spectacular in a series of efforts to take control of the means of his fictional production. After finishing *The Beasts of Tarzan*, for example, Burroughs submitted the manuscript to two publishers simultaneously, telegraphing between the two houses to get the best deal.[47] In April 1915 he published an article called "Syndication" in the *Bulletin*, the newsletter of the Authors' League of America. Since many authors were not getting proper remuneration for syndication, and indeed were often signing away second serial rights, Burroughs proposed that the league organize a clearinghouse through which members could arrange their serial rights.[48] Although some members expressed interest, the plan never panned out; it was clear that Burroughs's sense of expanding authors' control over the publication sphere made many league members uncomfortable. When ultimately he embodied his resistance to the publishing order in Edgar Rice Burroughs, Inc., he set an important precedent for creators of popular characters with multimedia sales potential.

The stock market crash of 1929 did little to damage the overall financial stability of the Burroughs and Weston families. The Westons' assets were primarily invested in land, and Burroughs had stable capital in his own literary output. But as the flurry of letters in 1929–30 shows, financial matters sometimes put a strain on their friendship. However successful Burroughs was at fiction writing, he had not become much more of a businessman than he had been at the turn of the century. His investments in real estate, a movie production company, and a golf course all floundered during this time. In retrospect, his proposal to the Westons for a joint venture in the Los Angeles Metropolitan Airport and Apache Motors (which was developing an airplane engine) seems spectacularly ill-timed. When the airport investments began to fail, Weston reassured Burroughs that their friendship and their business arrangements were separate spheres, insisting that "personally" the loss of profitability was no more emotionally disturbing than a gambling loss. Weston's financial involvement with Burroughs was in fact more complicated than he declared it to be. Maggie's money was also invested in the companies, which meant jointly negotiating their strategy and assessing Burroughs's skills as an investment adviser. Burroughs, for his part, offered up his chagrin time and time again at having proposed the venture, and allocated much of his secretary Ralph Rothmund's time to damage control. In the end, it was as much Rothmund's competence and the acknowledgment of the general investment downturn that kept the friendship healthy during this time.

Friendship Endangered and World War II

Although shared failure in business ventures did not interrupt the friendship between the Westons and the Burroughses, family matters did. For more than five years, from 1934 until 1939, Burroughs and Weston did not write to each other.

In March 1934 Burroughs announced, "I suppose you have got to know it some time, so I might as well tell you that we are not living together. Emma is still at the beach, and my address is Tarzana."[49] The Westons were in California at the time, and apparently changed their travel plans, avoiding Ed but probably visiting Emma. The separation and eventual divorce appear to have taken the Westons by surprise. It is unlikely that they knew that Burroughs had already begun to court Florence Gilbert Dearholt, a married woman who was herself about to be divorced.[50] (The two were married in April 1935 and divorced in

1942.) Irwin Porges suggests that Emma's excessive drinking was the main reason for the split, but there is little hard evidence of the factors that lay behind the separation. Certainly the Westons were not convinced that the breakup was necessary; when Ed did not reply to a letter from Weston (unfortunately missing) responding to the news, Bert did not write him again until 1939—even though he had prompted Ed during silences earlier in their relationship.

Included in this collection is a letter from Bert Weston to a mutual Burroughs family friend, Charles Rosenberger. Though the letter was not sent to Burroughs, it exists only in his handwriting; apparently Burroughs copied it—either with or without Rosenberger's permission—from Weston's original. (Burroughs evidently copied only the parts of the letter pertaining to their relationship.) The letter is a painfully candid expression of Weston's frustration; he and Margaret were torn between supporting Emma, acknowledging Ed's claims, and upholding their own familial and marital ideals. Though the language of unqualified friendship that Burroughs and Weston used to rekindle their communication in 1939 may seem stilted ("And now, what about you and me? You have made for yourself a new 'incarnation.' . . . Will I fit into it?"), the fact that Burroughs copied and kept the Rosenberger letter—which, in a sense, continued their communication despite the silencing of their direct contact—speaks to the depth of emotion that underlay the relationship.[51]

The letter also speaks the inseparability of that relationship from the men's marriages and family lives. The friendship included the men's wives in fundamental ways. The letters between them were read to the wives, and often to the whole family. Bert wrote letters addressed to Emma and the children, and Maggie and Ed Burroughs wrote to one another; these letters have been included to give a fuller sense of the communication flow among members of the two families. The divorce opened up a topic that Burroughs could not discuss in depth with Weston by mail. When they had reunited, Burroughs wrote, "I am writing you thus, as I have never written anyone else, because I value your friendship; and because I hope that some day you will meet Florence."[52] Burroughs here leverages the intimacy of his relationship with Weston—as far as we know, he had still not related in writing his reasons for breaking up with Emma—in the hope of bringing Florence into the shared dynamic of their friendship. Weston made a similar maneuver when he wrote in 1939, "My experience makes me believe that one's marital affairs are very much one's own business, and for that reason, what inhell could I do when you just quit writing to me?"[53] As the letter to Rosenberger demonstrates, this comment is disingenuous; Weston had, in fact, inquired into and then pronounced upon Burroughs's "marital affairs" immediately after the separation. The divorce with Emma thus threw the boundaries of the friendship into relief: perhaps ironically, it was the extension of their friendship to their families that resulted in silences and created boundaries *within* the friendship.

Burroughs may have wanted the Westons to get to know Florence, but that became unfeasible when Burroughs, Florence, and her two children (Lee and Caryl Lee) moved to Hawaii in 1940. Financially, Burroughs had suffered from the outbreak of World War II; European royalties from his fiction and films were a significant part of his income, and there was no resolution in sight. Still furiously writing, Burroughs began to drink heavily in the somewhat constricted social sphere of Hawaii—partly as a result of which Florence and the children left him in March 1941. Burroughs concealed the separation from Weston in his 20 March letter: "Florence and the children returned to the mainland on last Friday's boat: they arrive home tomorrow. It is so difficult to get reservations and the possibility of war with Japan so definite that we thought it best to get them off while we could. I shall finish up my business here and follow in about a month."[54] Concerned with his father's physical and emotional health, Hulbert Burroughs came for a prolonged visit. On 7 December the two men witnessed the attack on Pearl Harbor—and Burroughs finally found himself on the front lines.

The U.S. Army asked Burroughs to write stories for local radio and periodicals, and he received solicitations from several other public sources to act as a correspondent. But it was clear that his heart was set on being a correspondent for a major news source, and he quickly got credentials from the United Press. Early on, Burroughs traveled to New Caledonia and Australia, but few of his reports were published because the navy refused to recognize his credentials. Burroughs fumed about the denial, framing it as an insult to his manhood, in a letter to Senator

Hiram Johnson of California that, fortunately, he never sent. Once the miscommunication had been sorted out, Burroughs wrote frequently, traveling in 1944 to the Gilbert and Marshall Islands.

When the war ended, Burroughs returned to California suffering from angina and still drinking. Their correspondence was frequent during the men's final years. The Westons, whose capital and land investments had left them financially stable and whose children had begun to settle down, kept up their travel schedule. Having heard of Burroughs's health problems (he would also be diagnosed with Parkinson's disease in 1949), the Westons visited him in California in March 1947. Bert would later write that it had been a "great day" and that Ed looked "much the same": "After all the . . . things you have gone through during the war . . . you are the damndest man I have ever known also the most colorful and most lovable. . . . When I saw you 3/28/47 I wanted to pound on your back, hug you and perhaps hold your hand."[55] By early 1950 Burroughs was too sick to correspond, but Weston got messages to him through his secretary Rothmund. Burroughs died — in bed with the comics — on 19 March 1950; Weston followed in 1951.[56]

Seen in hindsight and through the lens of the ideology of manhood that, historians tell us, characterized their society, Burroughs and Weston traced inverse trajectories of masculine fulfillment. Early on, Weston represented the promises of national manhood — athlete and scholar, Yale engineer, Spanish-American War veteran, marrying up in society. Burroughs at that time found it difficult to reproduce the self-application that had put his father into the upper middle class. He was unable to get into college, got stuck in Arizona when he joined the military, and found himself bouncing from job to job. But things changed when Burroughs's fiction began to take off. By 1923 Weston's Nebraska Corn Mills business was failing and he found himself more and more at Maggie's command. In that same year Burroughs consummated his quest for an individualized version of manhood by incorporating, uniting family, self, and work in Edgar Rice Burroughs, Inc. In their later lives, Weston found himself in somewhat unwilling retirement — happy with his social life and with his role as an emotional beacon for his male friends, but sardonic about the inability of "old dob-

5. Burroughs-Weston reunion, California, 1947, photographer unknown
(possibly Hulbert Burroughs). From left to right: Herbert T. Weston, Collins
Weston, Mabel Weston, Margaret Weston, Marion T. Burroughs (wife of
Hulbert, seated in chair), Joan Burroughs Pierce (standing), unidentified
woman (possibly Joanne Anselmo), Edgar Rice Burroughs.
Courtesy Edgar Rice Burroughs, Inc.

bers" like himself to speak authoritatively on public affairs. Burroughs,
though, only gained more public voice; a year after Weston's comment,
he became a correspondent for United Press in the Pacific theater and
kept publishing until his death. This brief sketch is an artificial map
of the men's relationship to national sex and gender ideals—a more
complex picture follows—but viewing the threads of their lives from
the standpoint of their contemporaries is useful to illustrate how the
emotional, conflicted, negotiated relationship portrayed in the letters
worked against idealized gender narratives.

Brother Men:
Male Friendship, the Nation, and the Self

An influential body of scholarly work on gender in America discusses the changing mechanics and political implications of private and emotional life. Among others, Lauren Berlant, Dana Nelson, Joel Pfister, Priscilla Wald, and Chris Castiglia have historicized emotion and illuminated the relationship between the private and public spheres, showing how affect and the private have come to be a source of authority in politics. Their work combined with that of scholars like Gail Bederman and Amy Kaplan who are interested in the relationship between the logics of masculinity and imperialism in the United States has produced a sophisticated sense of the weight of identity-formation in sustaining and promoting social and political structures that are premised on subjugation or differentiation.[57]

Scholars studying Burroughs, and especially Tarzan, have followed these broad contours. John Kasson's *Houdini, Tarzan, and the Perfect Man* explores manhood as experienced by Burroughs and his readers, seeing self-metamorphosis as the characteristic motif of the creator's approach to popular manhood. Bederman and Eric Cheyfitz come down hard on Tarzan, arguing that the narrative encodes or allegorizes a violently racist U.S. foreign policy. While both Bederman and Cheyfitz make sophisticated arguments that avoid attributing determining power to any single cultural formation (such as authorship), they imply that Burroughs's fiction is more than merely a symptom or epiphenomenon of ambient cultural forces. Because Tarzan has been a mass success in multiple media, it is assumed to have had more agency in shaping cultural politics than has less popular fiction. Other discussions of Burroughs's work have seen more nuance. Marianna Torgovnick insists on the complexity of the relationship between the utopian urge behind much of Burroughs's fiction and the conservative work performed by primitivism in popular fiction. Bill Brown argues that in many ways Burroughs's vision of American imperialism was in fact a nostalgic—almost humanistic—one when compared with the already sophisticated means by which the United States had begun to subordinate other American countries in the years before World War I.[58]

For the most part, these discussions have been built on readings of Burroughs's fiction or what is known about his writing career. The letters, photographs, and histories of the friendship between Burroughs and Weston offer new evidence and complicate our understanding of the formulation of the relationship between intimate and national selves. Here I read the letters in three interlocking early-twentieth-century contexts: race, imperialism and xenophobia, and masculine subjectivity. The intimacy of the letters can add to our understanding of manhood in two ways. First, it suggests that aging significantly influences how men embody ideals of manhood. Second, the multilayered performance of the intersubjective self portrayed in this correspondence helps explain how the "local," or intimate, masculinities of "lifelong side-partners" may work in a *spectrum* of homosocial attachments from the physical to the imagined (that is, the national). The terms on which men like Weston and Burroughs established friendships were capable of jamming the transmission of masculinist ideology.

It is true that letters used as the main body of evidence for historical arguments may put too intimate a "spin" on the issue.[59] In an effort to offset this tendency, I offer other evidence—for example, images and the biographies delineated above—to make a case for the presence of an intimate tension and creativity that may have constituted the experience of manhood at the beginning of the twentieth century. It is worth remembering, particularly with a figure like Burroughs (who often mingled friendship and business), what Erving Goffman argues about the characteristic dynamics of middle-class self-presentation: "The general notion that we make a presentation of ourselves to others is hardly novel; what ought to be stressed . . . is that the very structure of the self can be seen in terms of how we arrange for such performances in our Anglo-American society." For Goffman, "the individual was divided by implication into two basic parts: he was viewed as a *performer*, a harried fabricator of impressions involved in the all-too-human task of staging a performance; [and] he was viewed as a *character*, a figure, typically a fine one, whose spirit, strength, and other sterling qualities the performance was designed to evoke."[60] As his letter to Charles Rosenberger of August 1934 shows, Weston was aware that Burroughs's letters were on one level a performance by a character; no doubt the same perception guided Burroughs's readings of Weston's messages. As we read friendship, interest, concern, and excitement at mutual recognition in these letters, we must keep in mind that these men could, and almost certainly did, employ a decoding mechanism of discernment and suspicion. At all levels, then—from the relationship between an individual man and a national ideal to the practice of reading a letter from a close friend—what Joan Wallach Scott says of identity holds true: "gender identification, although it always appears coherent and fixed, is, in fact, highly unstable."[61]

Weston and Burroughs were, of course, products of a racialized nation. As middle-class men with families and multiple businesses, they invested in the racism and classism that had helped their families get leverage before they were born. We should nevertheless keep sight of the fact that racism and classism are learned, and are revised or sometimes even rejected over the course of a lifetime. Both men's writings include evidence of the stresses and contradictions that racialism forced into their imagination of what it meant to be a man.

Theodore Roosevelt, the idol of both men and the emblem of masculine ideology for many historians, was one of the leading proponents and public theorists of racialism in the United States. In *The Winning of the West*, Roosevelt claims that it is "of incalculable importance that America, Australia, and Siberia should pass out of the hands of the red, black, and yellow aboriginal owners, and become the heritage of the dominant world races." Gauging all too accurately his audience of men struggling, in difficult financial times, to establish a place in the economy, Roosevelt leverages anxiety about self-application against visions of racial equality. Those who resist his formulation are "too selfish and indolent, too lacking in imagination, to understand the race-importance of the work," he says, while "the rude, fierce settler who drives the savage from the land lays all civilized mankind under a debt to him."[62] Compelling as this case might have been at the time, it was difficult for men like Weston and Burroughs to enact this cult of bullying with any consistency.

While a virulent racism structures many of Burroughs's Tarzan novels, some of his other treatments of race are more problematical.[63] In 1899 a parody of Rudyard Kipling's "The White Man's Burden" (1899) appeared in the newspaper of Pocatello, Idaho, the small town where Burroughs was living at the time. Kipling's poem uses the term *burden* in a range of potential meanings, as Bederman explains, "to urge white males to take up the racial burden of civilization's advancement."[64] "Send forth the best ye breed," Kipling writes.

> Go bind your sons to exile
> To serve your captives' need;
> To wait in heavy harness,
> on fluttered folk and wild —
> Your new-caught, sullen peoples,
> Half-devil and half-child.

Attacking the blind spots of Kipling's poem, "The Black Man's Burden (a Parody)" introduces a radical shift in the narrative point of view, as evidenced in this section:

> Take up the white man's burden;
> And learn by what you've lost
> That white men called as counsel
> Means black man pays the cost.
> Your right to fertile acres
> Their priests will teach you well
> Have gained your fathers only
> A desert claim in hell.[65]

Burroughs's approach here suggests that a focus on the cultural work of his fiction might be more productive than locating a particular kind of racism in Burroughs himself. The lure of generic fiction writing for Burroughs was in large part its structural and rhetorical workflow. Once he had set out the terms of an essay, a poem, a short story, he tended to follow its accompanying affective logic to its conclusion. Sometimes, as if having realized that the compulsion of the narrative had led him beyond the authority his text could bear, Burroughs undermined his own critique with a self-deprecating conclusion. Thus the racist logic of popular fantasy forms often worked hand in hand with whatever quotidian racism Burroughs had developed by the time he began his career as an author. While it is true, then, that the power of parody often led him, in the attitude of contradiction, to trenchant critiques of imperialism, racism, or capitalism, we would be missing the point if we took these progressive moments as indicators of how Burroughs processed difficult questions about race or empire.[66]

In many ways, Weston's views on race and ethnicity were more coherent and less progressive than were Burroughs's. A letter to Burroughs from 1918 suggests how enmeshed Weston was in middle-class notions of racial decay and linguistic hierarchization:

> Anyone with an ounce of intelligence now knows that the vanishing from the face of the earth of the Hollerzollern [Hohenzollern] Hapsburg idea is as sure and certain as the change of the seasons. The kais [Kaiser Wilhelm] and gang know they are gone coons, and for that very reason they will fight on. They know that just as soon as the Allies commence to take charge of things in the dear ole papaland that the status of kais & co will be exactly the same as that of a buck-nigger in Mississippi who has outraged a white female.[67]

Strangely, in a letter that implicitly vaunts the American way over European violence and corruption, Weston turns to that persistent and notorious failure of American democracy, the racialized lynch mob. This passage shows a remarkable deployment of the logic of white racial domination in the United States to address fears about international politics. Weston applies theories of racial degeneration nurtured in white anxieties about Native Americans not to Germans generally but to the "idea" of Kaiser Wilhelm's government. In a kind of wishful translation of more immediate American social problems into the European conflict, Weston metaphorizes the Kaiser's cabal as a black gang, as "coons." As if to regain control, he then turns to simile, arguing for Germany's imminent defeat by comparison to the foregone product of the lynching algorithm. At a time when racial violence was increasing in the United States, sometimes to the point of fetishization, Weston's comment leaves violent white supremacy unquestioned.[68]

Weston was as conflicted as most white Americans were about ethnicity. His correspondence with friends in New York and Chicago occasionally reveals a strong anti-Semitism. And late in his life he was unable even to credit recent immigrants with national origins, as in his account of a trip to New York in 1939:

> It is well for me to go there and spend a week with Margt's brokers, sort of getting their view point and letting the Corn Belt stink blow partially

off of me. But NY is a sort of a horror to me. It is now mostly inhabited by the scum of Middle Europe. There used to be mostly Jews, Irish and Italians on the streets, but now there are hordes of mis-shapen, under-nurished queer folk, who look as tho they had crawled up out of filth, like unclean worms. Last time I was there, I went up on the tower of the Empire Building, as I always do. It was a wonderful day and visibility was 100%. I looked for perhaps 40 miles in every direction. And I thought of the seething millions within one man's vision who had been trans-planted from backward Middle Europe, and concentrated into this area, where none had a chance to know much about what it was all about.[69]

Weston's ascent of the Empire State Building is a panoptic fantasy of transcendence and mastery—but one haunted by a sense that there is something wrong here, something to be corrected; immigrants might need "a chance to know" more about what they have gotten into. Stand-ing on the heights of "Empire," as it were, Weston works himself into a state of "horror," where 100 percent visibility means only the recog-nition that the magnetism of the United States has drawn to its shores "mis-shapen, under-nurished queer folk." The realization that immi-grants do not "know much" is representable only in a passage that high-lights Weston's own limitations, his own marginality (including his de-pendence on the brokers' "view point"); the "stink" of the Corn Belt can only ever be "partially" removed.

As the fluidity of race and empire in Weston's comments about New York make clear, anxieties about white male domination and U.S. im-perialism were imagined in terms of each other. Kasson helps put Bur-roughs and Weston's experience in perspective:

Burroughs's generation had grown up during the great wave of Euro-pean imperial expansion, when a fifth of the world's landmass (excluding Antarctica) and a tenth of its population had been seized by European powers, great and small. Britain, whose national symbol, appropriately, was the lion, claimed the largest share: one-quarter of the land and one-third of the people on the globe. With the United States' own frontier ex-hausted, the excitement of a new global land rush with immense prizes to the victors was hard for many Americans to resist.[70]

As Westerners, Burroughs's and Weston's lives offer a powerful ex-ample of the transition from a time when nationhood and manhood were related through territorial expansion to a time when manhood was defined in relationship to the construction of an intercontinental empire—the emergence of the United States as a global colonial power.[71] The Spanish-American War was the first test of Burroughs's and Weston's faith in the man-making power of imperialism. In 1900, Senator Albert Jeremiah Beveridge justified his argument that the United States should annex the Philippines by claiming that it would mean "opportunity for all the glorious young manhood of the republic—the most virile, ambitious, impatient, militant manhood the world has ever seen."[72] Amy Kaplan observes that although "the Spanish-American War was viewed as a chivalric liberation of Cuba and the Philippines from a tyrannical old-world empire," Beveridge's statement "welcomed the war's conquests as a rescue mission for American manhood, from the equally threatening forces of a modern industrial democracy."[73] Certainly we can view the eager attempts by Weston and Burroughs to serve in the war in the light of this ideology. But Beveridge's exhortation protests too much against a recent military past that, as far as men like Weston and Burroughs were concerned, offered all too *few* suggestions that American men were "virile" or "militant."

Military service in World War I also turned out to be an *ignis fatuus* for the two friends—but Burroughs, at least, could turn to fiction to play out his fantasies about imperial manhood. Torgovnick points out that the Tarzan books "gave enduring cultural life to the idea that civilizations in Africa were of white origin. They helped shape popular (mis)conceptions of Africa and its (non)past. In using the motif of the lost, white civilization, Burroughs inscribed and reinscribed a trope central to the imperialist enterprise he was in so many ways critical of."[74] While he usually advocated self-determination for other countries, Burroughs was criticized at home and abroad, by readers and editors alike, for his persistent xenophobia. Like his racism, his xenophobia was in part a product of the ambient white ethnic violence of the time. Harvey Green points out that "[f]ilmmakers produced scores of works with such titles as *The Claws of the Hun*, and the biggest industry stars—Mary Pickford and Douglas Fairbanks—toured the country to sell war bonds to their adoring fans."[75]

On the one hand, then, Weston's and Burroughs's credentials as male chauvinists and imperialists are incontrovertible. But in reading their letters it is important to keep at least two things in mind. First, their relationship to man-making international conflict was one of disappointment and failure (until Pearl Harbor—after which it remained vicarious for Weston). Second, and more significant, the shifting tone of their comments is key: they tease each other, are self-deprecatory, and alternate between the morose and the bubbly.[76] The possible meanings of their exchanges—and of any particular turn of phrase—are multifold when read through the fluidity of irony, parody, and seriousness ubiquitous in the correspondence. With his editors also, particularly Thomas Metcalf and Robert Davis at Munsey, Burroughs took a tone by turns tongue-in-cheek and sharply businesslike, suggestive of the openness to irony each man had to sustain while reading the other's text.

Weston, for example, feeling their age, reminded Burroughs in 1940 during a protracted, self-righteous exchange about national politics that "[c]onditions have so changed since the War I that old dobbers cant realize that these changes are really hear. Old Dobers want to go back to Old Times. That can never happen. So what the country needs is a man who has grown up and made a success under these New conditions."[77] Burroughs often recognized his tendency toward tunnel vision. A passage from a letter on international politics during World War II reveals the worst xenophobic and fascist tendencies in his reactionary thinking. Yet almost in the same breath, sensing his bombast (though not quite, perhaps, his hypocrisy), Burroughs systematically deconstructs his own authority, first by irony and then by recommending a text that will help Weston share his sense of a loss of authority:

> Having successfully disposed of most World problems which seem to be confusing all statesmen and other lesser minds, I now approach one of our own—the insidious boring from within by Communists, Fascists, and Nazis in this country. I should proclaim membership in any of these organizations high treason. I'd kick out all alien members by deportation without trial. I'd exile all American members who would not renounce their allegiance to these organizations and swear renewed allegiance to the United States, and I'd finger-print every one of them and put them on ten years probation, requiring them to report to some authority periodically. And I'd start in on the Reds in the Administration. I understand that there are over two thousand of them in key positions.
>
> Have you ever read Pitkin's A Short Introduction to the History of

Human Stupidity? [. . .] The one trouble with that book is that while it conclusively demonstrates the stupidity of every one else, it also convinces you of your own stupidity, which leaves you in something of a mental mess after expounding such gems of wisdom as this letter contains. [. . .] It is all very confusing and depressing.[78]

Self-undermining rhetorical maneuvers, emotional ups and downs, and swings from seriousness to jocularity and sometimes double entendre are the affective and rhetorical modes of these communications. It may be unfair to claim a final, transcendent stance for either Weston or Burroughs on race, ethnicity, or imperialism.[79]

As Kasson points out, the specter of internationalism held other challenges for men of the United States: "Above all, perceptions of manliness were drastically altered by the new dynamics created by vast corporate power and immense concentrations of wealth. Fundamental to traditional concepts of American manhood had been autonomy and independence, which had to be recast in a tightly integrated economy of national and international markets." Certainly Weston and Burroughs participated in what historians have called the developing "culture of professionalism" that gave shape to male public experience in the decades following Reconstruction. But while they belonged to that culture, their letters also trace out, implicitly, a critique of its valorization of systematicity and a man's place in it. And ultimately, both men sought ways of establishing themselves if not beyond capital, certainly beyond the corporate culture that appeared necessary to sustain it.[80]

Kasson emphasizes process in his discussion of early-twentieth-century manhood. The process of male transformation became significant at a time when masculinity had evolved fully into "being one's own man": there was no perfect man to imitate, because one could not simply follow models without being mocked. But there was a *way* of becoming a man that aspirants struggled to experience to a greater or lesser degree. Kasson points out that the appeal of early professional bodybuilder Eugen Sandow—who Burroughs and Weston probably saw perform in 1893 across the street from the Chicago Exposition—lay in the fact that he claimed to be "an original, a man who stood apart from the crowd."[81] Speaking of the end of Sandow's career, Kasson implies that this was, in a sense, the golden age of spectacular manhood: "From the lost world of manly strength and heroism, he sank into the modern world, where there were no longer originals, only copies." But that was just the beginning of a reconceptualization of spectacular manhood, a new mechanism of individuation at the highest levels of publicity. To imagine that the culture machine was thereafter incapable of making men in the modern world is to ignore the triumphs of self-promoters like Ernest Hemingway and F. Scott Fitzgerald, William Faulkner and Jackson Pollock, Muhammad Ali and the Kennedys. Certainly Burroughs felt this pressure to "sell" himself. Kasson goes on to argue that Burroughs's *Tarzan of the Apes* "gave powerful narrative force to a widespread sense that modern technological civilization created restrictions, frustrations, ordinariness that entailed special losses for men. Like Wister and London, Theodore Roosevelt and Frederick Jackson Turner . . . Burroughs celebrated untamed masculine individualism."[82] But we might ask how this story (read perhaps most often by boys) played out in the daily lives of men. The letters included here suggest that Burroughs was anything but untamed, and perhaps not even the individualist that he depicted Tarzan to be. Even Tarzan's metamorphosis, after all, involves taming: learning not to kill people, learning the right way to relate sexually to white women. This story was as interesting to young men of Weston's cohort as was its proffered release from ordinariness.

Returning to a key moment of taming for Weston—his time at Yale—offers an opportunity to watch him learning the logics of intimacy, male friendship, and subjective development. While at college, Weston continued to take photographs of himself and of his friends as he had at MMA. Three of these images seem particularly dense with meanings for manhood. In the first photograph (fig. 6), Weston stands in his room at Yale, showing off both his college accomplishments and associations (sword belt and sash from MMA to his right, Yale class of '98 pillow to his left) and his interior decoration skills. The room can be viewed as divided into two realms of individual experience based on four terms: on the left, work and family; on the right, leisure and public life. To Weston's right is his neat desk, complete with textbooks, ink and pen stands, visor, and ink rag. Above his desk are arranged a number of objects, including a calendar, several pictures of Weston's family, and a photo of his MMA football team. To his left are his bed and (barely visible) another wall display. This display includes a cascade of pictures of women—possibly acquaintances, but equally possibly actresses—terminated at the bottom by a picture of a man. Prominent on the wall, as mentioned earlier, is an elegantly framed reproduction of the famous White City image from the Chicago Columbian Exposition. Standing at the center of all of these things, figuring himself as in a sense the product of them, is Weston, whose filial devotion, hard work, high aims, and potential for reproductive heterosexuality are all on display in his room (and beyond, in this photograph) as much for his male companions at Yale as for his own contemplation.[83] The photograph itself constitutes evidence of Weston's willingness to perform his "self," both for posterity (including his own, post-Yale self) and for potential consumption through the circulation of the photograph. It is likely also that this room was shared by two students, and that Weston's corner was thus always on display.

The second of the three images is a silly combination of school-chum pride and domestic daintiness—formally, a mixture of the group portrait and still life genres (fig. 7). On the left, as in the previous image, is another Yale-pillow-covered bed. A mandolin, a symbol of fellowship, lies on the bed; in the right foreground are a chafing dish, tea setting, and warmer. Katherine Snyder has argued that cooking with the chafing dish—the fin-de-siècle equivalent of the microwave—was a locus of male companionship and performative domestic labor; its inclusion in this carefully composed image would have reinforced, for nineteenth-century viewers, the message of male fellowship encoded here.[84] The dressing-screen (also visible in fig. 8) acts as an enormous dress, making the men into one five-headed, rose-bedecked being. Once again, the labor of constructing a space that both expresses individual sensibility and enables companionate masculinity, a communal male Yaleness in this case, constitutes much of what is on display.

The third image can be read as a stunning literalization of the relationship among physical self-culture, companionship, and public manhood (fig. 8). Supporting the white-collar public man (with his watch fob and wool pants) is the sporting, physically fit athlete he could be during his leisure hours. But here, compensating for the fact that not all middle-class workingmen could claim this kind of fitness, is a suggestion that fitness as a shared ideal could be a resource for a community

6. Herbert T. Weston in his room at Yale, New Haven, Connecticut, circa 1897, photographer unknown. 7. Unidentified Yale students, New Haven, Connecticut, circa 1897, photographer unknown (probably Herbert T. Weston). *Both from the Weston Family Collection.*

8. Three unidentified Yale students,
New Haven, Connecticut, circa 1897, photographer
unknown (probably Herbert T. Weston).
Weston Family Collection.

of male friends. The hyperbolic "1000 lbs" that one friend can lift can be shared by all as an ideal physical capacity. Reading somewhat hyperbolically, in tune with the ludic mood of this image, we might say that we have here men embodying a Marxian base-superstructure model whose unifying premise is not capital but friendship—a kind of economic athleticism. The masculine, muscular ideal supports the notion of the public businessman, whereas in economic actuality the opposite relation holds sway.

Costume play in front of the camera did not end with graduation from Yale. Images from the reunions of the class of 1898 show the broader connections this masculine comradeship had with notions of imperial destiny and manly leadership. These photographs also suggest the way these notions could be constructed, perhaps paradoxically, by what might be considered a feminized performance. At their sexennial and decennial reunions this class of engineers and finance managers dressed up in costumes that borrowed a sense of masculine superiority and achievement from cultures implicated and subjugated by the imperial project of the United States (figs. 9 and 10).[85] Frederick Taylor Gause, the committee member assigned to write up the sexennial, described the orientalist gowns and parasols of that year: "They may not have been handsome, but at least they were loose, cool and effective. Effective, not only in looks, for they kept the Class well together. One felt ashamed to be seen alone in such garb."[86] "Loose, cool and effective"—like the ideal man? Gause here suggests, though in jest, the deeper power of this kind of ritual performance (one for which a photographer had been specifically hired) of individualism dissolved into fraternity: it promoted, even coerced into being, a physical unity that it had been designed only to represent to others. (Class here moves synecdochically as well, from uniting the small Class of '98 to keeping the middle class at large "well together.") Certainly some resistance to the exercise, suggesting the real effort it took to sell companionate manhood on this scale, is evident both in the prose recounting the stories of the reunions and in the body language and facial expressions of the men photographed. Yet the power of the spectacle to attract others to the "fold" is suggested in the ten-year reunion photo (fig. 10) both by the larger group of reunionists and by the many non-Yale men (and women) at the margins of the image, writing themselves into the record alongside the play-Mexican '98s.

The associations of exercise, education, and professionalism in these images evoke Dana Nelson's argument that national manhood substituted self-discipline for its promise of fraternalism:

> The federal plan offered men a reassuring unity in the brotherly exercise of rational managerial authority. But the precondition for the white man's authorization as a civic manager would be his ability to model the ideal of national unity in his own person: to train his own self-difference into a rationally ordered singularity. [. . .] Rather than conceptualizing (equalizing) friendships between men as a model for democracy, national manhood embodied democracy *in* the competitive, self-subordinating individual.[87]

When we look at actual peoples' enactment (and in this case recording) of fellowship, we see that *local* manhood—here both the diachronic, imagined-as-eternal "Yale man" and the specific, synchronic version of

9. Yale class of 1898 sexennial reunion photo, New Haven, Connecticut, 1904, photographer unknown. 10. Yale class of 1898 decennial reunion photo, New Haven, Connecticut, 1908, photographer unknown. From the *Decennial Record of the Class of 1898, Sheffield Scientific School*, comp. Joseph W. Alsop (New Haven: Tuttle, Morehouse and Taylor, 1908).

it enacted by the class of '98—powerfully shaped the ways in which men performed their masculinity. Late in the nineteenth century, national manhood had adapted to conceptualize friendships as a model for democracy, even if agency (responsibility that one could claim, or tout) was ultimately to be embodied in a single person. It is this complicated spectrum of national ideality and real emotional hailing that confronted men like Weston and Burroughs as they were entering positions of economic and cultural authority.

As they aged, things changed. Most of the correspondence remaining from the Weston collection is from the men's middle and old age. They were still extremely mobile and active during these years—in 1926, when he was fifty, Weston estimated that he and his wife spent eleven weeks away from home, which he considered a low number. The Burroughses were famously peripatetic, even after Ed's divorce and remarriage. Moreover, and more interesting for the increasingly complex study of ageism and critical gerontology, is the fact that from the earliest letters on, a collaborative hyperbolization of aging characterizes the men's friendship—not merely as a response to their being slightly too old to fight in World War I, but as a sustained mechanism of creating common interests and identification: in a 1918 letter, for example, Burroughs writes: "I think it would be a very nice thing, Bert, for you and I, now that we have reached old age, to settle down together for our last few days in a spot not too far removed from the Los Angeles Athletic Club and where we might also have our saddle horses and the other things that appeal to us in common."[88]

These men experienced firsthand what historians have described as the transition to a heterosocial model of public sociability in which middle-class families began to consider mixed-sex social gatherings the norm. Burroughs and Weston retained, however, a strong sense of homosocial commitment, gendered behavioral ideals, and a valuation of themselves based on their own economic competitiveness. As the passage just quoted shows, they talked about moving to the West together, setting up adjacent ranches, hiring someone to teach their children—a homosocial western romance. A generous portion of their emotional well-being was sustained by mutual contemplation of the future and a desire for sustained male sociality. Kevin White argues that in the early twentieth century the "presentation of self became vital in an arena where peers determined among themselves what constituted valued masculinity."[89] In order to construct themselves, men needed not only corporate masculinities but local ones as well, shaped less within the family than in male emotional society—either face-to-face or mediated by communications technologies.[90]

For much of his life, even into old age, Weston was fascinated by people who had some kind of agency that he lacked. His relationships with women often threw this into relief. The letters reproduced here explore at some length his relationship with Margaret and her social and economic power, but a minor moment in a letter from 1933 dramatizes his dilemma as it was provoked in an otherwise leisurely social encounter. Never a good gambler and struggling to learn the family's new favorite game, Contract Bridge ("I continue to refuse to attempt Contract," he wrote in a 1930 letter), Weston finds a mentor:

> We have a married old maid in this village who has seriously taken this so-called Contract, in the last two years. And this barren matron has learned it!
>
> I have had just one seance with her, and she opened up a vision to me that I did not know even existed before! [. . .]
>
> She eased into me, not that she had any idea of what these things are, that Modern Contract, is simply a matter of Combinations and Permutations, just simple mathematics!
>
> I checked this natural born school-teacher, and, after five hours of various hands, I found she was never off more than one (1) trick, and that her well-learned Combinations and Permutations were right, to a gnat's eye brow.

As exclamation succeeds exclamation, Weston's amazement at the "natural born" mathematical skills of a "barren matron" gains paradoxical weight. Evident elsewhere in the correspondence, particularly in the discussions of Tarzan, is Weston's awe of Burroughs's creativity, his "spark." Weston here finds himself in a state of Darwinian envy, caught between the old maid who has decoded Contract (which he has been unable to do and so has refused to play) and Burroughs, whose creativity seems an equally "natural" resource. Weston cannot be coldly logical, but he cannot freewheel either, cannot make people happy regardless of the cost—a hesitation made clear elsewhere in the same letter when

Weston explains his refusal to visit California that year (1933): "If we went to SoCalif, as we would like to," he reports, "I know d——d well, that Margt's soft heart, and my none too sound trustee-ship, would weaken, and it would cost her plenty, to help our poor busted friends in SoCalif.!"[91]

In Burroughs's case, ironically, it may have been in the 1923 founding of Edgar Rice Burroughs, Inc. (when he was forty-eight), that he found the best expression of the innovative manhood that seemed requisite. If Weston was searching for natural resources, Burroughs equally struggled with discipline and playfulness. Neither the order of the army nor that of the "grasping and soulless corporation" answered his imagination of himself.[92] Burroughs knew that the businessman's masculinity was a charade, a construction; in his unpublished autobiography he writes that while "Stace-Burroughs Company was flourishing we were doing considerable advertising in magazines, many of which were the all-fiction variety, possibly because our brand of advertising might come under that designation."[93] That he went on to incorporate himself was in a sense the apotheosis of this self-making: the corporation, after all, is a kind of fictionalized individual with metaphorical "interests" but real assets. Burroughs could not convince himself that he was a "man" by what he thought of as unique yet recognizable terms until he had made Edgar Rice Burroughs into ERB, Inc.[94]

Burroughs's fictions had very real consequences in national and international politics; certainly fictional, juridical, and legislative representations exist in a mutually constructing circuit. But to push humans to imagine better, more sympathetic selves, we have to reveal and explain the processes by which men have come to live with their asymmetrical power, how they justify to themselves the inequalities they see in the world around them. Burroughs was *selling* one version of masculinity, a primitive one, which he framed in an exaggerated, fictional form; he declared no intention of reconciling it with or making it a model for actual men or boys. He lived by another, negotiated manhood, in which, until he had made his own way in the sense both of achieving economic independence *and* of taking what control of the means of literary production he could—legally by incorporation and domestically by purchasing a ranch that ultimately produced cultural, not agricultural products—he did not feel at home. Burroughs rejected the discourses of high literature or modernism and made literal (or at least legal) his status of author as a producer of goods for the marketplace by incorporation.[95] But this self-incorporation emblematized the dilemmas of manhood as much as it represented one man's solution.

Tarzan lovers will recognize the title of this book as coming from chapter 23 of *Tarzan of the Apes*, in which Tarzan and Paul D'Arnot write messages to one another. The phrase "Brother Men" captures a popular fiction of manhood, a national fictive kinship of men who are imaginary brothers, suspending their individual identities in ways both conscious and unknowing. The story as we have received it from historians is that American men took strenuous individualism and phantasmic brotherly citizenship as their models for manhood, and that these self-images, catalyzed by imperial greed, violence, and racism, were the fundamental ingredients of an irresistible gender-potion. But perhaps we can imagine a "corresponding" image of male association. The formulation of "side-partners" speaks to a more local—a more intimate and performative—communion of interests, a sphere characterized by the emotional assurance needed to ensure frank arguments about and negotiations of both familial and political questions. It raises too, in the multiple meanings of "partners," the fluidity of economic and emotional relationships, persisting into the age of long-distance synchronous communication and the nuclear middle-class family.

This introduction is at most a prelude. The correspondence reprinted here is a rich resource that offers mystery enough for a wide range of inquiries—about visual culture and media technologies, consumerism, the history of the family, the history of authorship and readership, the development of the West, and the development of Nebraska and California, among many others. Fans of Burroughs and students of history and representation alike will see much in what follows that is invisible to me. But merely from the standpoint of airing the archive, much more work is needed; the textual and visual richness of this collection is the tip of the iceberg. Other parts of Burroughs's vast correspondence and the multimedia panorama of his representations, when brought to light, will show that Tarzan was only one small part of Burroughs's negotiation of modern culture.

Note on the Text

Readers will notice that I have preserved spelling and typographical errors, underlining, and marginal comments. After 1926, Burroughs dictated most of his letters and got considerable help with spelling from his secretaries (whose initialed signatures have likewise been preserved). Weston, on the other hand, wrote or typed all of his letters himself, expressively manipulating spelling, usage, and formatting, fiddling with capitalization and punctuation, in many ways approximating the "emoticons" of today's email and instant messaging communications. This makes it difficult not merely to say precisely when he has made a spelling error but what in fact would *constitute* a spelling error. In the interest of retaining the most fertile interpretive possibilities, I have left Weston's spelling and punctuation irregularities, probably much to the chagrin of my copyeditor. When even the superficial meaning is obscured and it appears that a typographical error is involved, I suggest the most likely reading in a footnote. Italics have not been added to titles of books or radio programs mentioned in the letters.

That being said, some textual features are not preserved here. To improve readability and avoid distracting the reader I have standardized the format of the letters so that letterhead, location, and date appear in the upper right; paragraphs are indented; and so on. Notations of typewritten overstrike corrections as well as crossed-out corrections — handwritten or typewritten — have been removed unless they were very obviously related to the contents of the letters. Page numbering has been excluded. Although Burroughs persistently underlined the word *and* in his handwritten letters, that underlining does not appear here. Casual spacing and spacing errors have not been preserved unless they are characteristically expressive. Weston, for example, always concatenates the phrase "of course," and often concatenates ones like "how in hell" as well; these usages have been preserved.

Finally, since both men kept carbons of their letters, there are, strictly speaking, two versions of most of the letters—the carbon in the collection of one author and the sent letter, which may have corrections or postscripts added, in the collection of the other. When the record is relatively complete, responses by the men to each other's letters suggest that such corrections were slight, and postscripts infrequent or short. Still, since there is no such thing as a definitive re-presentation of such a correspondence, it is best to indicate this limitation and more broadly to point out that since the men kept these carbons for their records, in fact *both* versions were authoritative because each, sender or recipient, regarded his copy as equally significant.

Correspondence

[Letterhead: Sweetser-Burroughs Mining Co.,
Geo. T. Burroughs, Jr., Pres., Walter S. Sparks, Vice-Pres.,
Lewis H. Sweetser, Sec'y., Henry S. Burroughs, Treas., Minidoka, Idaho]
Parma, Idaho
Dec 30 1903[1]

My Dear Bert;—

We wish to thank you and Margaret for the lovely bug you sent us, but why, O why, did Margaret blast my fond dream by writing to Emma and calling it "that ugly dragon"?[2] We thought it was an "antique" and I have been pointing it out with pride to all my friends and allowing as how they might now perceive a real antique, they having lived in the sage brush all their lives and not had an opportunity to mingle with the elite and learn how to furnish their homes from a second hand store.

But, though our joy and pride is some what disfigured by Margaret's letter we still feel that the Gila monster means much to us for it tells us that we were in your Christmas thoughts and so among the favored possessors of your friendship. Anyway the worm holds the honored position at the feet of Emma's Japanese devil with the dinner bells. Wishing you both the happiest and most prosperous of New Years and hoping that the grasping and soulless corporation will give you passes via Parmie, we are,

Your very good friends,
Emma and Ed.

March 22 1906

My dear Bert ————————

Why, but you're careless. Who would ever have thought it! And you always used to be so orderly, Bertram — just look at the mess you've made now! I am very thankful that $\underline{2}$ am neat.

TO YELL TO YALE TO HELL

Anyhow, Emma and I are awful glad and envy you both a whole lot. Of course we are young yet.

I certainly do remember Tom Wood. Lord Godfrey,

11. Edgar Rice Burroughs to Herbert T. Weston, 22 March 1906.
Weston Family Collection.

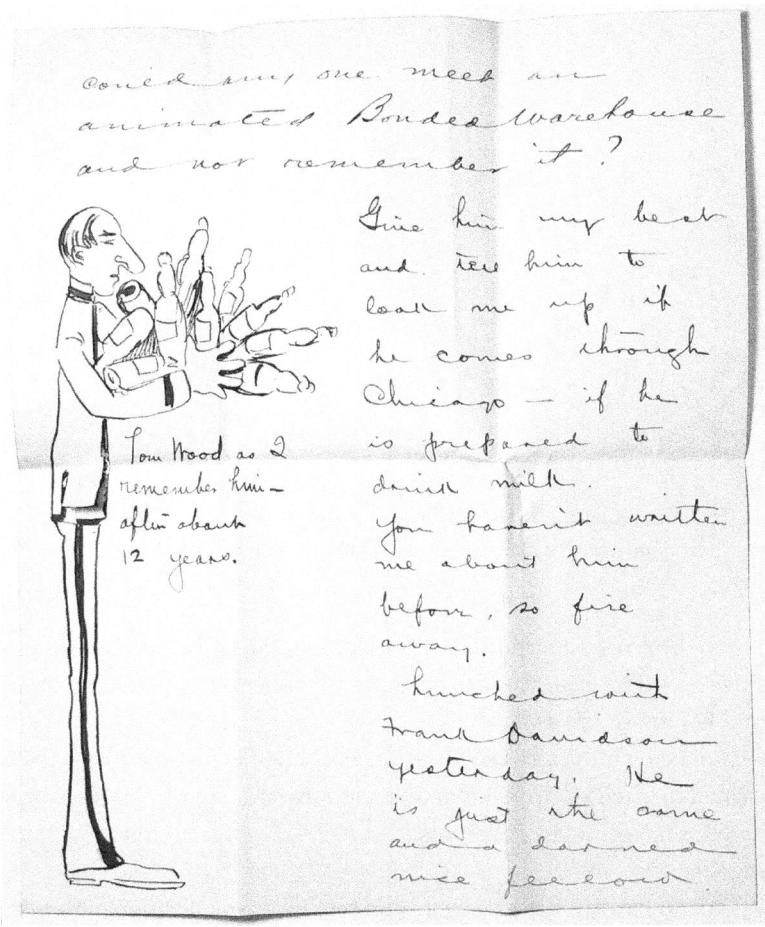

12. Burroughs to Weston, 22 March 1906. *Weston Family Collection.*

March 22 1906

My dear Bert—

My, but you're careless. Who would ever have thought it! And you always used to be so orderly, Bertram—just look at the muss you've made now! I am very thankful that I am neat. Anyhow, Emma and I are awful glad and envy you both a whole lot. Of course we are young yet.[3]

I certainly do remember Tom Wood. Lord Godfrey, could any one meet an animated Bonded Warehouse and not remember it?

13. Emma Burroughs and Edgar Rice Burroughs to the Weston Family,
postcard, 23 December 1907. *Weston Family Collection.*

Give him my best and tell him to look me up if he comes through
Chicago — if he is prepared to drink milk. You haven't written me about
him before, so fire away.

Lunched with Frank Davidson yesterday. He is just the same and a
darned nice fellow. We eat together about twice a month. Frank is running his father-in-law's business J. H. Bell & Co.; Tea, Coffee, and Spice
merchants.

I am embarrassed at your question relative to my position with E. S.
Winslow Co. However, I am constrained to remark that I am Office Boy.
Will send you a bunch of literature tomorrow <u>and</u> can say that we have
the <u>only real thing</u> in our line.

If you will forgive me for this letter I will write you again.

Shall I send you a pair of ferrets?

Ed

[Written vertically down the left side] Emma joins me in love to Margaret, yourself and John Alexander Dowie Weston.

Uncertainty as to the movements of a certain stock has decided Santa Claus to remain where he is for an indefinite period. We are therefore sending you only our best wishes for A Merry Christmas and A Happy New Year

A poor excuse is better than none

Emma & Ed

[Letterhead: BURROUGHS . . .
82 Sherman Street, Chicago, Illinois]
March 12 1908

My dear Bert:

We were tickled to death to get your telegram today.[4] Glad it is a girl. Nothing like girls anyway. Anyone can have boys. Hope everything goes as well as it did when Collins came and that the little girl is just as good looking (how could she help being) and just as healthy.

Was the baby born on the 12th? If she was it was just two months to a day from JOAN's birth. JOAN is a son-of-gun, she is THE BOSS of the ranch. She is spoiled, ruined, curdled. But what do we care. We are proud of it.

If you have time to run on here for a week I can tell you several things about babies. Several more things than I could have told you two months ago and even then I was a wiz on babes. I know more about babies than the man who invented them. I can tell a baby where ever I see one. No one can fool me. I am getting so that I stop and inspect every baby I see on the street. I can tell how old they are without looking at their teeth. Many mothers with large families are coming to me for advice. So are fathers without any families.

Dont wait eight years before you write. Emma wants details.

She hasn't had time to get down town yet to buy Jane an auto but hopes to this week.

She joins me in the best ever to the whole Weston family.

Yours,

Ed.

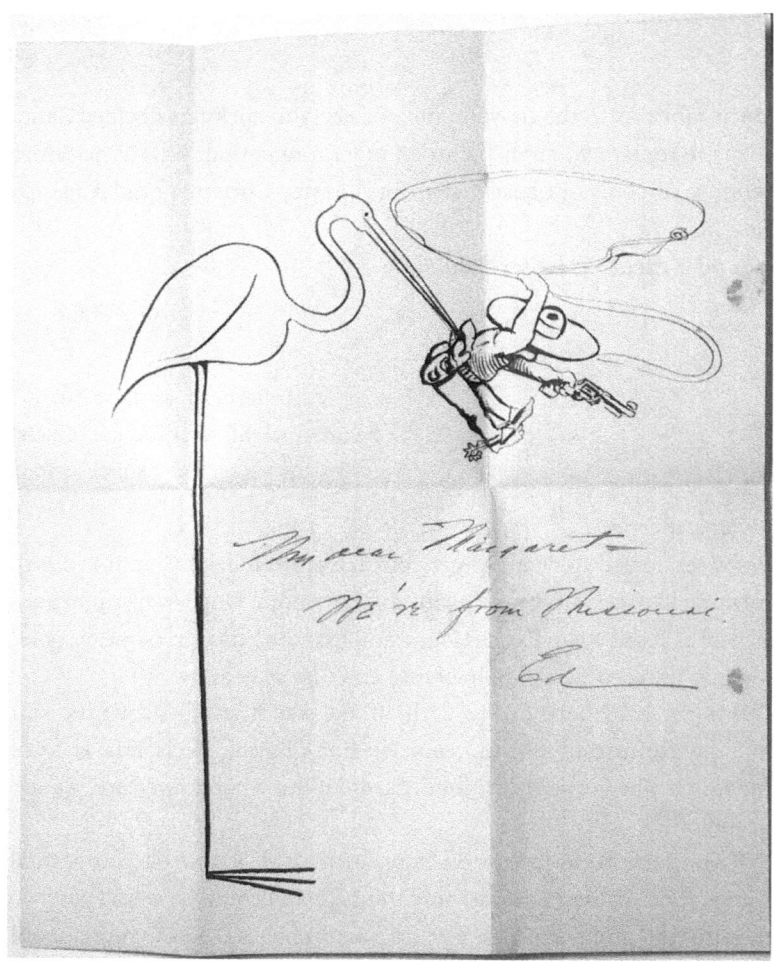

14. "My dear Margaret—We're from Missouri. Ed." Edgar Rice Burroughs to Margaret Weston, 29 March 1908. *Weston Family Collection.*

194 Park Ave.

Chicago, Ill.

March 29 1908.

Dear Bert:

Sure I change Joan. If you dont know how to do it I will tell you. Insert eight safety pins in your face, grasp infant firmly by hind legs, place three cornered piece of cloth beneath stage entrance, put on shoe that has fallen off during scuffle, grasp one end of one corner of didy with teeth unoccupied by safety pins, take the other two corners in one hand, drop them and put on the other shoe, do it all over again, in the mean time say goo-goo and giggle-goggle. After pinning all securely feel of baby. You will find her wet again by this time and should immediately commence to change her again. Repeat.

If you require any further information on this subject, wire me. I am very full of information on this subject. In fact I know more than most old maids.

Did we tell you that we are taking a house across the street from here? Next time you come though, if you dont come too soon, we will be able to give you a place to roost so that you wont have to go to the Grand Pacific. *[Margin insert in ERB's handwriting: "It has burned down."]* We are going in slowly and hope to be set by Fall. Have some hard wood floors to lay and seven dollars worth of furniture to buy and then we should like to have you come and call.

I have nothing to say this time as I drained myself the other day. Will send you a copy of a scientific article I wrote on babies. Cant send it now as I have to make another copy first.

Emma, JOAN, Rajah and the canaries join me in love to you, Margaret, Collins, JANE and the collie.[5]

Yours,
Ed.

6415 Augusta Street, Oak Park, Ill.
June 24 1914

Dear Bert:
Found your letter about Margaret passing though here, on my return from New York this morning. So when you write tell her how it was that I didn't come to the train to see her. You might also mention that as you didn't mail your letter of advice until 5:30 PM Friday there wasn't such a hell of a swell chance of my getting it in time anyhow. It came Monday, after I had left for the train.

No, Bertie, it aint a toupee—it's just the elevation. Now a southern exposure would have been something else again.[6]

I am glad that Collins likes the story. I always kind of felt that your children would be real bright, Margaret has such a good head.[7]

Had a nice letter from General Charles King to-day.[8] I have always kept in touch with him, and as I love him just as I did as a kid I sent him a copy of Tarzan. When you are here on that visit you promise don't let me forget to show you his letter. It will be right beside one Weston's among my Pet little treasures.

Tell Margaret that I had no grouch — I was merely attempting to look intelligent.

Speaking of pictures. When I met Robt. H. Davis of Munsey's in N.Y. yesterday about the first thing he said to me was: "For God's sake send The World another picture of yourself — that thing they are running makes you look like ——".[9] I didn't catch the last word; but, thinks I, if its that bad it must be awrful.

We cannot believe that you really contemplate stopping off to see us. It seems too gosh dinged good to be true. If you disappoint us this time I shall can your memory hermetically. And make it more than one day — you can certainly spare us more than that. Let us know a little way ahead, as we are figuring on doing a few short touring stunts and don't want to be away when you are due.

Sunday we are going to drive up to Coldwater, Michigan, where a couple of Emma's sisters live. Shall be there about a week.

You wont have to sleep with the dog, and as the baby sleeps with Emma there is nothing left but my bed, which you will find quite comfortable until Joan and Hulbert wake across the hall about 5 AM[10]

Emma joins me in love to you all,

Ed

1020 North Boulevard, Oak Park, Ill.
June 22, 1918

H. T. Weston, Esq., Beatrice, Neb.

Dear Bert: —
I was mighty sorry to learn from your letter received today that Margaret is afflicted with neuritis. It is a mighty painful disease as I know

from seven years experience with it.[11] I am pretty well shut of it now and it may interest you to know that my improvement immediately followed the taking of a medicine which I obtained while in Coldwater the 1st of March.

I do not take much stock in patent medicines but after a fellow has had neuritis for seven years he would take almost anything to be rid of it. — I even tried Christian Science once. — This dope which I obtained is put up by a druggist in Coldwater from a prescription given to one of the Coldwater plutes[12] by a traveling salesman — but where the traveling salesman got the prescription, deponent sayeth not. Anyhow, it cost one and one half bucks per bottle and is absolutely guaranteed to be harmless. Dr. Earle pooh-poohs the idea that it helped me and so do I; however it was a remarkable coincidence that immediately after commencing to take it the pain left me for the first time in years and I have been steadily improving since. To show what a narrow minded chump a man can be, I quit taking it because they doubled the price . . .

[page 2 missing]

saved the little fellow's life. I would not have had it happen for anything as all the dogs in the World are not worth such an accident as this. Emma and the children are so attached to Tarzan and Emma feels so safe when I am away evenings if she has Tarzan with her, that unless I am forced to, I shall not get rid of him, but I am keeping him strongly muzzled or chained up all the time when he is out.[13]

I wish that we could have some of your heat here. While we have had some hot days, the weather had been what most people would call delightful although too cool for me. Just as soon as the Home Guard have defeated Germany, I am going to beat it for Los Angeles or preferably the center of the Mojave Desert.[14] Next to Yuma, The Needles is one of the nicest places in the World, the temperature never falling below three or four hundred degrees in the shade.

With love to Margaret and the rest of you in which Emma and the children join, I am,

Yours,

Ed

Mr. H. P. Weston, Beatrice, Nebr.

Dear Bert:—

I found yours of the 16th on my return from two weeks at the civilian's training camp at Geneva Lake and yesterday I autographed a set of Tarzan books at McClurg's and told them to ship them to Miss Jones.

Inasmuch as you are so hectic to pay for them, I will send you the bill as soon as I receive it, or at least the amount of it as since I get a discount, I will have to pay it personally. I have already donated many books to the camp libraries and as you suggest, it would be considerable of a burden to continue the practice at my own expense to any considerable extent although I should be very glad indeed to do so, and therefore I thank you for your offer to help me out on this lot.

I put in a very interesting and profitable two weeks at Camp Steever and have at least brought back to my Company a new spirit and considerable more pep than I had before, for I must admit that I was growing rather stale with no new methods or plans for training.[15]

We expect to drive up there again next week as I wish to see the Battalion from the outside. Immediately following our camp, a new bunch of men came in and by the middle of next week they ought to be in fairly good shape for observation.

We have not been away much this Summer. Spent ten days at Coldwater which will probably be the limit of our outings for pleasure and now that the fuel administration has asked us not to use our cars on Sundays, we wont even get our little week-end ride which we shall all miss. However, it is a very small thing to give up for the cause and if it is necessary, I am personally very glad to forego even more than that.

I have a bunch of mail to answer and Emma is due in ten minutes to take me down town so I will have to close with love to all in which Emma and the children would join were they here.

Yours,

Ed

Mr. H. T. Weston, Beatrice, Nebraska.

Dear Bert:—

Was glad to read what Miss Jones said about the Tarzan stories, also to know that Margaret caught you keeping the boys up so late at night.

What with backing her new car into the neighbors' front yards and losing the family jewels I am inclined to think that Margaret Medorah is slipping.[16] Of course it can't be old age; but if I were in her place I should watch my step.

Speaking of rain, I wish we could swap climates with you. We are getting our November rains now and at present are in the midst of one which looks very much like an all-day proposition.

Tomorrow we are planning on driving to Geneva Lake and Camp Steever as I wish to see the Battalion from the outside which was impossible while I was in it myself. I spent two weeks there, from August 12th to 26th with six other men from my Company. There were eight of us in a tent, all Oak Park men and we had a mighty fine time. They worked us pretty hard and there were periods during which my old joints refused to function, especially after they had kept us up half the night for field maneuvers and trench work.

Not being able to dress in three minutes, I always took advantage of the permission granted swimmers to turn out for the Reveille formation in bathingsuits and after five or ten minutes of setting-up exercises, took a plunge in the lake. This and the afternoon swim were the greatest pleasures of the camp.

Geneva is a deep, clear-water lake. The water is never warm and the swimming is fine. It is one of the deepest lakes of its size in the country and goes right off within a few feet of the shore into deep water. At one place Government soundings show it to be 1027 ft. deep but I did not go down to verify the report.

I derived considerable benefit from the training, especially in the matter of the new spirit of military instruction. I believe three months intensive training in an officer's training camp would make me a regular guy again as I feel that I was after my five years at Orchard Lake.[17]

I notice in the new draft law that bald headed men with three children are to be put into A-1 class so I suppose you and I will soon be in the front line trenches.[18]

Harry's wife and daughter are being examined on an average of once every six days for over-seas service with the Red Cross or Y.M.C.A., or Knights of Columbus or something, I have forgotten which.[19] Every time they pass one examination they are sent along up to some superior she-officer who re-examines them, evidently not taking the word of inferiors as to their fitness. They have both been doing canteen work for a long time and Nellie stands very high indeed with the powers that be who are familiar with her work. She is peculiarly adapted to that part of it which brings her into contact with the boys as she is wonderfully sweet and motherly in her way. Evelyn has completed the course for over-seas long distance telephony and has become a fluent French conversationalist. I shall be very proud indeed when two of the lady members of the family are at the front and the men here in America.

You ask about my various addresses. 1020 North Blvd. is my office address where I now maintain more or less regular office hours from 9:00 to 5:30.

My best love to Margaret and the boys in which Emma and the children join, and my sincerest sympathy for you for being so damned old and decrepit that you cannot fight for your country.

Yours,

Ed

First Battalion, Second Infantry, Illinois Reserve Militia
1020 North Boulevard, Oak Park, Ill.
October 12, 1918

Mr. H. T. Weston, Beatrice, Nebraska.

Dear Bert: —

Inclosed is a clipping I received yesterday from Frank Davidson which I thought might interest you as you doubtless remember Naylor who I think was in the band at Orchard Lake. You need not return the clipping.

I hope you are all well and that the Flu has not found any of you yet.[20]

Hulbert has been in bed for two or three days with some of the symptoms but if he has Spanish Influenza it is a very light case. The other children so far have escaped it. Emma has had a sore throat for several days but no temperature and she is getting the upper hand of her throat now.

Did Miss Jones send you a copy of the camp paper recording your gift to the library? I have not yet received an itemized statement from McClurg's for these books so could not tell you what they cost but please lose no sleep over it for as soon as I find out I will hasten to comply with your wishes.

It may interest Margaret Medora to know that I am now a major (in the Home Guard.) Today I have to ride a truck horse in a Liberty Loan parade downtown. I never hear of one of these parades without recalling the Labor Day parades of past years when the Grand Marshal of the Ancient Order of Hod Carriers rode a brewery wagon horse and wore rubber boots. That is just the way I shall feel today. I suppose the stable that furnishes the officers mounts will pass me out some frightful looking skate.

I bought the children a pony a week or ten days ago and since Hulbert has been sick I have been exercising her. She is a little polo pony, a mighty nice little animal, a five-year-old and as kind and sweet-tempered as a kitten. Joan, Hulbert and Jack have been taking riding lessons and have done very well but Joan lacks the nerve to ride on the street alone and Jack is too small. I have a horse or should have one on the way from Wyoming and when he comes I expect to derive a great deal of pleasure as well as physical benefit from riding with the children. Emma is going to take lessons also and pretty soon we will junk the automobiles and all ride horse back which would be a darned sight better for our health and much less wasteful of gasoline.

Love to all in which Emma and the children join,

Yours,

Ed

[Letterhead: Nebraska Corn Mills Incorporated,
Exclusive Corn Millers, Lincoln, Nebraska]
Beatrice, Nebr.
10/22/18

Dear Ed;

Major, I salute you!!! And a good little major I'll bet you are, and it is a doggoned pity you are not majoring over in Flanders where you'd be a credit to yourself, tribe and country, and not merely herding the "Park Ave Rifles" around.

Yes, Mary L Jones, did send me the paper with all about you and Tarzan, and everything. I barely glanced at it myself, was called away, and when I got back the paper was GONE, and never was seen again. This was when the Collinses were here, and I did not dare to start anything.[21] I'm sorry. All I read was the inscriptions you had written, which I thought well of.

Herewith, from the last Digest, which you may have seen. I congratulate you, and believe me I would feel mighty good in your place.

I am sorry to hear that Hulbert had even a light case of the Flu. Hope all the rest of you avoided it entirely. So far we all have (I whistled and tapped wood then!) and are all in fine shape, but one can t tell a doggoned thing about there that accursed malady will hit. Everything is shut up tight here, schools, curches, movies, everything. That may help, and we are mighty glad to have the boys out of school, but the disease seems to be raging anyway.

I remember Naylor very well. Did not know he went into the Service. What ever became of your much-admired-one Tyner? He ought to be a general or something.

I'm classified; Serial No484, Class G-1. I suppose that is as close as I'll ever get to the Service.[22]

Do you think the filthy hun is going to lie down and make a quick and complete surrender? Or is he going to have to take a complete and thorough licking? What is your guess?

Yours,
[HTW]

1020 North Boulevard, Oak Park, Ill.

October 22, 1918

Dear Bert:—

I inclose memorandum of books sent to Camp Kearney as per your request.

Why don't you write?

Yours,

Ed

Incl.

[A book list, handwritten on ERB's office letterhead, was enclosed.]

Memorandum:

1 Tarzan of the Apes	50
1 Son of Tarzan	78
1 Return of Tarzan	50
1 Beasts of Tarzan	50
1 Tarzan & the Jewels of Opar	81
Express Charges	45
	3.54

IF ATTACHED TO REMITTANCE NO RECEIPT DESIRED.

10/24/19 [23]

Dear Ed;

This hour has arrived the Bill for the Books, for which I thank you, and for which I send Chi Draft. Also please to bear in mind when the financial burden gets too heavy for you, I'd like to help out of further placing of this Tarzan stuff where it will do the most good.

As there was nothing but the statement, I trust that that young Hulbert is over his "cold" and that none of you have experienced anything resembling the Flu. No Weston as yet shows any symptom—for which we than God, but keep our powder dry. The best way, I judge, is not to get it at all. I also whistle and rap on wood everytime I tell anyone we have it not, because it seems to just light anywhere, irrespective of rank, disposition, or preventative measures, and whenever I get home I look all four over carefully for symptoms.

I was a good deal delighted with Wilson's letter to the kais this morning.[24] I detected no symptom of a weasel-word in that communication. It seemed straight. I can see where there is small chance for further stalling on the part of Solf, or whoever is on the other end of the line. Looks like either complete surrender, or fight.

I trust I am utterly wrong, but my guess is that the damned prussian will fight on till the army is destroyed, and then I think the civil population will snipe, and poison wells, etc.etc. You see for half a century those square heads have had it dinged and drilled into them for 23 out of every 24 hours, that the kais is IT, that the kais and nothing but the kais amounts toadamn. And it has taken—they are a low order anyway, and that sort of stuff is duck-soup for them, and they have lapped it up to such an extent that to the average german, the kais is more to him than his religion, than his family—even than himself.

I credit the kais and his gang with a certain degree of intelligence. Anyone with an ounce of intelligence now knows that the vanishing from the face of the earth of the Hollerzollern Hapsburg idea is as sure and certain as the change of the seasons. The kais and gang know they are gone coons, and for that very reason they will fight on. They know that just as soon as the Allies commence to take charge of things in the dear ole papaland that the status of kais & co will be exactly the same as that of a buck-nigger in Mississippi who has outraged a white female.[25] Therefore they will sacrifice the last man and the last mark to put of this, for them, evil day. And 80% of those wooden headed people will back them up. Turkey will fall, Austria may drop by the way-side, but Prussia fights misguidedly to the last man—and for why? Simply to protect the Prrusian military autocrats from being treated by an outraged world as the common criminals which they have proven themselves to be a thousand times over!

Damn the kaiser!!!!

How do you get along on the livery horse leading the Bond parade?

Yrs
[HTW]

1020 North Boulevard, Oak Park, Ill.

October 25, 1918

Mr. H. T. Weston, Beatrice, Nebr.

Dear Bert:—

Thanks for yours of the 22nd. Am glad you have escaped the Flu. Joan complains of a sore throat today but has no temperature and is up and around the house. The others are all well.

Thank you for the clipping from the Literary Digest. I knew about this some time since and also that the librarians being purely high-brow have not heretofore admitted that anybody wished to read fiction. That article in the Daily News has done me a lot of good in a business way and insures a continued demand for my stories. I wish, however, that about twenty million people would fall for my Martian stories, too. Then I would not have to worry for another four or five years.

Serial No. 484, Class G-1. You must be a regular guy. I did not know there were any classifications as far away from the front as G. If they put me in that class, I should go down and jump in the lake.

It looks very much as though the filthy Hun would have to lie down and surrender within the next six months but I think he will only do it after a complete and thorough licking unless a gleam of intelligence manifests itself among the German people to the end that they rise up in their wrath and massacre the entire darned military class.

Love to all in which Emma joins,

Yours,

Ed

1020 North Boulevard, Oak Park, Ill.

October 26, 1918

Mr. H. T. Weston, Beatrice, Nebr.

Dear Bert:—

Yours with draft inclosed received. Many thanks. I note your offer to pay for other books for soldiers and if the need arises, I shall be very glad to call on you.

No, we are all free of any Flu symtoms at the present time. The weather is abominable just now, having been raining or threatening to rain for the past three days. I do not know what effect it has had on the epidemic conditions but I imagine it would increase the number of pneumonia cases and fatalities.

If you were delighted with Wilson's letter to the Kaiser, what do you think of his appeal to the American people to vote the Democratic ticket? They could stand me up against a stone wall in the morning for what I think about it.

Anent that livery horse, I had my worry all for nothing. As a matter of fact, I rode about the only real horse in the parade and there were several hundreds of them. A North Shore riding master let me take one of his star performers, a prize winning jumper nearly sixteen hands high and beautiful to look upon. He elicited applause all along the line of march for he certainly was a beauty. And now said riding master wishes to sell him to me for 600 bucks. I almost fell for it but not quite.

As I have to beat it down town in about three minutes, I will close, with best to you all,

Yours,

Ed

1020 North Boulevard, Oak Park, Ill.
December 5, 1918

Mr. H. T. Weston, Beatrice, Nebr.

Dear Bert: —

What has become of you? Emma suggests that you have gone to California for the Winter. I hope that such is the case as it is very possible that we shall be there ourselves in the course of a few months. We are going to try to find a ranch somewhere near Los Angeles where I expect to give up the prosaic vocation of writing fiction for the more romantic one of raising swine.

I wish you would write and let me know how you all are and if you really have gone to California as you spoke of last year.

Emma is laid up with something akin to grippe, being her second attack this Fall. It doesn't seem to be anything serious, nor was the first attack. Jack and Hulbert each had the same thing some time ago but so far Joan and I have escaped.

With love to you all in which Emma and the children join, I am,

Yours,

Ed

December 7th 1918

Dear Ed:

Promptness is its own reward. I have just had yours and hasten to reply.

No — we are not in Calif., nor are we thinking of going there anywhere soon. If you locate on your hog-ranch, we will come and visit you next summer, arriving early in same summer, or about when school is "out".

For your private information — the real reason we are not in Calif right now, is because the bottom has fallen out of the corn milling business.[26] That and because, when the grand-pas commenced to be drafted, I, being in class 1, finally got permish to apply, and expected to go to Camp Taylor up till the 11th of Nov. At that date the Flu was upon us so strong that anyone with a family of more than two would have been a phoole to attempt travel.

Except for the above things, we were certainly going to Calif. Now we sort'o think we will hit for there just as soon as the boys are out of school. Try to try it for a year. If we like it we may stay there, but some-way, I do not think, or rather I do think, that one born and brought up in this accursed Nebraska climate, where there are greater extremes of temperature than any other place in the world, there the wind blows more and harder, and where there are fewer days that are livable — I suspect that year in and year out Calif. with its perfection, would pall on meh. Besides, Calif is an old mans paradise, and I'm not an old man — except in my appearance. Reference; Margaret!!

Collins had the Flu. So the MD said. I have seen him sick in exactly the same way with a plain pure bilious attack. However, this vicinity is simply rotten with flu. Death rate way way up, etc.etc., and so Collins had a true Flu treatment, and is now up and with no complications

69

whatever, and without being but little inconvenienced by the experience. I took care of him all the time, slept in the room with him, etc.etc. The rest of the family did not see him at all. None of us had it.

I have had the Rosenow shots-in-the-arm. All my family also. It may do no good, but the fact remains that on USA contingent, of 10,000 who went over-seas, were so treated before leaving the USA. They were stationed in a hot-bed of Flu in France. Not one case of pneumonia in the whole 10,000. In these times it is worth $75 to me to know that the chances of any of us having pneumonia are very remote. Also I was greatly exposed to the Flu while helping the draft-board, and the arm-shots and a good deal of whiskey stood between me and IT.

The farm or ranch appeals to me also. However, I look upon a farm as a factory. If I go farming, I'll run the damnedthing not with any idea of getting back to nature, but from the point of view making it produce so much stuff for a 5 year average. I have been considering seriously farming. I think I would light in Canada. After two years, I figure I could run a large plant in Canada, make it pay from 10 to 25% in the investment, and have to be on the job only 4 months out of the year—60 days in the spring and 60 days in the fall. I'd then have 8 mo per year to loaf (my speciality!), play golf with you, and spend my money. I would also have a place, where, if my boys did not "do well" at college, and along the lines they pick out for themselves, I could say, "All right, old Top, back to the farm for thee!"

I know that all of the men of my age, if any one of them had put in the same degree of intelligence, and the same amount of labor on a factory-farm, every doggoned one of them would have been ahellofa sight better off right now. Some few have farmed, and they "have done well". They are also absolutely independent. No one tells them even remotely where to head in.

As you may have heard, I have three sons. Were they old enough to start in for themselves right now, I'd rather have them tackle farming than anything I know of.

It is very very hard for me to get along with Pres. Wilson, Mrs Wilson the 2d, and Colonel House, all three out of the USA. A major friend of mine back from the army says, that to his knowledge not a single officer will ever vote the democratic ticket again. That sounded all right to me, until I got to thinking, that so far as I know, no democrat went into the army at all—except by the draft route!!

It is very hard for me to realize that the War is over. Out here we saw mighty little of it anyway. It was all mental with us. I cannot adjust for an hour or two in the morning. I have to figure it all out over and over again that the WAR IS OVER!

Margaret has a Franklin 4 passanger. She drives it and that relieves me a good deal from the Chaeuff act. It is a nice little female car, and has many good things about it. I would not choose it for my handsome self—though in the mud it beats anything I have ever driven even a 4d. I personally now have a Cole-8. I tried to get a Marmon but could not. Got a good trade on this Cle and took it. It may be better than I think. I know that I'll never drive it as fast as it will run. It has a whole lot of zoom to it, and that is the one thing I seem to require. I loath a loggy car—such as the Cadilac.

I hope Emma and the rest of you will not trifle further with any indisposition this winter. This Flu is no joke. The thing is to stay off of it. I congratulate you and Joan upon keeping away.

While Collins had to stay in bed, he read and I read to him endlessly of the Tarzan books. As a matter of fact the more I read those book the more I think of them. Collins detests Jane Porter. He thinks Tarzan was mightily stung when he married her. I do not know but what he was right. I should say that Tarzan was rather the choicer vessel.

Yours,

[HTW]

1020 North Boulevard, Oak Park, Ill.

December 9, 1918

Mr. H. T. Weston, Beatrice, Nebraska.

Dear Bert:—

Many thanks for your good letter of December 7th. It is fine to know that you are all well and have so far dodged the Flu. I imagine Collins had about the same thing that Emma and the boys had. The doctor called it Flu, but when there is an epidemic of anything, that is always the easiest way out of it for the doctor. Diagnosis is at best uncertain and difficult. I was asking our family physician about this yesterday and he had to admit that the Coroner makes the most successful diagnoses.

I certainly hope that you decide to try California while we are there. You will not like it at first. It is the experience of a great many people that they return to California a second and often a third time before they finally decide that they wish to live there permanently.

You will soon be disillusioned as to the "perfection" of California's climate. It can be just as rotten as anywhere and really during the rainy season it is abominable. The greatest trouble with southern California is that it has been over-touted and a man goes there for the first time with the expectation of dropping into the Garden of Eden whereas the fact is that southern California is nothing more than desert land, certain spots in which have been reclaimed. The soil is enough to make a man from the Mississippi Valley laugh himself to death, but on the other hand it has for me the advantages of a longer period of sunshine than this climate and the lure of mountains and ocean. I would never go to California to make a fortune although I expect to make money out of hog-raising. There is, however, some satisfaction in leading a decent sort of outdoor existance in a pleasant climate and that is what I am most interested in.

I think it would be a very nice thing, Bert, for you and I, now that we have reached old age, to settle down together for our last few days in a spot not too far removed from the Los Angeles Athletic Club and where we might also have our saddle horses and the other things that appeal to us in common. What does Margaret Medorah think of the California proposition?

There is, of course, the question of educating the children which is giving me considerable concern. They are getting along nicely in school here although they are not very far advanced inasmuch as we have never attempted to push them and none of them is an intellectual prodigy. Out there if we have a ranch twenty-five or thirty miles from Los Angeles, it will probably mean that we will have to have a governess for them as it would be too much of a trip to take them in every morning and bring them back in the afternoon.

What can you tell me about the best place to get corn for finishing hogs in California? Could it be shipped from Nebraska reasonably? You know you can get your hogs pretty nearly ready for market on alfalfa and so cheaply that you can afford to ship corn in for finishing and it seems to me that Nebraska ought to be about as close to California as any of the corn states. How about it?

Yours,
Ed

If you got the adjoining farm we could build a little school house and prorate the professors salary.

Beatrice
Dec 13th 1918

Dear Edgar Rice:
Yours of the 9th interests me extremely. In re corn! We ship 1000s of bu yearly to the Coast and elsewhere west. You are a good guesser— Neb is the Last Chance for corn. Except when we have crop failures, no other territory can compete with us on corn or corn products into the Pac. Coast and NW territory. Also Nebr corn, generally is better than any other corn in the world. Exporters often pay us a premium on account of our corn grading perfect quality, and exporters are the most choosey of all coru-buyers.

When you get to pouring the fattener into your piggies, I'll tell you more about feeding. There is nothing whatever I do not know about the feeding of hogs etc. I suppose I have forgotten more about feeding and feeds than most feeders of 40 years experience know. My middle name is Feed, and instead of a Jr or Esq after my name, it reads FE— meaning Feed Expert. Incidently, I'll say, if we should go to Calif for a year, it is likely I should use a part of my time—that part which friend Wife could spare from my nurse–bell-boy duties—to selling feed.

Do you know that west of McCook Nebraska, that not a doggoned fattening feed is raised? You can get size and even bulk out of the western feeds, but you kaint get marketable flesh.

I know nothing whatever about Calif. I know less about hog manufacturing in that locality. Plenty of alfalf at a low price, with a warm climate, and a quick forced finish with corn or hominy feed, might work fine. As a general rule, however, a factory is handicapped if located too far from the source of raw material supply. Have you considered the cholera hazard?

You ask me regarding Margt's views in re Calif. I thought she was for it—in fact I thought she had rather planned the years stay with the idea of remaining if satisfactory. The other day however, in a croud, she lectured to this effect. That Calif was my idea, that if she went it would be entirely on my account. That she thought she ought not go just as far as possible away from her Father & Mother. This was news to me. Hereto fore I have been lead to believe that what she wanted to do was to get about as far as possible away from long visits made by Mere et Pere C.

Friend Wife has always rather intimated that she was abused living in a small rural corn belt bergh. There is nothing particularly to keep me here. More than a year ago, I told her I was willing to go live any-where under the sun she might choose—provided only that she would try said place for a year, before making (or permitting her father) to make large investment in residence, etc. until she was SURE she had what she wanted. Then a few weeks later, I actually had a man (with money) ask me to make a price on the house. He would have bought at a reasonable figure. Do you think Margt would make a price on her house, her home? No by much!! She was affronted at the idea that the man and I should think she would part with it. I have told her, if she wants to try it in Westchester County, or on Long Island, so as to be near her parents (a certainly natural thing) that I'm perfectly willing. I insist upon a more or less rural suburb however, as I do not want three extremely active boys cooped up in a city. We have a considerable in-vestment in our house here, but that could be shot as not more than a 5000 loss, and whats 5 to the only child of CWC?

I am willing to freely admit that Nebraska has the worst climate for living purposes in the world. The wind blows like hell here for at least 300 days out of the year. The thermometer has a range from 118 above to 36 below. I have seen the dnmd mercury go up 30 degrees in 31 min-utes, and drop 60 degrees in 74 minutes. The humidity varies all the way from zero to a fog so you cant see the garage. It is ahellof a climate if there ever was one, and there is simply no arguement on that score.

On the other hand, barring climate, it is a bully place to raise boys.

The schools are rather better than the average public schools. My sister and we live on $^1/_2$ a block, and the other $^1/_2$ block is pasture for the ponies, and the kids can do as theydamn please there in. They dig caves, make race tracks, gardens, hold trench warfare, and every thing, $^1/_4$ mile west, is Indian Creek. There they can trap and fish. 1 $^1/_2$" east is Bear " " " " " " [i.e., "1 $^1/_2$ miles east is Bear Creek. There they can trap and fish" — Ed.], and also go in swimming without danger of drowning. 1 mile S-W is the River, mill-pond 150 feet by 4 miles long—motor boats, canoeing, deep water swimming, and all that sort of thing, which is remarkable in this part of the Middle West. Everyone in town and most everyone in the county know my kids. They are as safe as kids can be. They can have ponies, dogs, guns, and raisehell generally almost as though they were on a farm.

For adults there is nothing here except what one produces oneself. Before the quarantine, we had a movie house that showed the same stuff currently with the releases in Chicago (I know from reading May Tinee in the Trib)—and that is all. No real theaters. Rather inferior preachers in the churches. We can boat on the River, play golf, motor. The people here are just exactly like the people anywhere else—neither better nor worse. I have noted in living various places, that types are duplicated in every community. There are only a limited number of types, and we have them here just as you have them in OPark, and exactly as they exist in NY. Few have made any real money in Beatrice. A good many have saved it.

Out of my youth, I have retained only 5 side-partners. You, Holbert, Sanders, Thomas, and Lloyd.[27] Lloyd is Colonel of the 10th FA, and I never see him anyway. Thomas is for ever located in NY. You, Holbert and Sanders are going to live in So.Calif.

Margt likes the CITY, and what it supplies. The shops, the theaters, the bright lights, cafes, clatter, noise, etc. I like the country, the open spaces, and that sort of thing. The city is nothing in my fair young life—except for short rapid shots at it. Margt likes the ocean, I like the mountains and the sage brush country.

It sort of seemed to me, that if we located somewhere—say in So Pasadena—within $^1/_2$ an hour by trolley or motor of LosA, that we would be cleaning up on what everyone of us were really looking for. Good rural normal surroundings for the Boys, good schools. A quiet place to live and sleep, with a good live city with plenty doing withing grabbing distance. The sea, with bathing (and the Triangle & Mack Sennet Girls) within half an hours drive west, and the maountains, with all the trimmings an hour east.[28] I'm doggoned, if it does not appear to me as though So Calif was just made and a-waiting for the Weston-outfit.

And then there would [be] three of my life-long side-partners located there too. And that is a funny thing—I am quite sure that Margaret takes a lot more interest in you & family, and in Holbert & family, than she does in any of her own personal friends.

I have often wondered how you would get along with any of these other men and their families. Whether, because you all intensely interest me, if any of you would appeal to each other. Probably not. It would be interesting to see however.

This is some little discourse. Very personal. Much of the GREAT-I-AM stuff. However, there is onedamnednice thing about a letter. It does not have to be read!! If one hooks his finger in your botton-hole and talks and talks, you have to listen or resort to violence, but with a letter, a simple twist of the wrist lays it down!!

Yrs,

[HTW]

1020 North Boulevard, Oak Park, Ill.

January 13, 1919

Mr. H. T. Weston, Beatrice, Nebraska.

Dear Bert:—

As you may have suspected I received your letter of December 13th some time ago but what with Christmas, the holidays, birthdays, business and getting ready to move to California, etcetera, and so forth, I have not replied.

We leave here January 31st for L.A. A friend of mine while looking around for a possible farm site for me discovered 28 acres near Burbank which is a little north west of Los Angeles and from the map I should judge about the same distance from it as Pasadena. It would be mighty nice if you people could come out there and settle. While I can imagine that Beatrice must be a wonderful place to live, it is also within the range of possibilities that you might find some points of interest in southern California, especially during the Winter.

I cannot tell you what our address there will be as I have not yet heard from the manager of the Alvarado Hotel where I have asked that accomodations be reserved and inasmuch as we will land there in the heart of the tourist season, it is likely that we will have difficulty in getting accomodations. However, a letter addressed to me in care of the Los Angeles Athletic Club will always reach me as I will notify them as soon as I am located.

Emma and the children are well at the present writing and join me in love to you all and in the hope that you all likewise are in good health.

Yours,

Ed

Jan 15th 1919

Dear Edgar Rice:

Yesterday I started a letter to you, and could not finish and today I get yours of the 13th. Mark Twain says if you want some one to write you, write them, and the letters will cross en route. Anyway ours would have if I had written—and Mr Clemens is again proved a great and good man—also wise.

You movement to L.A. listens mighty good to me. I wish we were about to duplicate your action. I see no very good reason why the Westons should not locate in Calif—or at least try it out—but I gather it is not to be for the present anyway.

I have explained to you the strange incompatability of Margt and her parents. Last summer, after they had been here with us some months and each had worn the other to a frazzle, Margt planned to go to Calif this Fall, and try it a year anyway, and possibly locate. I had started in July to try to get into the army, and would have been called to Camp Taylor, but the Flu prevented, and until Nov 11th it looked as tho I might go any day. Then the Flu hit hard, and no one dared travel for fear of being taken en route, and by the time that was relieved, Margt began to have dutiful feelings toward her parents—to forget the nervous strain of last summer, and to decide, with her parents old and in ill health (Mrs Collins is you know) that she had no right, nor would it be decent for her to remove herself to the opposite end of the USA. All of which was true enough—but which same good argument appealed to her not at all last Fall after our visitors had recently departed.

Right now we do not know whatinhell we are going to be doing during the next year. I myself think it would be ill-advised to put 3,000 miles between us and the Collinses, because in the natural course of things those two elderly persons will need the aid of the younger generation before very long.

I feel very sure that it would be a fine thing all around for the Westons and the Collinses to all go to Calif, but I think there is little chance of that being pulled off. I know Mrs Collins ill health would be benefitted in that climate, for it is cold damp weather that gets her worse than anything else. To me the life the Collinses live in Bklyn is simply hell, and I dont see how they stand it year after year. Both Mr and Mrs would have a infinitely better time the year round in Calif. Why they stay put in Bklyn is more than any sane man can fathom.

I should make a guess that next summer will find us all famlied up either in the Adriondacks (spelling doubtful) or on Long Island. My choice personally, next to L.A. is Colo Spgs—but my vote cuts little or no ice whatsoever. It may be an indication of insanity, but I am crazy about Colo Spgs. The climate there makes me feel as tho I had had 2 drinks all the time—and believe me that is more than a mere something in these drouth times!!

The Flu has removed itself from our Midst. Collins is the only one of the Weston Family who had it (thank Gawd!) but it took a terrible toll in this burgh.

I always knew that Roosevelt had me in the palm of his hand, but until his death I never suspected that I also had a personal feeling for the man. His going has put a real crimp in me. It is said that no man is necessary—but to my way of thinking, we could much better spare the next ten greatest men in the USA. Honestly I dont know whatinhell we are going to do without THE Colonel![29]

The corn milling business is more rotten than ever in its history—and that is going some!! They have taken all our war profits in taxes—

they have raised our frt rates, not 25%, but from 45% to 65%, they are admitting Argentine corn to the USA, they cut out wheat substitutes over night, and they have let the sates again say what size sax to use, and have left us with thousands of dollars worth of 5 10 & 25 lbs sax on our hands—which we cannot use and are a loss. D——n the Kaiser! Also D——N the—But, nay—the gates of Leavenworth still yawn!!

Yrs

[HTW]

1020 North Boulevard, Oak Park, Ill.

January 17, 1919

Mr. H. T. Weston, Beatrice, Nebr.

Dear Bert:—

Your letter of the 15th just received.

That business of southern California being so much farther from Brooklyn than Nebraska is more in your mind's eye than a reality. Beatrice can't be much more than a day and a half nearer Brooklyn than Los Angeles. We are moving three days further away from our people who are also well advanced in years but we do not feel that we are lacking in filial affection or sense of duty.

It would not take a great deal longer to get from Los Angeles to Brooklyn than to get from Beatrice to Brooklyn and then there is the indisputable fact that there is nothing on earth to prevent Mr. and Mrs. Collins from living in southern California if they care to be near Margaret Medorah.

Every time we go away, and we have gone a great many times, there is always that same suggestion that we shall never see our surviving parents again but we always do. Of course the time will come some day when they will go or possibly one of us will go first but it seems to me that it is not very cheerful to be always assuming that the grim reaper is at our elbow.

Mrs. Hulbert lives at Coldwater, 150 miles from Chicago. She could easily sicken and die before Emma could reach her but we are not expecting her to do so.[30]

79

As a matter of fact, I believe that if you and Margaret really wished to live in southern California and moved there, that Mr. and Mrs. Collins would eventually follow you and finally like it better than Brooklyn. A friend of mine was telling me of a seventy-nine year old aunt of his who had lived in St. Louis all her life and believes it the finest place on earth to live, always being unable to understand how anyone could live elsewhere, yet she is now picking up and moving with all her family to southern California.

I wish it might be that you people could come out there where we could see each other occasionally.

The car has just called for me and I shall have to quit. Love to all in which Emma and the children join,

Yours,

Ed

P.S. Tell Margaret that I know its none of my business.

[*Woman's World* magazine letterhead]

January 20th, 1919.

Dear Mr. Weston: —

Mr. Edgar Rice Burroughs is to leave Chicago permanently for California the first of February. The White Paper Club has planned a farewell dinner to be given at the Hotel LaSalle, at seven o'clock on Saturday, January twenty-fifth.

The committee issues a very cordial invitation to you.

Will you please send in your acceptance to Mr. James Quirk.

Very truly yours,

Hiram M Greene

Chairman of Committee.

Mr. Herbert T. Weston, Beatrice, Nebr.

My dear Mr Quirk,
Upon my return home tonight, I find The White Paper Club's invitation to a farewell dinner to Mr Burroughs.

I am sorry indeed not to be able to attend the dinner, and thank you very much for the cordial invitation.

Sincerely,
[HTW]

Jan 25th 1919

Dear Ed;
Right now the White Paper outfit is farewelling you! I trust that you are conducting yourself with your usual propriety and poise. I should like to have been present and see you take leave of your peers, and I think it very decent of you to have given me the opportunity, by having an invitation sent to me—but, Lord, Lord,—no chance for meh to get off on any purely pleasure-hounding expidetion like that. Also I was in Lincoln, and did not get notice in time, even if I could have otherwise come.

I dont know how much of a recluse you have been but if you have been out among 'em much, they will be darned sorry to have you wend your way westward.

Before I forget it. You know Margt had one hellofa time with her arm—neuritis, sort of like yours I guess. Nothing seemed to help it much. Finally, somehow or other her dentist X-rayed her teeth (you know too she has close to perfect teeth, and has never found the slightest thing wrong with 'em)—and the dentist found the faintest sort of a blurr on the plate—thought it was silly, but bored in, and found an abcess with a puss content about equal to $1/2$ a pin head. This was cured entirely up, and her arm has improved ever since, until it is almost normal again. In fact her arm now does not hurt at all, and the only thing left is that she cant reach up her back as far as of yore. Now I do not know whether that little abcess had anything to do with it, but the fact remains that with that gone the trouble <u>left</u>! In any event it wont kill you or break you to have your teeth X-rayed.

You will be a-starting when you get this. I wish I were going to see you en route, but I suppose you are going your beloved Sante Fe, and Via KC, and that is out of my beat. If by any mischance whatever you happen to go through Lincoln or Omaha—wire me and I'll meet you and ride an hour or so along with you. I'd like mighty well to see you, because imdamned if I know when I ever will see you again now that you are locating in Calif.

The last letter you wrote was truth clearly stated from beginning to end. I think that Margt realized this when she read it, though it rather fired her, and she threatened to sit down and write you instan-tus—which ofcourse she did not do. I think she does not know in the least herself what she is going to do with her family next summer. She sprung one today; towit; that along in June or July, we'd pile all the kids into the Cole, and beat it for Colo with just one steamer trunk (no golf clubs) and would take a cabin in the mts, and put in from 4 to 10 weeks doing our own work, getting back to nature, and closely associating with our boys—and that does not sound so bad at that—though I fear me it would pall on some of us as time went on.

Anyway, write me pronto when you get settled on your hog-ranch, and good luck on the trip, and great joy always in your new habitat.

Yrs

[HTW]

Tarzana Ranch, Van Nuys, Calif.

March 14 1919

Dear Bert—

It has been a long time since I have heard from you or written you and much has happened in my young life in the interim—I don't know what that means but it seems to sound all right.

I hope that you and Margaret and the kids are all well and happy and that you are still thinking seriously of coming to California.

We arrived in Los Angeles Feby 3rd and immediately started out looking for a ranch. Had about given up hope of finding what we wanted when we discovered that we could get the country estate of the late Genl Harrison Grey Otis at a very reasonable figure.

We have been moving in and settling for the past two weeks and expect to go in ourselves tomorrow. In the mean time we have been living in a furnished house in Hollywood.

Tarzana is a very delightful place. We have 540 acres on the State Highway—a boulevard running from Los Angeles to San Francisco—in the San Fernando Valley foothills of the Santa Monica Mountains. The place is 23 miles from L.A. shopping district and thirteen miles from the ocean—by auto road. The house stands on top of a hill about half a mile from the boulevard and has—as nearly as I can count them—eighteen rooms & six baths. It is of Spanish architecture built around a patios in which are many flowers & shrubs. The hill comprises some fifteen acres set out in flowers, shrubs & trees. I think there are some two thousand trees of several hundred varieties—many of which were brought from Asia & Africa.

Half a mile up the canyon are the foreman's house, bunk houses, barns, corrals, etc. I acquired 500 head of pure bred Angora (mohair) goats, five horses, a cow, forty hens, and a bum dog, beside farm implements and $8000°° worth of iron & concrete water piping. There is an abundance of water and I almost forgot a 12 acre grove of olive, lemon, apricot & orange trees, beside 250 English Walnut trees.

I know you wont mind hearing all this because I am tremendously interested in it. It really is a very decent sort of dump. The house commands a view of the mountains and a lovely valley of farms & groves, beyond which are other mountains with snow capped peaks in the distance.

At this time of year the hills are green with new grass—about July they will turn brown again.

The range into which Tarzana runs is very wild. It stretches south of us to the Pacific. We have already seen coyote & deer on the place & the foreman trapped a bob-cat a few weeks ago. Things come down and carry the kids out of the corrals in broad day-light. Deeper in there are mountain lion. I think Collins & Jeff would like it here. I have bought a couple of .22 cal. rifles for Hulbert and myself beside my .25 Remington and automatics, so we are going to do some hunting. Jack has an air rifle with which he expects to hunt Kangaroo-rats and lions and I am going to get them each a pony.

We are looking forward to having a bully life on the place. There is plenty of room for a golf course—and a mighty sporty one too. Also expect to put in a swimming pool and tennis court. My principal business later will be hog raising—from bred Berkshires; but I am going to go slow on that.

I wish you lived near me—there are wonderful sites for houses or ranches on both sides of us and, Bert, it is a dandy place to live. Of course it has its draw backs as all places have; but yet I cannot imagine a more nearly perfect place, taking everything into consideration. Just now it is raining like Billy-be-damned and is, consequently, cold and disagreeable, but tomorrow or next day I may be perspiring in my shirt sleeves—you know what I mean.

Sue Ball's father called me up yesterday. He and Mrs. Ball are living here in Hollywood. I am going around to call on them soon.

If you are not now entirely sick of the Burroughs Tribe & their affairs write me—and be sure and tell us all about the Westons.

Yours,

Ed

March 21st 1919

Dear Ed:

Yours was mighty interesting to us. Gad Zooks! Little did I know when you suggested some months ago that I should join you "ranching" in Calif. that you were going to branch out like the Star Spangled Banner, take on a line of Mil Flores, and run the Triangle Girls a close second as one of the show stuff of the Sunny Land of Native Sons.

The blow was softened however, by the fact that my sister takes a LosAngoles paper and in a Sunday edition she ran across an elaborate discription you you and your new place.[31]

It must be bully. It listens just exactly ideal to me from here. I can see no reason why you and yours should not now go on indefinitely in perfect contentment—which after all is what we all are after. You state that it has its draw-backs. I'd like to know whatinhell they are—unless possibly the aroma from the goats.

Speaking of goats, hogs and such. Gage County is the most go-getting agricultural community anyway west of the Mo River in the Middle West. We have live stock associations, milk testing groups, and all that sort of thing. And the truth is that it is just pouring the coin into this vicinity. Why, Great Gawd, the other day a farmer lad sold a 140 lb boar for $2,100.00!!!!!!!!! And to think, it cost little more to raise that boar than to raise a runt!! Even ole Dick Grant, the local architect, and not a very good one, got a little better than $1,100.00 for a seven months old Holstien bull calf. Anitithell? Its getting to be a quality and not quainty proposition. Why I suppose you can selective breed along for ten years or so, and get an ole billy goat that will be worth his weight in platinum.

I envy you your new lay-out. The farm is the only place to be in these times anyway, and besides you have a wonderful place to live along with it—and again, I'd like to know whatinhell are them drawbacks you speak of so glibly???

Margt departed Wednesday upon her yearly pilgrimage to the effete east. She cloud not hardly bear to go. In fact, during the last 24 hours she went really off her feed, and 2 hrs before the train left I had the MD pass on her. He said it was almost entirely her nervous state at leaving.

Item; When it seemed quite necessary that I live here in Beatrice, all the time in spots, Margt used to be very sure that any-thing-oh-Lord to get away from this corn-belt village. This (in spots) seemed to her the last place, the most undesireable residence under the sun. Two years ago, I told her to pick any old place and we would move. I urged it in fact. And now by heck! she is a hot ramping booster for Beatrice, and she gives any one hellandrepeat who even intimates that this is not the best climate and the best place to live on earth. It has even come that she has to be fairly driven off to make her required yearly visit to her fond Bklyn parents. And, yet, ofcourse there is nothing whatever in the theory of the contrariness of human nature!!!

Our plans for next summer are just exactly nothing. Margt and her Father will no doubt frame up something, and that something will turn out to be the worst yet, and put Margt close to the squirrel-house due simply and only to the fact that she and her parents get on each others nerves to an unbelievable extent.

Personally, my idea is to get to running a farm-factory some place and some how and some time, on account of being able to place the Three Weston Boys eventually where they will [be] out from under (as far as possible) Bolshevics, Wilsons and such.

I would playhell ranching in Calif. I could hardly afford to buy one of those furthermost rocky canyons of the Mil Flores, nee Tarzana. I want something not involving a liberty loan investment, and that would pay dividends upon the few scheckels put in.

Canada wheat land is the nearest thing I have run across, but there is no denying that that is the most unGodly place in the western hemisphere to live. I wish I were cave-man enough to just pull up and hit for Saskatchewan anyoldway, but while needy in the present generation, I am weak-kneed enough to feel that with Margt sole heir to the ole man's RR bonds, that I have hardly the right to disrupt her way of living, and to stick the whole tribe on a wind swept barren northern frontier, just because my inclination leads that way.[32]

My friend Bob Nickell, who has lived in Long Beach now for a year and who is returned for a visit, deposes and sayeth, that he has the same tires on his car that he left Beatrice with, and that he has driven on them some 18,000 miles, and that the reason is because of the wonderful roads in So Calif. That, like the $2,100 hog, does not seem possible.

We have had a wonderful run of luck this past winter. Col had the Flu, but with no serious results whatever, and all the rest of us have been unusually well (I whistled and rapped on wood to remove the jinks right then!) Right now there seems to be a good real of Flu re-occurance around here, but it apparently is not as severe as it was on the first round.

Jeff's pony, Mack, died about the first of the year. Got into the feed and over ate. Too bad.

The Boys have recently acquired another dog. It just "came". It is the funniest looking 5 months old pup I ever saw. However he has a wonderful disposition, and is possessed of the right sex, so has apparently won a home. There is much speculation as to just what kind and manner of dog he is. Nearly every sort of breed has been suggested—but I think that he is a booze-hound.

My business is absolutely rotten. Nothing in the history of the business ever was $1/10$th as bad. You see corn meal had been shoved down the peoples' throats for so long by Mr Hoover et al, that when the order was removed, those same pee-pul will not now accept anything made of corn as a gift.

We laid by some during the war it is true, but not a hellofa lot, due to close government supervision, and to tremendous taxes. We have aimed to tell the truth all through, and not attempted to fake our records or anything of that sort, and the result is that we actually pay more taxes than others whose profits were many times as great as ours.[33]

If I had it to do over again, under a democratic administration, I should select to be dishonest and rich, rather than on the square and poor, but the war is over and that is all past and gone so the NCMills is listed for all time in Honest but Foolish column. I very much doubt that we will come out, when its all over, as well off as we went in. Aint it hell? The—or rather A Farm for me!!

I read your letter to The Three. Their eyes fairly rolled! At lunch, much later, out of a clear sky, Jeff ventured; "Gee whiz, I'll bet he writes peachy Tarzan stories now. He and his kids will live around in those mountains, and he will know a lot more." And so on through the meal, hot interested discussion between all three of them about the life you'd live and the stories you emit.

You are a rotten sort of a friend in some ways. I had just finished dishing out to them Tarzan & The Jewels, and was up against it, and doggoned if I did not accidently run on to Tarzan Untamed in the Red Book.[34] Why inhell you dont let me know about such things I do not fathom. That is a bully title.

[Some text is missing, probably a third page, since there is no salutation to Emma and the children and HTW's customary "Yrs." is missing.—Ed.]

Tarzana Ranch, Van Nuys, Calif.
March 28, 1919

Mr. H. T. Weston, Beatrice, Nebraska.

Dear Bert:—

I was glad to have your letter of the 21st but sorry to learn that there is so little liklihood that you will be removing to southern California. The only way to get Margaret out here is to have her come and spend a few weeks each year for two or three years when she will probably be glad to get away from the Nebraska winters.

I am awful sorry about my not advising you of my stories. I fully intend to but I do not think of it and the chances are that I never will think of it when I should.

I hope Margaret has a good time in Brooklyn and that when she returns she will find you and the boys in good shape. Tell the latter that we now have over 250 kids and have only had four die which I think is a mighty good record. They are getting excellent attention. Neither Onthank nor I had ever seen a goat except at long distance before and just by applying a little common sense to the care of them we have made a record so far that I venture is almost unequaled.[35] It certainly has never been equaled in this herd before. We may, of course, run up against something in the future which we cannot foresee and lose the whole bunch but I am inclined to think that the goat is a mighty hardy animal. I have seen them born on a cold morning after a rain, on a cold, damp ground and in a few minutes they would be up wagging their tails and trying to nurse. If pigs are anywhere near as hardy as these goats we ought to make a fortune in Berkshires. Onthank and I figured out before we came out here that just with the natural increase we could start one sow and at the end of five years have a million pigs but inasmuch as we are going at it slowly, we intend to start with only five sows and at the end of five years God knows how many we will have. If you have any knowledge of the pig industry I should advise you to come out and buy the adjacent property and start in at once.

There is a beautiful site right next to mine that was offered me at $350.00 an acre which is about as low as anything in the valley but I am told that it could be bought much cheaper as real estate has not been moving very lively since the war began. It runs back into the hills just as mine does and in front is a knoll similar to mine on which a residence could be built commanding a view of this whole broad valley and surrounding mountains. Why don't you get Papa Collins to at least buy the property for Margaret as in the course of five or ten years it will be worth at least a thousand dollars an acre, at a very conservative estimate.

Yours,

Ed

Dear Ed;

In your sunny Calif—and we with now just one week of cold rainy weather, enough to make any man fight any grandmother.

It is quite remarkable what a large part this man Tarzan has with us. It seems to me that my sons talk Tarzan to me as much as they used to talk the kaiser. He is very real to them. In this Tarzan Untamed, Collins said: "Gee Whiz—I'm glad that Jane Clayton is dead!!" Jane never was any favorite of his.

My chief side-kick here is one Charles Brewster—late Major in the USA. Privately I term Charles Old Ironsides—he filling all the bill for that character.

When war hove into view, he left a $6,000 per year law practice, a bride and three children and just WENT. Ofcourse he did not get over—any man past 40 was safer in the army than he was in civil life—and that nearly broke his heart, but his ability was recognized, and he was kept in the USA training drafts, having at one time 4,000 men under him tho only a captain.

Anyway, this same Charles—who incidently belongs to the brain trust—became a good deal interested in Tarzan, and I have been feeding him the six (6) Tarzan books we have in stock. The other night, to Mag and me he said; "What sort of a chap is this Burroughs any way? Here this Tarzan consistently fights lions, gorrilias and what not with his bare hands, and kills them causually and often. At times he even runs the mighty elephant around and around, and yet just any spindle-shanked slab-sided woman can knock him on the head and make him feed out of the hand."

I would hate to tell you what Margt said to him in way of explaination. Anyway, after while Charles said to her; "Yes, and he knows you and Bert very well too, does nt he? And he has seen you together a lot?"

Margt returned from her yearly "visit" about a week ago. It is determined that we remain in Beatrice this summer, and her Paw and Maw will be with us about July 1st.

I have a new dog (acquired while Margt was away). His name is Morning View Sergeant. It would have been Morning View Tarzan but I presumed that that purp of yours had been registered, and I wanted no conflict of names. Sergeant's father is Vicory Crack as is also his grandfather on his mother's side. I suspect that at 18 months he will be absolutely the best Ariedale in the USA. His litter brother his breeder will not sell at all. I think Sergeant just as good a dog in every way or possibly better, except that his nose is about $1/2$ white—but this seems to be getting black, and he may out grow it. If I can ever get him still for even $1/50$ of a second I'll send you a picture of this newest addition to the Weston family. Serg, by the way, will be 6 months old May 1st.

With your start of 5 sows I suppose you have 300 pigs by this time. I hope so anyway. I believe I would like pigs rather better than goats. I loath sheep, and a goat is a sort of 1st cousin. I am very much interested in your ranch venture—much more so probably than you know. I hope you will drop me a few owrds now and then and let me know how matters break.

Corn milling business is still extremely rotten. Absolutely nothing coming in, and everything going out. This last advance in corn did us no good, as we do not speculate. The Omaha bunch cleared up between 5 & 6,000,000. We would like to specualte but everytime we do, they crack us. There is nothing it it for us. I sometimes suspect that corn-milling is a thing of the dim and distant—the glorious—past. I wish I knew where with a small investment and much sweat of my honest and sloping brow I could emit ten to 15 thousand dollars per year. I suppose I ought to go to Saskatchewan and raise wheat—but it is the doggonedest place in the western hemisphere to live.

What are you going to do after July 1st, or thereabouts?[36] I have suspected that Genl Otis stored vast cellars under that 29 roomed house with barrels and barrels of vintage—and that the vintage went with the ranch????

Nothing like that here! I'm down to my last 4 gals of real whisky. Bootlegger stuff is now worth 100 per case, and rot-gut at that.

I have dallied a little with what can be done with a raisin and a little yeast. I must say that the results were not electrifying. We may come to that sort of stuff eventually, but it does not seem possible.

You have nt any sure fire receipts, have you? Things are getting critical around here.

Some are laying up their hopes on dandilion wine. That may be all right, and Gawd knows there are plenty of dandelions around this part of Nebraska, but the best wine therefrom I have been against tasted like a slightly sweetened coal tar vinigar, and contained about as much pep as a deep breath on the front porch on a July morning.

Let me hear about the goats and the piggies, and even a few words about the Burroughses would be indeed welcome. Love to all from all

Yrs

[HTW]

Tarzana Ranch, Van Nuys, Calif.
May 8 1919

Dear Bert:

I wonder what Margaret Medora said to the major. He asked her, you will recall, what sort of a chap I am. Margaret is more or less candid; but she has always been too polite to tell me what she really thinks of me, though I always have had my misgivings since I wrote that under-clothes letter to her—back when the world was young.

You say Tarzan has a large part with you. Same here. We eat and sleep Tarzan—I ought to be tired of him; but I'm not, nor do the children seem to be. Emma, again, is too polite to say if she feels otherwise. The dog is named Tarzan, the place is Tarzana and a guy bobbed up day before yesterday with the plan of a whole village he wished to plant in my front yard—school, city hall, banks, business houses, motion picture theater—and it was labelled: City of Tarzana, which sounds like a steam-boat.

There have been three motion picture men up in the past two days talking Tarzan films. I guess our move to sunny southern Cal will prove profitable from the m.p. standpoint as I am nearer to where they do it. I hope so as I need the money—it costs something to be a successful farmer.

My beans are up, baby limas; my corn is up, Orange County Prolific; my apricots are heavy on the limbs; my new alfalfa is also up, Hairy Peruvian. I thought some of drilling in safety razors with it. My barley is nearly all cut and the binders have started on it. The tractor is discing field #15 preparatory to hanging out potatoes, or should it be sowing or planting? Over three hundred kids frolic in the field. I do not know

91

the name of my apricots or I should have mentioned it. With the barley off we shall plant Milo Maize on about one hundred acres. I am going to plant Milo Maize because it is the only other thing I haven't planted that I can recall the name of.

I note the dorg, Sergeant Top o' the Morning. I have acquired three dogs in additon to Tarzan. There is Don, a mongrel sheep dog who was on the place and stayed. There is Jack, a full blood sheep dog, I bought to make the goats nervous, and Lobo, another sheep dog, that a Spaniard gave me. Lobo I love. Emma says he has soulful eyes. A wag would call him a sad dog. He is six months old and appears to have been born without any friends; but there is something about the little cuss that gets under my skin.

I must close now and run my ranch for a few minutes. I get streaks like that and am real busy.

Yours,
Ed

June 3d 1919

Dear Ed:

I'm taking the liberty of sticking this in with Collins' epistle to Joan, and thereby saving 3¢—which is something in these days.

I have news for you. It may not excite you very much, but it thrills me!!

Next week I leave for New Haven to put on the last WET reunion show that probably ever will be!!!

I have three side partners that I retained out of Yale—and starting about 60 days ago they began to write me daily about this Great and Last Party, and then ten days ago they began telegraphing—and every darned communication was more alluring than the last.

As a matter of fact there are at least 20 good reasons why I should not go—and I'd passed it up mentally, until my little bride Maggie raised up—before she got through she made it appear that it was my everlasting duty to go, even tho I robbed a bank for funds, shamefully neglacted my children, let my business gotohell, etc.etc.

And so I am going.

Seth Thomas I ofcourse see every time I go east. Murry Sanders stops here occasionally on his east-and-west flits — but Herb Herr — Ach Gott! the last time I saw that Bird, I was less than half as old as I am now. Aint it hell?

And then the last wire I got says Chas Lloyd (Col of the 10th Artillery) will be home and there. It listens most too good to be true.

All this is very thrilling to me — also it is my first lone joy trip in 16 years. Also I rather expect to be in NY the night of June 30th 1919!!!!![37]

One thing I'll miss like hell, and that is not seeing you Burroughses in Chi. That had got to be such a habit, and such a bully one, that it makes a mighty big hole in the pleasant prospect.

I see in Col's letter he gives the glad tiddings that his "ma & pa got run into". Indeed yes, and from now on no light weight cars for me! A 4d roadster going just as fast as it could go hit us a 45 degree belt just ahead of the rear mud guard. It dented my foot board and crumpled the mud guard, and jarred us a very little. The 4d turned pretty nearly in-side-out. No one hurt through.

The bird had rain on his shield, and absolutely did not see us at all. I tried to go over the curb, but he caught me first. If we had had a light car he would have come on right in. A hellofa thing to happen. I'll say Maggie is a sport. He lit practically in her lap, 4d and all, and she never turned a hair nor even got pale.

There is a 31 year old bird back here now from So Calif. Been there a year on a/c his health which is inclined toward the TB route. If ½ what he says is true, it is a shame wasting time and money tarrying else-where. But there is nothing stirring the HTwestons — not for a time, anyway.

How are the goats? I read a whole lot about goats in
[page break; lines missing]
. . . good part of the lamb we get from the KC packing houses is really kid. It also intimated that all goats were good for commercially was to follow sheep and eat what they left.

This returned TB from So Calif whom I have already referred to, vol-unteered to me that your joint never cost less than ½ a million and prob-ably a whole lot more. I'm disappointed in you. Most of my old cottage-pudding-chums have always been in the plut class—which same was more or less embarrassing to me through no fault of theirs. I had figured you as a life-long pretty-much-the-same class as my poor self, and now this TB blanks my hopes. But then I thought I was going to develope into something of a near plut myself a year ago—but hellno! After the dear ole administration had spurred us into ever lasting machinery for corn flour, etc. they carelessly slip the war from under us—and then, by heck, they tax us so that we are now trying to give our plants away. This is a hard life!

We are having absolutely nothing but rain and cold here. Fire in the furnace the past three days. I suppose it will break all at once and go to 115 in the shade with hot winds. Ahellofa climate.

My two oldest passed in school this year without being pounded on the back or working at home. That is a great satisfaction to me, and is going to do much to ease me into a peaceful old age if they keep it up. They aint much like their dad.

Love to all.

Yrs,

[HTW]

Edgar Rice Burroughs, Inc.

306 Hohm Building, Sixth and Western

Los Angeles, Calif.

August 16th 1926/sj[38]

Dear Bert:

Your letter has gone unanswered for a long time because of the fact that we have recently moved from town back to the Ranch, having built a small cottage on the subdivision, and I have been neglecting everything in order to get things settled here so that we could take it easy again.[39]

I am sorry that Joan and I missed you, Margaret and Collins in the east as we should certainly have enjoyed seeing you all.

I remember Carter very well and Alberts only vaguely.[40] I did not think that there was any feeling between the P.D.Q's and the Sigma

Q's—as a matter of fact I had forgotten all about the P.D.Q's until I received your letter.

I do not see why you always give up coming to California as you have every year for the last seven or eight years. Possibly if you would not plan on coming some year, then you would give up not planning on coming and come—a very brilliant idea.

My new address is Tarzana Ranch, Reseda, California. The Hohm Building address is my office address; S. New Hampshire and S. Gramercy Place are in the discard.

Yours,
Ed

Mr. Herbert T. Weston, Beatrice, Neb.

Your fifty-year old benevolent mug looks down upon me from my study wall as I write.

You have done well to retain your school-girl complexion.

Reseda, Calif.
January 3, 1927/ww[41]

Mr. H. T. Weston, Beatrice, Nebraska

Dear Bert:

We were delighted to learn through the medium of your much appreciated holiday greeting card, that you are planning on visiting sunny Southern Cal this spring. Of course you had to wait for eight years until we had moved into a house so small that it precludes the possibility of having you with us while you are here. Heretofore, we have had large homes and ample room. Now, we have a little 2 x 4 dump that is about half large enough for our own requirements, but there is a lot of outdoors surrounding it, so that when you are here we can at least offer you plenty of breathing space.

I cannot tell you how delighted we are to think that you really are coming out at last. Except for the wind, March should be a lovely month, but from what I have heard of Nebraska, winds should mean nothing in your life.

Are you bringing any of the boys with you? While we are all interested in an answer to this, the children entered a special request for this
information, together with the hope that you are bringing them all.

Are you planning on driving out, and are you going to stay long
enough to really enjoy it? We most assuredly hope so.

We are mighty disappointed to think that we cannot put you up at
our house, as all the time that we were at Tarzana we were hoping that
you would visit us, for then we had more than enough room. However,
we can be together in the day-time, and if you have no definite plans
as to where you expect to stop, I hope that you will let us help you. Unless you want to be right down in the heart of the city, there are lovely
hotels in Hollywood and also Beverly Hills, which locations are not only
nearer us, but far more desirable in most respects than the hotels in the
congested district of the city. If you are going to stay for a reasonably
long time and would rather have a furnished apartment or bungalow,
we can get either one for you.

Emma and the children join me in love to you all.

Yours,

Ed

Beatrice, Nebr.

1/6/27

Dear Ed Rice:

How are the Burroughses? Last I heard you were back on the ranch,
the ole home place, and I'll bet are draned glad of it! The more I see of
cities (and I have been in NY and Chi much the past year) the better I
like the rural sections.

In '26 Margt and I decided it was up to us to "stay home". I counted
up the other day and we were absent from our vine and fig leaf just
short of 11 weeks all together.[42] Much of this necessary.

Have not made Calif yet, but if theings go well, and Mrs Collins
continues strong as at present, we aim to slip that way along about St
Patrick's Day, or thereabouts.[43]

It was some Holidays with us, with Collins and Jefferson B both present. Col has been back since last Sunday and Jeff goes back for his 5 month stretch next Sunday, so it will quiet down once more.[44]

We have been in Chicago a whole lot recently. Since you left there, I have avoided that place like a pest, but have had to be there, and will admit that I am getting to like it. Better that NY. One thing, CHI is not too d——d big. In Ny it is getting to be a weeks job to see two people in one day.

Last time in Chicago I met some of the best gun-men. Not in a business way fortunately, but in a purely social manner. Jack McSweeny for one, and Jack Orr for another.

We saw the Army Navy game. I know you sniff at that festive game in your old age, but it is my modest opinion that there has been nothing finer in these USA since the Boys pulled away from Great Brittian in 76. This was somewhat on a smaller scale perhaps, but it gave an oldster like me an awful kick to see those 30 odd young lads from all over the country, and from every concievable previous condition of severitude, give every ounce they had to beat each other into the mud, and then come out tied. We were with Col Lloyd (who would now be Chief of Artillery if he had not been gassed all to h——l in France) and Seth Thomas & wives, and had seats on the 50 yd line just back of the West Point outfit and I am free to confess had a perfectly lovely party from A to Z, Honestly, I did not know that anyone past 50 could have as good a time.

Have had no word from Sue Ball recently. I Suspect he May be somewhat Peeved at me. He has an office in Omaha and I guess stays there much of the time. I played in the state golf tournament there last summer and did not see him, though I phoned his numbers several times. Anyway he sent me no Xmas greetings this year. Too bad, though someway he and I seem to have not so much in common any more.

Saw Roy Alberts again at Culver this Fall, and the Alberts and Westons put on a pleasant party indeed. They are nice quiet folk. Mrs Alberts and Margaret are amusingly alike in several ways, and I rather suspect that Roy and I are too.

I note your 4th paragraph in yours of Aug 16th 1926. A clever suggestion, and I call your attention to the fact that Margaret and I are not planning to go to California ever, but I am simply warning you that we may call you up from the Ambassador, or whatever the joint is along about the Ides of Mch., and you can motor over, or whatever you now do in Cal., and look us over. Look for two plump middle aged ones, one bald!

Yours,

[HTW]

Reseda, Calif.
January 12, 1927/ww

Mr. H.T. Weston, Beatrice, Nebraska

Dear Bert:

Your letter of the 6th must have crossed mine.

You do me an injustice in suggesting that I am too old to enjoy a football game. As a matter of fact, I am keener for the games of today than for those of our time. It seems to me that they are much more interesting from the spectator's point of view.[45] We saw the Notre Dame–u.s.c. game and the Stanford-Alabama game, in addition to one or two others. Would have seen more if I had been able to spend the time.

From present appearance, our interest in football may be still further augmented by the liklihood of our having an All-American Center in the family, Joan being very much interested in a very large young man who was accorded that honor several years ago.[46]

We received a Christmas card from Woodruff, but I have not seen him for several years.

Emma remarked that she wishes you were coming in February, during the Horse Show, as she thought that you would enjoy it. For the past four or five years, in fact ever since the establishment of the present Horse Show organization here, we have attended every performance, with the exception of matinees, when we turn the box over to the children for their friends. If you and Margaret are at all interested in fine horses, it might be worth your while to come a month earlier, as we will have one of the finest shows here that is held in the United States. The greatest saddle mare in the World is owned here, and we have pulled down first place in fine harness and five-gaited classes all over the United States with California-owned horses. The Show starts February 5th and runs until the 12th, inclusive. It is really a very brilliant affair, and draws people from all over the United States and Canada.

Whenever you come, be sure and let us know which road and train you will arrive on so that we can meet you, as otherwise you might get lost in a large city. With love to Margaret and yourself, in which Emma joins, I am

Yours,
Ed

[Card paper-clipped to letter:]
   New Address
   Edgar Rice Burroughs, Inc.

[added, by typewriter, "& Edgar Rice Burroughs"]
   Mail: Tarzana, Reseda, California
   Telephone: Owensmouth 220
   Express: Owensmouth, California
   Telegrams (Western Union): Owensmouth, Calif.
   Cable: Burroughs, Owensmouth, Calif.]

April 13th 1927

Dear Edgar Rice:

Here-with dope on the Lincoln car: The car you would get would be like ours, except it would not have disk wheels, and the extras over the standard 7 pass sedan would be; wheels, or rather tires, carried in wells on the foot boards, 1 extra tire, rim and cover, and trunk rack in the back. The list price on this Lincoln f o b Omaha is $5394.30. I can buy it for $4544.30, or a saving of $850 over list.

There is $1,000 profit to the dealer on this car, but Ford makes all Lincoln dealers give $150 service on all Lincolns. It is called "4 months free service" and is figured at $150.

Our dealer here tells me that he would have to make this 150 good to your Lincoln service man out there, and he suggests this plan if you but the car: I to buy it for myself for my own use in Calif. You to be along and drive it out there for me, and incidently use it till I arrive. It would have my Nebraska license, and would be my car. Then after a few months, and I could not come to Calif I could sell it to you. See?

The importance of this is that Ford requires that all Lincolns be followed up and reported upon, and your Lincoln would have a "Home" out there, get the regular service, etc. and with the title of the car being with me, the Nebraska license, number, etc. no question would come up.

Alec tells me that it is best to figure it will take 30 days before you can be sure of a Lincoln ordered.

Margt and I were in Lincoln last night dining with our Son and his girl. Left the Cornhusker at 11 pm exactly: we were home (just 40 miles) at 11:50 exactly.[47] It was dark and I did not realize I was going so fast. I could not see the speedometer, and you simply do not recognize 60 miles per hour in a Lincoln. I think you all would be entirely satisfied with a Lincoln. It is no better car than that big Twelve of yours, but it is more modern.

And then think of the kick we would get out of having you come and get it!! Also remember you can drive her 70 miles per hour the first hour, so you would have no loafing to do en route home.

I know that koin means little in your young life, but $850 would make it easy for you to come to dere ole Beetrice on the Blew, and still save money, and we would be so mighty glad to have you and Emma here.[48] You could look us over under our own vine and fig-tree, and possibly that would at last explain some of the queer things about us. Remember my Father and my Mother's family settled this town, and I am the ole Original Sin if there are any. Also I'd like to get your ideas on the Weston Boys. We like em pretty well ourselves, but we need sound ideas as to what to do with them.

This is a new t-writer, and I find I am not so good on it. It is one of these portables, and I bought it along with a new regular for the reason that I got it cheap, buying two at once, and then I want it to take to Calif with me.

We had a wonderful time out there. I am surprised that folk averaging 50 years old could have so good a time. I wish we could have staid longer, but anyway even 16 days was more than worth it. I judge we were there at just the right time, as yesterdays paper said you had been having real weather ever since we left. It poured that day we pulled out till we crossed the mountains.

I got the silly idea someway that we would be at the Canyon the 2d day out from LA instead of the 1st day out. We were getting much needed sleep when they commenced to rear around, ring our bell, etc. Finally I oozed out of the upper berth with the idea of finding out what was the big idea, and found we were due in the Canyon in 13 minutes!! There was some tall hurrying around that stateroom as we were right out of our peaceful slumbers! At that, we were nt the last ones off the train.

We caught a perfect day at the Canyon, and were crazy about it. I think that one day was a-plenty for Margt, but I would like to stay there several days sometime and let it sort of soak in. A few times I have seen the ocean that gave me somewhat the same kick, but never any thing else.

Gene Tunney was on our train from Williams west. At Colo Spgs he got off and there was a gang meeting him. They were taking his picture and sort of ganging around. Margt blew up to him, gave him a whirl, shook his hand, etc. I dont know just what she said to him, but he blushed like a bashful kid, and from them on they were pals. Too bad they could not have met earlier on the trip.[49]

I was a good deal impressed by this Tunney, in that he does not appear at all like a prize fighter, but rather as a sort of a bashful football player—sort of kiddish. I'll admit that I am sure if Mr Dempsey is at all right he will knock his youthful appearing block off.

Mrs Collins had the real flu. She had the very best care (probably better than if we had been home with our preconcieved ideas) and came out of it in fine shape. She is still somewhat depleted, but is in fine spirits and is going to make a complete recovery. Our MD, and in fact everyone around the place, took wonderful care of her.

The boys were delighted with the photographs and books. By the way Edgar Rice, I read Norman of Torn the first day out en route home. If it hadnt been for your name at the top of the pages I would not have known it was step-sister to the Tarzans and the Mars books. A jab or two of philosophy which I have not observed in Burroughs Books. Is this a change of style, an experiment, or full freedom of mature experience and observation? Incidently, I enjoyed the book very much. We all are a lot obliged for the books and photographs. They help much to make the Weston home happy.

I have been busier than a bird dog since getting home, or I would have written sooner—which I certainly should have done—because you people did certainly give us a real joy spot in our lives. It had been so long since I had foregathered with you, and it was fine to find you better than ever. As I may have intimated once or twice, people mean a lot more to me than things or places. I get more that way the older I get, and I just could not have a better time than to just jimmy around with you Burroughses. I think your children are peaches. I wish I could have seen more of them. I will, next time we are that way. This was such a rush trip all through. What I would like to do would be to hang around the Burroughs Wyoming ranch house for a few days (I could sleep in the 4d truck)[50] and have you pay no attention to me, and watch you come and go, read your books, play with the rats, be bitten by Lobo and Jet, ride a horse and shoot a little golf. Not strenuous perhaps, but joy enough for me!

Seems to me there is something I wanted specially to tell you, but I cant think of it now.

I do hope you take on a Lincoln car and come and get it, though I'd let the car go, if you will just come and get it. You seem so satisfied with it out there, that I know you would have to have some real urge to get you this far east. Think over that 850 saving!! Also how mighty glad we would be to have you come this way.

Much love to all Burroughses from all Westons,

Yrs,

[HTW]

Tarzan & the Golden Lion was here the week before we got home.

Reseda, Calif.

April 26, 1927/bw

Mr. Herbert T. Weston, Beatrice, Nebraska

Dear Bert:

I have had two letters from you that I have not acknowledged, both of which I greatly enjoyed.

I have given up the idea of buying a new car this year, at least, but I want you to know how very much I appreciate the opportunity you and Margaret offered me to save some money on a Lincoln.

There are, however, so many things I wish to do around the tract in the way of building and improvement, that I do not feel that it is absolutely necessary that I should have a new car now, inasmuch as I find that I can put the old one in good shape for a matter of some $300.00.

Glad you struck the Canyon on a good day. I was recently talking with somebody who knew someone who arrived there a short while ago in a fog, spent a day in the fog, and came home in the fog, seeing nothing.

Gene Tunney does not raise my temperature one-tenth of one degree, and I think if he ever gets into the ring with Jack Dempsey again, and if Dempsey is in proper condition, Mr. Tunney is apt to land in somebody's lap.

You will get a laugh out of the latest possibility that looms upon the horizon, which is a monkey farm, to be located here at Tarzana. It will be patterned after Gay's Lion Farm. Since the matter has come up, I have been making the personal acquaintance of a various assortment of monkeys. Yesterday I called on quite a bunch of them over at the Selig Zoo, meeting for the first time three or four orang-outangs who arrived from Singapore Saturday or Sunday. One of them was filled with vast content if I merely stood and held his hand. Joan wanted me to buy him, but when I told her that I thought they cost from five hundred to one thousand dollars, she changed her mind.

Emma and the children join me in love to you all.

Yours,

Ed

July 12th 1927

Dear Ed;

Here in a clipping that Jeff snagged out of a Detroit Free Press some time ago. Yeah, they take the Press there too! Except for Fred Strong the names are a little too old for me, but probably not for you.

We are pulling out tomorrow for Minnesota. The Lincoln and the

Big 6 Touring car full of baggage. It is about 600 miles north and the first 350 are unpleasant motoring, drifting north with the wind. From there on it is a fine moist country. We will be for a month or so at the Birchmont Hotel, Bemidji, Minn.

Margaret had Jeff in Lincoln recently. He was in the book department of a large apartment store, and did not come and did not come. Finally she looked him up, and found him delivering a lecture to one of the sales girls, his subject being, Edgar Rice Burroughs, Creator of Tarzan. Margt said he had this girl dizzy. Mart also intimated the girl was young and a good deal of a peach.

Jeff has come along a good deal in the past $^1/_2$ year. In the last 18 months the poor kid had grown $4^7/_8$ inches in hieght, which has nt left him time for much else. 2 inches taller than I am and weighs 165.

We have had a fine spring and summer here. Are going to have the best crop for years and years. The last few days have been hotter than the 7 hinges, but that is good corn weather so we loyal ones pretend to like it.

Have you a little camera in your Home? Movie? Eventually, why not now? I can buy that stuff for you at 33% discount, and you would enjoy the carefully edited fil-ums of the Tribe Weston at Work & Play.

I wish we were about to head for Calif instead of Minn.!

Much love to you all.

Yours,
[HTW]

Reseda, Calif.
July 19, 1927/br[51]

Mr. H. T. Weston, c/o Birchmont Hotel,
Bemidji, Minnesota.

Dear Bert:

I was delighted to have your letter of the 12th and hope that you all enjoyed your trip to Bemidji, which is a Hell of a name for a town.

I was tremendously interested in the Free Press clipping concerning Orchard Lake. Do you wish me to return it? It occurs to me that it would be a wonderful thing if we could form some sort of an association of Orchard Lakers and try to bring pressure to bear upon the state of Michigan to the end that it might establish a state institution to be known as The Michigan Military Academy and if possible locate it at Orchard Lake. What do you think about it, or don't you?

I cannot say that I am very hectic about the amateur motion picture camera idea. I have purchased so many things that the family was hectic about only to find that they were nine day wonders. I now have three projecting machines and seven hundred and twenty eight thousand miles of film which are never used.

Emma and the children join me in love to you all.

Yours,

Ed

Reseda, Calif.
July 30th, 1927/br

Mr. H. T. Weston, c/o Birchmont Beach Hotel,
Bemidji, Minnesota.

Dear Bert:

I suppose you are perfectly right about there being no chance that the state of Michigan will support a military school and I am damn sure that I wont, it being just a little more than I can do to support a family.

I know how you and Margaret must have felt following the boys' auto accident. You know Hulbert had a similar one when a lady stopped her Ford head on in front of him and he put her and her mother in the hospital.

I am afraid you will have hard work convincing me that I will ever become greatly enthused over the home made movies.

Every once in a while we destroy a bunch of photographs that were taken several years ago and which now make us appear ridiculous. What's the use of leaving something to posterity that will make them ashamed of our poor taste and sorry for our lack of intelligence? Caesar, Napoleon and George Washington would be no great heroes if we had 16 mm movies of them.

We are all glad that you are having such a good time and wish that we were rich enough to take a vacation. It must be grand to be wealthy. Emma and the children join me in love to you all.

Yours,

Ed

defunct!!⁵²

Beatrice, Nebr.

9/11/27

Dear Ed and other Burroughs who whappen around:
I am much embarrassed—so is Margt—to say nothing of Collins, our First Born.

I suspect that Col is a good deal like his dad, age for age, weight for weight, only more so. Some letters which you will receive are self-evident. No one knows howinhell this happened, not exactly. I suppose the first line of this paragraph is the nearest explination. I repeat that I am much embarrased and also very regretful, for Col is nt a bad sort.

We got back from Bemidji just two weeks too soon. It has been hotter than the 7 hinges around about here since we returned and after our sojourn in the frozen north, we notice it. They say it is mighty good for the corn!! Mebbeso!!! Tiz doggoned hard on humans.

We found Bemidji, and our layout there all and more than we had hoped. There is an undoubted charm to Northern Minnesota. We liked it so well that Margt got gay one day and dickered for a cottage. However, when we got to talking it over, we wisely concluded if we locate with an investment for summers, it will probably be on the coast of Maine. Minn is charming, but Maine has all Minn has and then skins it 40 ways from a Jack—chiefly on account of the North Atlantic Ocean which is there abouts, and I will say that that same Ocean is the best Ocean I ever saw.

They (or rather I suppose I should say WE) are going to have the biggest all around crop ever known in this county this year. The weather the entire year has been ideal for aforesaid crap. Gawd knows we need it. I trust that both Maggie's and my stores will leave the red far behind the next 12 months.

The Lincoln is a great car. We all felt like kissing ours all summer. Worth the money I should say, IF you can afford them. However, poor man that I am individually, if I were going to invest in a car tomorrow for my personal use, t'would be a Studebaker.

My niece, Sally Weston Simmons, increased the population of Pasadena—as per schedule—on Sept 1st, with a nice little Helen Jane.[53]

Col is already at the U of N on what they call Rush Week. Jeff leaves for dere ole Culver tomorrow. Herb breaks into the 9th grade also on the morrow. That darned Jeff grew another $^7/_8$ inch while we were away. He is a large lad!!

I yearn for So Calif. I think I could put in my remaining 8 or 10 years very happily, situated out there somewhere, where I could ride in the a.m., golf in the p.m., and sleep 13 hours of your cool nights.

Much love from all of us,

Yours
[HTW]

This summer I read the damndest story of yours in a Mag called Amazing Stories and I'll admit AMAZING was Right!!

Reseda, Calif.
September 17, 1927/br

Mr. H. T. Weston, Beatrice, Nebraska.

Dear Bert:
Yours of the 11th arrived yesterday, also letters from Collins for Joan and myself. Tell him not to lose any sleep over the delay in acknowledging the photos. Having two boys of my own and once having been a boy myself, I realize what a heck of a chore it is writing letters, especially to total strangers.

Am glad you enjoyed your trip to Bemidji.

Emma, the three children and I just returned from a trip to the North Rim of the Grand Canyon, Kaibab Forest, Zion Canyon and Bryce

Canyon in northern Arizona and southern Utah. The enclosed snap-shots will give you an idea of our transport. Emma and I piloted my roadster with the trailer, and Hulbert and the children trailed along in the dust in his Buick. Please note the snappy canopy over the rumble seat of Hubert's roadster which showed in both pictures. This made riding in the rumble seat a real joy, which it is not ordinarily when one has to endure sun and wind continually.

Emma and Joan occupied a nice bed in the trailer. The tent, behind which Hulbert is standing, is our old beach tent which we used for a dressing tent. Hulbert, Jack and I slept on folding cots in the open. We really had a bully time.

I gather that you do not care for THE MASTER MIND OF MARS and probably agree with the correspondent who took the trouble to write to some British colonial paper to say that the Burroughs' stories were the silliest things he had ever read. The clipping came in the same mail that brought your letter.

I will admit that the Lincoln is all that you say it is, but I still think that the old twin is a pretty fine car.

Everyone here is getting ready to welcome Lindbergh, who arrives Tuesday. I think I have never admired anyone as much since Teddy Roosevelt, but I would not go downtown and be milled around by a million people to see the almighty. However, I expect we shall have an even greater treat as he will probably fly over Tarzana, which lies directly beneath the air mail route to San Francisco.[54]

Please congratulate Helen Jane on the remarkable sagacity she dis-played in having elected to be born on my birthday.

Emma and the children join me in love to all of you.

Yours,

Ed

Shall mail this tomorrow to give you one of the special Lindbergh cancellation stamps

Ed

15. Two photographs included in Edgar Rice Burroughs to Herbert T. Weston, 17 September 1927, Utah or Arizona, photographer unknown. *Bottom photo, left to right*: Edgar Rice Burroughs, Hulbert Burroughs, and Emma Burroughs. *Weston Family Collection.*

Mr. H. T. Weston, Beatrice, Nebraska.

Dear Bert:

I was interested in your letter and your account of your visit with Att Conner.

Did I ever tell you about Mattison coming to see me a couple of months ago? I do not know whether you recall him or not. He was a rather husky, red headed fellow and an old boy, I think, when I was a plebe. I had not seen him or even thought of him for some thirty five years. He came upon me quite unexpectedly and I called him by name instantly, notwithstanding the fact that I hold the record for world's rottenest memory for names and faces. He did not open up much, so I do not know what he is doing or how he is prospering, but I imagine as he was touring around California that he is not a total loss financially.

Yes, I saw the Tunney-Dempsey fight pictures. I think Tunney could have gotten up before the count of ten, but I think he would have gone right down again for a count of about one hundred and fifty.[55]

I believe that Dempsey will come back if he gets another chance within a year. I have a great deal of faith in him, not so much in his supremacy as a scientific boxer, but in the fact that he is essentially a fighting machine.

Did I write you that Joan is playing in stock at Glendale? She played one week as leading woman, but since the return of the regular leading woman she has been playing ingenues. She is accumulating a great deal of valuable experience inasmuch as they put on a new play each week, rehearse six days a week and give fifteen performances weekly of each play—the rest of the time she has to herself.

Emma and the children join me in best to you all.

Yours,

Ed

Mr. H. T. Weston, Beatrice, Nebraska.

Dear Bert:

It was good to hear from you and to know that you are all well.

I am appalled by your schedule. If I had to face the possibility of that much travel during the next year, I should seriously consider passing out. I see you are electing to come to California during our bad weather, which is quite the usual thing for people to do.

I have only seen one football game this year — u.s.c. vs. u.c., but I have listened to several over the radio which is just as interesting and much easier on the feet.

Hulbert, Jack and I have been following the wrestlers quite a bit lately, but the game is so damn crooked that much of the kick is taken out of it. They say that every opponent who faces Stecher, the heavyweight champion, has to post a twenty five hundred dollar bond that he will not beat him, and the bouts certainly suggest that this may have foundations in truth. We saw him wrestle Zbyszko last night and in my opinion if Zbyszko had dared, he could have killed him. Of all the rotten excuses for a champion, I think Stecher the rottenest.[56]

We also attended the classical Dundee–Ace Hudkins fiasco last week. You have probably read something of it in the papers.[57]

If all the lousy crooks who make an easy living off the fighters and wrestlers could be eliminated, I think the public might enjoy some pretty good sport, but as it is going now it will not be long before boxing and wrestling will be stopped in California entirely.

Joan's company is playing "Buddies" this week. She has the part of the American sweetheart and has a cute little song, which she does well. She is improving a great deal as she gains experience.

Emma and the children join me in best to you all.

Yours,

Ed

Dear Edgar Rice;

I suspect that one of the chief drawbacks in living in Sunny Southern Calif is that sooner or later everyone you know or ever have known drops in on you. Some wize cracker, when I was in dere ole Yale drinkher down, said, that if you stood on the corner of 42d St and 5th Ave long enuff you would see everyone in the world. The vicinity of LosA is much the same way, only more so.

But speaking of red ants, Mattison was before my time. You had been building up the morale of the M MA some time before I arrived on the Shores of Orchard Lake, if you remember.

I have a recollection of the day I arrived, and you hard-boiled up to me and asked if I had ever played football. I blushingly replied that I had played two games as end on the Nebraska 'Varsity, and you almost kissed me!! This must have been two years after Mattison left the fold.

Margaret and I agree that it is wonderfully fine for Joan to do what she is doing. For a youngster of her age to have a real interest in life, other than merely frivoling around, and to get in and really work, and work hard, is certainly great stuff. We congratulate her, and you and Emma.

We had dinner in Lincoln tonight with Col. He impressed me chiefly as being such an infant. He must be a year or two older than Joan. That is much the same age considering she is a girl and he a boy, but I could nt help hoping and wishing that poor ole Col would develope an undoubted interest in something more or less worth while, as she has.

I'll say this for Son The I; the last $1/4$ at the University is about over, and to date he has held up well in his work. Col is a sweet sort of a kid, but is inclined to be Gawd-awful footless, like his dad.

Maggie and I are about to depart to Culver to look over JBW 2d. I am chiefly hoping he has nt grown much more. Those uniforms cost likehell: we had to outfit him anew in September: and besides, when a kid grows so d——d fast he has nt energy for a whole lot else.

I was much pleased to run on to another Tarzan Story in the December Blue Book. Lapped up the 1st installment with great interest! I hope for much of "the upper terraces". Like meeting up with an old friend.

We have had the best weather for the past 6 weeks that I ever saw. Golf in cotton clothes. Great stuff, and especially for Nebraska. We have about concluded that eventually our schedule will be; Dec 15 to Feb 15, Beatrice: Feb 15 to May 15, SoCal: May 15 to June15, Beatrice: June 15 to Sep 30, Maine: Sep 30 to Dec 15, Beatrice and points east following football games where they most interest us. Very fair—wot?

Much love from us both

Yours,

[HTW]

Reseda, Calif.

December 9, 1927/br

Mr. H. T. Weston, Beatrice, Nebraska.

Dear Bert:

Thanks for yours enclosing note and clipping from Woodruff. I am afraid he is off of me for life.

I was interested in your account of Ford Day. We had one here at the Ambassador ~~Hotel~~ Auditorium, which you will recall, and I understand that it was jammed full. Everyone here is buying Fords. I am going to get one myself, for if what they say about the new car is only 50% true, it should be worth twice what they ask for it.

We were quite disappointed with the outcome of the usc–Notre Dame game, but of course it was just one of those unfortunate breaks and does not reflect any upon our playing ability.

I saw usc trample all over Washington last Saturday. In the first two or three minutes of play it looked as though Washington was going to wade through our line for a series of touchdowns, but as soon as usc got on to their system they put a stop to the rushes. During the last half we were playing the second team against Washington and it was then that they got their two touchdowns. Morley Drury received the greatest ovation that I ever saw given to a football player when he went off the field after the first half, some sixty or seventy thousand people all stood up and yelled their heads off until he had left the field.

Consider this the annual Christmas Greeting, since we ceased sending cards last year. It grew to be a meaningless gesture. We had a list of names in a book, we ordered the Christmas cards a month ahead of time, some one else addressed the envelopes—that is Christmas sentiment for you. All our friends were vying with each other to outdo everyone in the expense and elaborateness of their Christmas Greetings. We decided that it was vulgar, shoddy and the bunk. Therefore, we cut it out.

Love to all in which Emma and the children join.

Yours,

Ed

Reseda, Calif.

December 14, 1927

Mr. H. T. Weston, Beatrice, Nebraska.

Dear Bert:

Thanks for yours calling our attention to Rex Beach's article in Liberty Magazine, the title of which indicates that it may be of interest to us, all except the "Fat".

Yours,

Ed

1/12/28

Dear Edgar Rice;

Herewith a selection of kodacs of the best lookers in my immediate family. These are the first "stills" I have seen in a long time taken by Weston. He runs mostly to movie stuff, but I think his technic is still fair!!

In some of the pictures Jeff 2d is making a desparate effort to look hard, and as he wants to look, which I judge is normal in a 16-year old. In others he looks as he really does look.

Have I told you about Jeff's mumps? No? Three weeks in the dere ole hospital and home on Dec 28th. 174 at the end of football season and 154 when he got home. Some mumps. However, he gathered 8 ³/₄ lbs at home, and went back the 10th apparently feeling fine.

He is crazy about the school. Thinks there never was any place like it, which is a d——d good thing.

Col had been around in the corn fields and corn dust some years, and I concieved the brilliant idea of sending him to NY on a 10 day trip for a Xmas present. I think I would have sent him to LA, but his present girl was in Pasadena. I think he had a good time in NY and I hope took on some ideas.

Margaret and I hope to break for the Southland in about another week, but you never can tell a d——d thing about whether we can get away or not. I feel no particular entheusiasm about this trek, as I know no one anywhere en route who has any interest for me. I may be nutts about the country when I get there, as I was about Southern California, but I suspect the people around LA supplied much more of the charm to me than did the country or climate.

If things go well, I think we will come to Calif later on, and we will probably take ole Herb out of school and bring him along. This public school is nt teaching him a d——d thing, and I'd take him to Cuba, only we are going to stay with M's cousin, and the servants are all Spinachios, and we could not cache Herb alone with them nights, while we rat around.

We have had a solid week all below zero here. It is very pleasant now, but it was bad enough during the Holidays.

This is one of my busy seasons. I have about four per year.

Hope you had a fine holidays, and that everything is going along the best in the world with all of you. I hate to think of Joan working so hard, but I do surely hope she is still playing when we get there. I have known few Thespians, and I'd get an awful kick out of seeing her do her stuff.

I suppose you are now asking $60,000 for your 3 cornered residence lot?

Love to all from Margaret and me

Yours
[HTW]

Mr. H. T. Weston, Beatrice, Nebraska.

Dear Bert:

We were mighty glad to have the pictures of Margaret and the boys. You certainly have a husky looking family.

Sorry Jeff has been laid up, but am glad that he is on the mend.

Joan is still working in stock, but do not know how much longer she will remain with this company as she is getting nothing from it except experience and a rather small salary—I mean there is no proper direction, which would be of such inestimable value to her at this time. We are, therefore, hoping to place her in a better company, if possible.

I am enclosing a picture of the whole family taken on Joan's twentieth birthday and, also, a picture of the store and office building that I built last Spring on Ventura Boulevard. The office is almost completely hidden by the black walnut tree. It is the old Spanish farm type of architecture. You will note the idea carried out in the ratty looking fence.

Hope you and Margaret have a wonderful time on your trip to Cuba. Emma and the children join me in love to you all.

Yours,

Ed

Reseda, Calif.

February 10, 1928/br

Mr. H. T. Weston, Beatrice, Nebraska.

Dear Bert:

We were glad to have your post card from Tampa. It arrived a few days after we had celebrated our 28th anniversary.

It must be great to be rich and be able to travel around the country and be crowded and jostled and stepped on and annoyed. Pity us poor farmer folks who have to stay peacefully at home and enjoy life in our simple minded way. However, when I get rich, if I ever do, I am going to travel as I believe that all young people should do this to improve their minds.

Emma and the children join me in love to you all.

Yours,

Ed

Reseda, Calif.

March 19, 1928/br

Mr. H. T. Weston, Beatrice, Nebraska.

Dear Bert:

Glad you got back from Cuba safely. We are all looking forward to seeing Margaret, you and Herb.

Yes, the St. Francis dam catastrophe was a terrible thing, but if it had been one of the dams above our valley or the Weed dam above Holly-wood the loss of life would have been many fold greater. The trouble is that no one knows the cause and the community is so full of rumors and guesses that there is considerable apprehension concerning all dams, though I believe this is more or less groundless.[58]

Knowing nothing whatsoever about the matter, I am still entitled to an opinion which is that continuous twenty four hour inspection of every dam should be required by law, as I cannot conceive of a break coming without some warning—a little stream of water must have grown in volume until the dam was sufficiently weakened to give way and a watchman on the job, if furnished with the proper means of giving warning signals, could have reduced the loss of life to a minimum.

Everything is moving about the same here. I am trying to work hard on new stories in the constant battle against the wolf of which you pluto-crats know nothing.

At present Joan is not working. She quit her job at Glendale think-ing that she was about to better herself, but found that conditions had been misrepresented to her. At Glendale they say that she can come back whenever she wishes, but she does not wish to take her old posi-tion away from the girl who is filling it and in the meantime we are trying to wriggle along without her forty dollars a week and, of course,

I could probably always find washing for Emma to do—at least I could if I were more energetic.

The family join me in best to you all.

Yours,

Ed

Ambassador Hotel

Los Angeles, Calif.

5/7/28

Dear Edgar Rice;

Doubtless you expected to get your little movie outfit this morning. So did I!

Here in dere ole LA there seem to be only jobbers in the Eastman stuff. 20% discount is what they allow, and that only.

Also, I have checked up the prices, and the latest machine (projector) costs more than I thought. Also the 1.9 lense $25 more than I thought.

Since I could not get this outfit right here, and since the prices were rather different than I had coyly suggested, I have not telegraphed for anything, and wont, till you pass on what it shall be.

What I have is as follows;

Cine-kodac B Model with 3.5 lense	100.00
Kadascope A Model	180.00
" Rewind Machine	7.00
	287.00
Less 30%	86.10
	200.90

This is a d——d good outfit and has been very satisfactory to us, but the Model A Kadascope is a big heavy thing and is not made to carry around any. Also, you cant reverse it, and run the film backward, Neither can you stop it on a still, because the film will melt. It has to be re-wound by hand. So far as merely showing the films, it is very good indeed. A powerful lamp, close focusing etc. I consider it a good deal better machine that that Bell & Howell I had in your office.

The best outfit I know of is as follows;

Cine Kodac Model B 1.9 lense	150	00
Kadascope Model B	300	00
" re-wind machine	7	00
	457	00
Less 30%	137	10
	320	00

This is the outfit I would buy, if I were buying. The 1.9 lense lets you take a picture in less than $1/3$d the light possible with the 3.5. While you do not use this a whole lot—this poor light—at times you would like mightily to have it—for interiors, dark cloudy days, late in the evening or early mornings. I admit that 90% of the time the 3.5 lense is fast enough, but when you do want the faster one, you want it badly.

The Kadascope B Model does not throw a bit better straight picture than the A Model I have, but is a $1/4$ the size and $1/2$ the weight; can be carried around. The A Model is to use in the house and to keep there. Then the B Model threads itself, and always correctly. Runs forward or backward, and you can stop it and show any one picture as a still as long as you please. This is often very very amusing, and is a good feature.

I dont know as you would get $120 more out of this really better outfit. If I had none at all, I'd buy the one on this page, but you notice I am using the one I have with a good deal of satisfaction, and will think some time before blowing myself for the better one, especially as they make no decent allowance on a trade-in. Hulbert says the Bell & Howell people are selling out, or something, and making some good prices. You might investigate what they have. All these machines are good. B & Hs or Eastmans. I like the Eastman best, not because I have one, but because after using both, there are more things about the Eastmans that I like; but Ralph Scott, for instance, would nt have anything but the Bell & Howell. If you can get real bargins on Bell Howells, they might suit you just as well.

I am glad to get you Eastman stuff at just what it costs us. Any of it, as much or little as you want. There is either 30 or 33$1/3$ off on the list price, plus the express charges.[59]

One thing, these 16 mms are really fool proof. Any one can take the pictures, provided the camera itself is helf still, and a reasonable attention is paid to the stops, tho this last is much less than in a still camera. Your projector will always work. Never will jam up as your standard machine did that night. It has to have a little oil occasionally, but that is ALL. We have never had the slightest trouble with ours in three years, and showing thousands and thousands of feet. I showed over 2,000 feet in your office the other night.

Look the situation over carefully and let me know.

Margt and I both had a wonderful time the other night. The Burroughs outfit certainly made the Big Hit with us.

yrs htw

Tarzana Ranch, Reseda, Calif.
May 9, 1928

Mr. H. T. Weston, c/o Ambassador Hotel,
3400 Wilshire Boulevard, Los Angeles.

Dear Bert:

Thanks for yours relative to the camera.

I certainly appreciate your kindness and am trying to make up my mind — not as to the outfit, but as to whether a poor, struggling, young author should make this investment at the moment.

We want to see you folks again soon.

Emma and the children join me in best to you all.

Yours,
Ed

Reseda, Calif.
June 1, 1928/br

Mr. H. T. Weston, Beatrice, Nebraska.

Dear Bert:

That was a mighty good letter of yours. I should have written you before had I not been trying to finish a Tarzan story, which is, at last, an accomplished fact.

You may get a night letter most any time asking you to get the movie outfit, but not at the moment. When we do get our projector, we shall certainly want to see your films and we shall send you ours, if you can stand them.

We know what it is to get home again after a trip. As a matter of fact that is always the best part of the trip to us.

I can't tell you how much we all enjoyed seeing you and Margaret again and especially in meeting Herbert. We hope that it will not be long before you are living out here and we can see the other boys in person, although we feel that we know them fairly well through motion pictures. Now if you will just buy one of these vitaphones we can hear them talk, too.[60]

Joan has about half talked me in to driving her to Flagstaff and Tuba, Arizona, next week with a friend of hers, as Jim is on location with the Fred Thompson Motion Picture Company there. Tuba is north of Flagstaff about fifty or sixty miles on the Mohave Indian Reservation and is so far out of the world that it has not even telegraphic connection therewith.

The cesspools are backing up into the front parlor again, so I must close and get down to my real business in life.

Yours,

Ed

Reseda, Calif.

June 26, 1928/br

Mr. H. T. Weston, Beatrice, Nebraska.

Dear Bert:

I have mislaid your letter relative to the motion picture camera.

I want to get an outfit such as you recommended, and if your offer still holds good I should like to avail myself of the discount, which I don't need to tell you will be appreciated.

What I want is a lense that will do the best work under the worst conditions, which I think is the one you recommended, and I should also like to buy at the same time twelve rolls of film.

Hulbert, Jack and Mr. Rosenberger and I are going on a camping trip up into Shasta County, leaving the last of this week, but if you will write and tell me the amount to send you Emma will take care of it, as either she or Mr. Rothmund will handle my mail while I am away.

Joan is going to be married about the eighth of August and we are anxious to get the camera and do a little experimenting so that we can get good pictures of her wedding, which will take place outdoors between the chicken yard and the corral.

When we get our machine we shall have to exchange films occasionally. I am sorry that I did not attend to this sooner, as I should like to have had the camera on my trip as I might have gotten something interesting.

Emma and the boys join me in love to you all.

Yours,
Ed

Reseda, Calif.
July 9, 1928/br

Mr. H. T. Weston, Beatrice, Nebraska.

Dear Bert:

Your the travelingest family I ever saw. I suggest that you put a miniature railroad track in your backyard with an engine and private car, so that whenever Margaret has the urge to travel she can do so with the least effort.

Hulbert, Jack, and I just returned from a fishing trip yesterday. We went up into Shasta County, in the northern part of the state, taking the two roadsters and a trailer. Charley Rosenberger went with us. We went up the west side of the Sierras, crossed over to Reno and came down on the east side. It was an interesting trip, but we didn't catch very many fish, though we saw a lot of nice, home grown mountains, including Shasta, Whitney and Lassen, the latter being the only active volcano in the United States. It erupted a few months ago, but failed to put on any show for us.

I think you're crazy to vote for Smith. The prohibition question is practically dead as far as the majority of Americans are concerned and even if it were not you and I and anyone with any property or financial interests of any sort would be crazy to upset the even tenor of a Republican administration, under which we have had the greatest prosperity the country has ever known. If you are pining to reduce your income and Margaret's, vote and work for the Democrats because that is all that you will succeed in doing, as the prohibition question, like Farm Relief and the Boulder Dam, is nothing more than a political issue which both parties will use as long as they can for purely political reasons.[61]

I was talking yesterday with a friend of mine, who ran for Governor of California a couple of years ago. He and his wife were at the house when we returned from our camping trip and he told me that conditions are quite serious and that although Hoover is the best trained presidential candidate that we have ever had in the history of the country, Republican leaders are very much concerned by the chances of a Democratic victory owing to Smith's strength in several of the Eastern states that control the majority of the electoral votes.

So if you have any political whooping to do for God's sake do it for Hoover and buy your booze from the bootlegger as of yore.

Emma and Joan are as busy as cranberry merchants preparing for the great event, which, from the amount of publicity that Joan has received, appears to be upon the verge of pushing Hoover and Smith over into the advertising section.

Next time you are out remind me to show you the clippings. I even received one, cut by one of my friends, from the Chicago Tribune today, and it all came out of a little squib that the real estate agent, from whom Joan and Jim bought their house, put in a local paper in Van Nuys. Every paper in town has been telephoning Joan and Eastern papers have been telegraphing FBO Studio for Jim's photograph. The New York Times had their local representative send their photographer to the ranch and the end is not yet, but the whole business is more or less embarrassing inasmuch as we had been planning on a very small, quiet wedding and had not intended to make any public announcement until the last minute. However, Joan is not at all peeved as she is in her element with publicity.

We certainly wish that you folks could be here for the wedding, though you probably would not enjoy it as it is going to be as dry as the Republican platform.

The last wedding I went to was in town and when we left things were going good, but I am told that the next morning there were guests, chauffeurs and policemen lying around on the ground recovering and I have made up my mind that Joan's wedding will be no drunken brawl.

Emma and the children join me in love to you all.

Yours,

Ed

[The following letter is undated but was probably received about 10 July 1928. — Ed.]

Dear Ed;

Your letter in re movie outfit came while we were in Chicago seeing that our second son was getting none the worst of it from the USA. I decided he was NOT.

Got back yesterday and am ordering today, as per letter (copy) enclosed. If they will ship from Frisco, it ought to save you quite a lot on express, but mebbeso they wont do it. Anyway you ought to get her in about a week or so.

This projector is exactly like mine, and I think it is a good a one as I have ever seen. It's one objection is that it is large and cant be carried in the vest pocket. But I think you will use same 99.99% of the time in your own home. They have another (the latest) $300 projector, but I cant see the 120 difference.

This camera has the 1.9 lense. Mine has the 3.5. I am going to have mone changed as you can take a picture with the 1.9 in $\frac{1}{3}$ as much light as with the 3.5. Read the directions and DONT over expose. You can ofcourse set the stop at anything down to $\frac{1}{32}$.

Am sending you 4-400 ft reels too. You need them (or will soon) and you might as well have the 33 $\frac{1}{4}$ off on them too.

In a hand kodac it is better to expose over, rather than under. In a movie the reverse is true. Under-expose slightly rather than overexpose. If you have anything of a mining engineer's mind you will readily see why this is; To-wit; A regular kodac negative can be "cut" lighter, and improved. In a movie film, the film you take is the film you show. They change it from a negative to a positive.

I have but one word of advice; HOLD THE MOVIE Camera STILL. Let the objects flit as they may, but hold the camera STILL. DONT MOVE THE CAMERA!!!

You will have to buy a screen. They make em in Calif. The best one known to man is one made out of beads, but in any event get the kind which suits you best. Far be it for me to pick your screen for you. I'd as soon try to pick a tooth-brush. I know the kind you ought to have, but NOT the kind you might want.

I think we will pull out for Bemidji on the 14th. It's certainly hot here. But at that, this is a regular ole summer resort as compared to Chicago.

When you get into this self-made-movie stuff, there may be a lot of little accessories you want, besides more film, and I'll be very glad to get em for you at the regular discount, any and all times. WHEN you get the stuff, send your check direct to The Owl Pharmacy, Beatrice, Nebraska.

I'll be much interested in your movie experiences, and I think we will get a heck of a kick out of trading fil-umms.

[Typed down the right margin of the page:] Ralph Cook Scott 2869 West 7th Street LosA can tell you how to get a bead screen. He is a hellofa good guy as well. A beatrice product, of whom we are very very fond.

Reseda, Calif.
July 10, 1928/br

Mr. H. T. Weston, Beatrice, Nebraska.

Dear Bert:
Yours enclosing bill for Cine-Kodac received. I cannot tell you how much I appreciate your kindness and the big saving you have effected for me.

I was also glad to have the pointers on using the machine. I suppose I shall make a terrible blob of it at first. Just as soon as we get something good, I shall shoot it on to you and let you see what a punk I am.

Emma is waiting outside the office for me now and I shall have to hurry.

Am sending check to The Owl Pharmacy in this mail.

Again thanking you and with love to all from all, I am

Yours,

Ed

Reseda, Calif.
July 23, 1928/br

Mr. H. T. Weston, c/o Birchmont Beach Hotel,
Bemidji, Minnesota.

Dear Bert:

Thanks for the clipping from the Chicago Tribune. It is quite usual that I receive my most desired clippings from my friends rather than from the clipping bureau that I pay to cut them for me, so I am always glad and grateful when anyone is good enough to send them on. In addition to this one that you sent we have received others from various parts of the country, as Joan and Jim broke into newspapers all over the United States.

We are all sorry that you folks cannot be at the wedding, but we shall take a picture of it and send the film on for your edification.

We have taken two reels and are waiting impatiently for the first one to be returned. I knew when I took it that I was doing everything wrong, so I am not expecting very good results. The principal trouble was that nothing that I wanted to take would stay in the finder for eight or ten seconds and so I was starting and stopping the thing for little short shots.

I want to tell you again how much we appreciate your kindness in getting this outfit for us. I have made a cabinet that looks like a smoking stand and holds everything pertaining to the outfit. I am going to take a picture of it and send to you.

Was glad to hear of your wonderful fire sale and only wish that we had been bright enough to choose Beatrice as a place of residence so that we could have each bought a twelve dollar slicker for one dollar apiece.

Is the projector that you sent us supposed to run the film backward and, if so, how?

Emma and the children join me in love to you all.

Yours,
Ed

Reseda, Calif.
August 13, 1928/br

Mr. H. T. Weston, c/o Birchmont Hotel,
Bemidji, Minnesota.

Dear Bert:

The wedding went off as per schedule and everyone seemed to think that it was a very lovely affair, principally because of its simplicity. Joan was married on the knoll at the east end of the lily ponds. It made a very pretty setting. They left the next morning in Jim's car for Indiana to visit his people and from there they are going to Coldwater and Chicago to see some of Emma's people and mine. We have had telegrams and letters from them en route and so far they have encountered nothing worse than an electrical storm in Arizona.

Your present came this morning. It was postmarked Beatrice, August 9th, so that if you do not hear from Joan until after she returns you will understand why and forgive her. For my part, let me thank you and Margaret for all of us. Being fond parents yourselves, you realize that whatever is done for the children is appreciated more by father and mother than the things that are done for them. I have not opened the package as I would not rob Joan of the thrill. For the past two weeks she has been in ecstasies and if her friends could have seen the joy their presents gave her, they would have been more than repaid, and it made no difference whether the gift was a dishtowel or a set of silver, Joan's enthusiasm was just as great.

After the ceremony they made their escape without being seen, and after driving around the Valley for several hours came back and hid under some trees down the road until after the last of the guests were gone when they came back to see us, which was mighty sweet of them, and the next morning they came home to breakfast and to say good-bye to us before they left for the East.

Emma and Hulbert left for Chicago and Coldwater Saturday. They are driving on in the "8". They pass rather near Beatrice and if you had been there they would have made the trip up to see you. They are going to the Sherman House in Chicago and after a few days there will probably go to Coldwater.

I rented an extra camera for the wedding and Jack and Mr. Rothmund took four reels, which was all that they could take before it got too dark. The conditions were bad as the sun was low in the west and several of the important shots had to be taken in that direction or not at all, but we are hoping that some of it will turn out well.

I had about eight rolls of kodak film and asked Chris, the stableman, who, according to his version, is the world's greatest photographer, to get snapshots for me. He succeeded in getting two, one of which is good. This was the only disappointment of the wedding as I had banked on having at least two or three dozen pictures.

As soon as you get home I will send you some of the Burroughs' films, if you care to see them, and certainly the one of the wedding if it is any good.

With the best to you all, I am

Yours,
Ed

Reseda, Calif.
August 28, 1928/br

Mr. H. T. Weston, Beatrice, Nebraska.

Dear Bert:

Received yours of August 22nd and suppose you are home by this time.

I think Emma and Hulbert will leave Chicago for home about the twenty-ninth or thirtieth. I am going to wire them today and will mention the fact that you and Margaret are home, so it is possible that they might drop in on you. It will depend, of course, on how hurried they feel about returning home.

They sent me two reels that they took in Chicago. We ran them last night, and I tell you it was wonderful to see some of my old friends and relatives and a couple of new in-laws and babies that I have never seen. I bought a screen yesterday from the Arrow people who make them—one of these glass bead screens, and it improved the projection fully 100% over the wrinkled sheet I had been using.

The Rosenbergers are thinking of getting a picture outfit such as you got for me. I have not told them that you effected a saving for me, but I thought if I could get it through you and make this saving without any embarrassment to you, I should like to do so, in the event that they decide to get an outfit. Do not hesitate a moment to say no, if it is not wholly to your best interests to do it, as I am vastly more interested in your peace of mind than I am in saving the Rosenbergers a couple of hundred dollars.

Did I tell you that I saw the new Eastman color film down at one of the Eastman stores recently? It is certainly wonderful and I know that that is the next thing that I am going to have to have.

Thanks for the clipping from the Beatrice paper. Too bad the N.E.A. bawled Jim's name up so, but I think it will make little or no difference as everyone in the business knows who he is anyway.

Drove by Margaret's lots the other day and noted that they are still there.

Give my love to all the family.

Yours,
Ed

Tarzana Ranch, Reseda, Calif.
Aug 31 1928

Dear Bert—
It sure was good of you to remember my birthday and there is none whose remembrance I appreciate more.

Jack & I are just leaving for Catalina over Labor Day.

Emma, Hulbert, Joan & Jim left Chicago Thursday (yesterday) I doubt if they can stop at Beatrice as I know Jim must get back.

Love to all

Ed

September 12, 1928/br

Mr. H. T. Weston, Beatrice, Nebraska.

Dear Bert:

I was much interested in your long letter of September 3rd. I know how you and Margaret must feel with all the boys gone but I do not agree with you that it is better for them to be away from home. The Lord knows during a lifetime we get little enough of proper influences, so when the home influences are good I believe the children should remain at home as long as possible.

I am glad that Herb is still rooting for me. He is a great kid and should have a highly developed mind, if he continues to read Tarzan books.

That portion of my family which drove East this summer was disappointed in not being able to stop off at Beatrice for a visit. They went way south of you, however, not passing through Lincoln. That would not have made any difference if they had had plenty of time, but Jim was anxious to get back to work as he has had many calls from many studios and they did not wish to separate on the home trip.

I imagine you will get a lot of pleasure out of your new Lincoln roadster, but for me I am afraid I am a dyed-in-the-wool Packard user. I must say, however, that during the last month, while Hulbert was away, I have driven his car much more and with greater pleasure than my own, but then the new 8's handle more easily than my own Twin, which is not an easy car to drive.

I am anxious to get your letter home and let Emma and the boys read about Micky. I sure got a great laugh out of him and you.

Did we have the new Tarzan while you were out here? He is a six months Old English Sheepdog, weighs fifty five pounds and is still going strong. I think he is one of the brightest dogs I ever saw, but, like all puppies, a damn nuisance and eleven times as much a nuisance as though he weighed only five pounds.

It is mighty good of you to offer to get the picture outfit for the Rosenbergers. I shall tell Charles about it immediately and hope that he gets one.

We have been at the beach for two days now, and as far as I am concerned I would just as soon be home. The damned ocean depresses me terribly and there has been fog, or haze, or mist, or something that made it impossible to see much further than spitting distance. Everything is grey and somber and gloomy. However, if Emma and the boys enjoy it, I can put up with it. And I do like the cooler weather, I shall have to admit that. I was certainly fed up on heat this summer. I believe we have never had such a hot year. Jack tells me that a couple of days before we went down to the beach it was 114 degrees in the shade at the house, which is some hot.

With love to you both in which Emma and the children would join were they here, I am

Yours,
Ed

Reseda, Calif.
September 18, 1928/br

Mr. H. T. Weston, Beatrice, Nebraska.

Dear Bert:
Received yours of the 13th telling me about the film. Many thanks.

We finally got the wedding pictures back yesterday and ran them last night. They are going to Jim's people, and when they come back I want to send them to you, if you care to run them.

I will try to get information about the Santa Monica Yacht Club. I do not know a darn thing about it.

Am glad that Herb likes it at Culver. I am sure that they will like him.

Like it down at the beach very much now and would like to live there.

Yours,
Ed

Tarzana Ranch, Reseda, Calif.
October 16, 1928

Mr. H. T. Weston, Beatrice, Nebraska.

Dear Bert:

Ed Featherstone, who is quite a yachtsman, doesn't know anything about the yacht club being promoted at Miramar other than he received some literature concerning it. If I get any more information, I will drop you a line.

Emma and the children join me in love to you all.

Yours,

Ed

Reseda, Calif.
November 16, 1928/br

Mr. H. T. Weston, Beatrice, Nebraska.

Dear Bert:

Pardon me while I light a Murad![62] I just found your letter of October 15th under a pile of magazines on my desk, but I hope that you will reinstate me on your calling list.

I am working on a story and worrying my fool head off over the back property, which several wealthy gentlemen are trying to steal from me now that El Caballero has busted, with the result that I am not entirely accountable for the things that I neglect doing.

I could not send you the wedding film as Jim's people have not yet returned it and nothing else we had was really worth sending, although I shall send some of the other stuff when I get the wedding film back and can send that.

I suppose that you are in the East now to see the Yale-Princeton game.

I figure from your letter that you will be back home about the first of December. Let me know exactly when, and if the wedding film is back I will shoot it on to you with some highly exciting scenes of horses galloping around the paddock, which seems to be about the only thing we can find to take on Tarzana.

Emma and the children join me in love to you all and in the hope that we shall see you out here in the near future.

Yours

Ed

P.S. Did you hear who was elected President?

December 12th 1928

Dear Edgar Rice;

Before I forget it, a kid, one Bradley, here in Beatrice, has had a letter from you. His dad was telling me about it yesterday, and said that Xmas now meant nothing to him. The fact that you mentioned Herb gave it the "personal touch", and completed this little kid's utter joy. I should think that not the least kick you get out of it is giving these little kids these real thrills. They lap up the Tarzans, and when you write to them, it is just like getting a letter from God, or at least The Holy Ghost.

I have carried a color movie thousands of miles, to Culver three times, etc.till my right arm is 2 inches longer than my left, and NEVER have I caught "bright sun light" between Beetrice and the Atlantic. Culver would make hot color pictures, with the military stuff, and further, 688 boys out of 700 there have regular apple cheeks. Gawd knows if I'll ever get sun-light there. I seem to be a sort of a storm center.

We have had a pleasant surprise. Jeff and Herb were due here next Sunday for the Holiday vacation. Monday night I got a wire from the school, saying they were closing early, due to the flu starting an epidemic there. So the Boys hit here yesterday. 5 days extra vacation!! Gawd, I never had any such luck when I was in school.

Culver is some school in some ways. The assembled the Corps at 10 a.m. At 2:30 pm they had all been observed, temperatures taken, etc.143 detained and the rest were on special trains heading east and west. I think few schools are as well organized.

You know, last year poor ole Jeff was 28 days in the hospital with mumps; missed Christmas at home, and was here only a week. It was a hellofa a Christmas for the whole family! With this flu so prevelant,

I was sure one of em would get it, and be delayed. We certainly are for them for closing early!!

I wish you would send your movie reels any time now. We will all be here, all are crazy to see them, and I'll get them back to you pronto.

We had quite a trek eastward. The Nebraska Army game was just what I looked for; a whalloping team poorly coached, beaten handily by a fair team beautifully coached. I saw a lot of Seth Thomas and his immediate tribe and though the years pass and pass, I continue to get the big kick out of that, just as I do out Edgar Rice & Family. Margaret does nt take much to Seth. Collins says it is because both Margt and Seth like to take charge and runn things, and there is a conflict. The bossing around that they give me has never worried me any.

I hate it in NY. Too d———d big and getting bigger. It always takes me two or three weeks to get over being nervous, and I never do get over being scared of subways, crossing streets, taxi-drivers and head waiters. I cant imagine anything worse than being sentenced to live right in Manhattan for life. Chicago is bad enough, but it is positively a country village compared to NY.

Sure, I observed the result of election. I got no thrill from it however, as I was told by some of my wise friends 5 weeks before election that Smith did not have a dead china-man's chance.

Perhaps a one party political situation is a good thing for a country. I doubt it. It never has been a healthy situation. I have no objection whatever to Mons Hoover. I even suspect that he is one of the 1/2 dozen greatest men in this country.

However, I am still disgusted with the platforms of the two parties (which platforms, I'll bet I can take, paragraph by paragraph, submit em to you, and that you cant tell 20% of the time which is which) and I think we should have a progressive and a conservative party. Since the parties declared for the same things, I was inclined to the man who would more nearly reflect the majority of the peepul. Smith has a fine public record. Smith has personality. Smith is the type who could go over the head of congress and force legislation by direct appeal to us poor dumb common voters.

Personally, I dont care a tinkers damn whether a man is a Catholic or a Babtist, whether he speaks Bostoneessee or Alabama nigger talk, whether his wife has the social graces, or eats with her knife, whether he drinks beer or champaigne. I would a little rather have him one way or another, but so long as his record is good, I can let the rest go. Truth to tell, Mr Lincoln was no Beau Brummel, either personally or as to family connection.

Smith, personally represented the progressive element to me, and inclined me toward to him. A real he-progressive leader is needed, in my opinion, for the good of the country in general. Hence and therefore I was strongly inclined to Mr Smith, because I like him personally but more as a protest to the one-party situation.

Howthesoever, I voted for Hoover!! On entirely selfish accounts! I did not see where Smith could collect aids to the conduct of the business of government who rated up with Mellon, Huges and a few of that type, and I feel that my job of running Margt's business for the next four years will be easier!! Now, what do you think of that? A regular Manhattan conscience!!

I ought to be ashamed of myself, and am. Ofcourse there was another very minor element that entered with me, when I ducked into the voting booth. Like millions of women, for the first time in her life, Margaret, the wife of my bosom, took an active interest in politics. Also, like billions of other females, she was an extremely hot Hooverite. She intimated to me that if I voted for Smith she would never speak to me again, and she can always tell someway, when I am lying to her. I just can't get by with it.

What are Hulbert and Jack doing? Are they both going to U of C, SoBr?[63] My recollection is, that they were about ready last spring, being rushed by the iniquitous frats, etc. I wish to Gawd that we dwelled so all ours could go to school within 10 miles of the home ranch.

Hope none of you have had flu. If you stay on Tarzana you probably wont have it. Margt and I take cold serums every so often which pretty well immunes us.

Hope your matters in re the Cabalero Club are coming along in a satisfactory way. I have typed so little recently that I find I am not so good. My two fingers cross and that together with my poor spelling makes a weak result!

If you don't hear from me again, a Merry Christmas and Holidays to you, and lots of love from us all.

Yours,

[HTW]

Reseda, Calif.
December 27, 1928/br

Mr. H. T. Weston, Beatrice, Nebraska.

Dear Bert:

I am finally getting the films off to you. There are two large reels of Joan's wedding and one large reel of assorted Tarzana pictures in which, I think, is the film you took of Joan and Hulbert on their horses a couple of years ago. Then there are two small reels. The one of Jack shooting his coyote includes an experiment in titling. It was my intention to cut and patch this part of the film so that the title would come where it belongs, but I have so far neglected to do so. Therefore, the title will come after the picture instead of before it.

The wedding picture was taken from 5:30 PM on. Some of the shots had to be taken directly into the sun, but at that time we had no reflectors which will account for some of the rotten results.

I am glad that the Bradley boy was pleased with my letter. It gives me a great deal of pleasure to hear from children and to know that they like my stories. An odd thing about my work is that my stories are written for adults and I have a very large adult following and that the only juvenile that I ever wrote, THE TARZAN TWINS, is practically my only flop. Trying to find out why has taught me a lesson. I have it from no less an authority than the president of A. C. McClurg & Company, who has been publishing books for many years, that from fifteen years up children read and enjoy adult literature. I made my mistake in THE TARZAN TWINS by doing what is known as "writing down" and succeeded only in reaching a mental level far below that of the young people I wished to appeal to. I think Kipling did the same thing in his "Just So" stories, for I know that as far as I was concerned they were the rottenest things he did.

We had a very satisfactory Christmas with all the children, including Jim and Joan, with us all day.

Emma and the children join me in best to you all.

Yours,

Ed

Jan 2d 1929

Dear Ed Rice;

Your film shipment came this morning. Very glad to have em, especially before the Boys go back to school, which is on the 6th. Will run them and send them back in a day or two.

This happens to be one of my busy seasons. About four times per year I have more things on my mind than a bird dog pup the first time out.

I have fitted up and made a desperate effort to make some colored movies. This is the worst possible season of the year for so doing, because the sun is so d———d low that it has little chemical quality, and while reasonably interesting, I must say I am not entirely nutts over colored movies—not as yet!

After the boys leave, I'll send some on to you, and you can run em and see if you are going to venture into this realm!

We have had a good Holidays. No flu as yet, and everyone pretty happy. It is going to [be] mighty lonely around here next Sunday night, and as for me, I'd be in favor of pulling out for Calif or Havana, IF we could—which we cant—not for a while anyway!

I weigh 1 lb less now than a year ago!! This is the first year in ten that I have not put on at the dere ole rate of about two pounds per year.

Love to you all,

Hastily,

[HTW]

Dear Ed;

Again you Burroughses have given us a wonderful time, only this time it was thewholedamnedfamily!

We ran the films tonight, and certainly there is much kick in them. Considering the stress of the day, and that you could not plan lights, that wedding series is a wonder.

Just to show you how mighty good it was: I have a sad complex at a wedding—dont care how much I am for it, or how much I may desire the happy union, when it is pulled off, it takes all my self-control to keep from howling like a wolf. There is no remote explanation to this; I'm just that way.

Tonight, viewing the Burroughs-Pierce wedding, in the cover of darkness, I surpressed many a tear—and this is a fact!

That must have been a lovely wedding. Wish we might have been there.

As the films ran along I wish you could have heard Herb's lecture to his brothers, who, as yet, have n't had the luck to meet up with the Burroughs Tribe. A complete detail of the character of each of the family! And there is quite a remarkable thing, he is for you strong, as a group and individually, which you will have to admit is unusual. From an unbiased, unaffected kid, I think that is a real he-compliment. Deserved certainly, for children and animals are apt to be true detectors of character.

Hulbert's coyness at certain times; the family exodus from the house. Any number of things gave us a great kick.

This may interest you; comments from Col and Jeff, the things at which they seemed rather surprised and to marvel over; Emma's youthful appearance, and your Doug Fairbanks like figger!!

I am certainly obliged to you for sending these films, and especially before the Weston Boys got away to school. Am going to try to get them off to you tomorrow, as I know there must be numerous times when you want to show them.

A letter from Culver today saying they had postponed the opening of the school from the 7th to the 14th. They got the dope on the flu all over the country, and it is the advice of the health authorities, not to collect 700 boys so soon. That gives Jeff & Herb just a month holiday. I wish you could have heard the celebration when the news came this morning!

I noticed the effect of the Calif haze in some of your pictures. I had that same thing in a number of mine. I suppose, coming through the haze, a number of the chemical rays of the sun light are lessened.

I used to try all sized stops, etc., but could nt get away from it. Wonder if your local dealers can give any corrective dope to get away from the sort of a sketchy effect that haze gives.

I have now had back 150 feet of color films taken since the boys got home. Am not cheering over them. Some are quite remarkably good, but at least half are not. I think that Calif haze would have the same effect as our low mid-winter sun, and dull the colors and distinctness. Also you shoot all pictures with the 1.9 opening and have to be right at a gnat's ear with your focus distance. Think I will stick mostly to Panchromatic which is some better than the straight film, and is worth the dollar more in price.

Listened to the Pasadena game New Year's with a good deal of interest. Must have been a great game. That near-touchdown, on his own goal by the Calif center was the most amazing thing I ever saw, or rather, listened to, or saw. I can understand how a boy all keyed up and playing over his head could easily, with an unusual opportunity, and making the supreme effort, could do a thing like that. I certainly felt sorry for that boy.[64]

Did nt we see Jack driving a snappy A Model Ford in the films? How does he like it?

Our best from all Westons to all Burroughses, and we are certainly obliged to you for sending the films!

Yours,
[HTW]

Mr. H. T. Weston, Beatrice, Nebraska.

Dear Bert:

The films arrived this morning and I greatly appreciated your returning them so promptly.

I am glad that you found them interesting, but I believe the fault that you attributed to California haze was due solely to the fact that some of my shots were taken too early in the morning and too late in the afternoon. As a matter of fact we have very little haze here in San Fernando Valley, the sun light being almost as clear as on the desert.

We are very proud, indeed, that Herb has judged us and found us not wanting. It is great to be liked by a regular fellow like Herb.

One thing about Riegels' remarkable play in the New Year's day game is that it has fixed his name indelibly upon the minds of hundreds of thousands of people, giving him much greater publicity than he could have obtained had he made a touchdown for his own team. As a matter of fact, his is the only name that I can recall on either of the teams. No one here seems to hold the play against him and I am sure that no one would wish for him even a small fraction of the punishment the poor boy must have suffered.

Emma and the children join me in best to you all.

Yours,

Ed

Reseda, Calif.

February 6, 1929/br

Mr. H. T. Weston, Beatrice, Nebraska.

Dear Bert:

The book on happiness from you and Margaret came by the morning's mail and I proceeded to read it through immediately. It is quite the most intelligent thing upon this subject that I have ever read and furnishes considerable food for thought for both young and old.

We are all well, and after reading the book I am very happy, although I do not know what I am happy about. I hope that Emma will read it today as she is without help at present and needs every possible incentive to happiness. Anyhow, she and I can be happy because we are not young, and the children happy because they are and also because they are not going to remain young for long—it is an absolutely unbeatable philosophy.

Yours happily,
Ed

Reseda, Calif.
February 15, 1929/br

Mr. H. T. Weston, Beatrice, Nebraska.

Dear Bert:

Yours of February 9th just received. Many thanks for your assistance in getting the enlarging machine for me. It is for Jack's birthday, which occurs shortly. I am glad you got the diffuser thing, although I am equally in the dark as to its purpose as you. The express agent called up to say that there was a kodak at Owensmouth for us, so I presume that it is the enlarger. Pretty quick work.

Congratulate Margaret for us on having attained years of discretion.

Some friends of ours were out the other night and brought two Culver reels. If you have not seen them, I suggest that you try and get hold of them while you are down there. They are issued by the Culver Publicity Department and show both the winter school and the summer school. We enjoyed them immensely.

Everything is about the same here with us. Emma is just recovering from a bad cold, but otherwise we are all right.

Again thanking you, I am, as ever

Yours,
Ed

Mr. and Mrs. H. T. Weston, Beatrice, Nebraska.

Dear Margaret and Bert:
We arrived home safely yesterday afternoon and found everything fine here.

We certainly enjoyed our visit with you and are glad to be able to visualize you as you all are in your beautiful home.

While the sun did not give us an opportunity to see Nebraska at its best, Emma and I were both impressed by the natural beauties that we were able to see.

Emma joins me in again thanking you for your hospitality, our only regret being that we did not see Herb and Jeff. I suppose they got home today and that you are all having a great time together.

We found that Jack had accumulated about seventy baby turkeys and a bunch of light brahmas while we were gone and this morning he showed me a turkhen that had just hatched.

The whole family joins me in love.

Yours,
Ed

June 10th 1929

Dear Edgar Rice;
Had your letter today. Glad you arrived home in good shape. Bet you were plenty glad to get there.

You certainly got a tough break here. This is actually the d——dest climate possible. Today, a week after you left, it is about 100 in the shade and a degree of humidity which is almost overpowering, with so quick a change from the recent chill.

Lin Sherwood, classmate, and life long friend (in fact we fought and bled together in the sa War!) has a daughter, who is the buddy of the two girls who ran you down. This Marion Sherwood is my favorite of all of her generation. She runs strictly to horses and dogs, and any kind of an animal, and is good at it. Besides is smart and extremely attractive.

She is broken hearted that she did not meet the Great Edgar Rice. It seems that she has read every Burroughs book, etc.etc.

I told her dad of your fine habit of replying to every kid letter you received, and urged him to urge her to write to you. She is somewhat shy, and may not do it, but if she does, give her stock a boost with a letter she will remember, will you? She is a peach, if there ever was one. You would have got a real kick out of her, and it is d——d shame the weather was so bad, and she did not come around. Normally she horsebacks by here two or three times a day, and I would surely have flagged her if the d——d rain had not kept her away.

The boys got home on schedule. Certainly looking and feeling fine. Herb came through with flying colors, but JB kept up his record, and flunked more or less.

They were much disappointed that you and Emma were not present. They, as had Margt & I, had hoped you could meet up. I got the low down on this Tarzan serial report you asked for. It seems that the universal opinion of the Culver Cadets was that the serial they saw was a sort of a sacrilege on the Tarzan of the book. They both told me that every guy they asked said the serial was rotten and worse, and the reason they hated it, was because it did not follow the Tarzan books, and was nothing like the books in anyway. Jeff ever went so far as to collect written opinions. I asked; "Why didn't you send them to Ed?" He said; "Gee, dad, some of those cracks would make Mr Burroughs sore." I got both of them to repeat some of "those cracks" and the result was complimentary to the books but sure poison to the serial.

The whole general opinion raged on the fact that a bully tale and a real hero was absurdly misrepresented, and they hotly resented it.

"They did not even get the names right". "Tarzan was never an old cripple with a vaccination mark and a gold tooth". "There never was any love stuff much in Tarzan, and if they had been, she would never have fallen for that big stiff even if she was rating nothing herself."

I saw two reels of this serial. I am inclined to believe the boys are right; that, whoever put it on, probably never read any of the books. I personally know twenty youths who are closer to my ideal of Tarzan than that ham actor who took the part. He certainly gave out nothing of the untamed young human animal.

Since you were here, I am amazed at the universal knowledge of

Tazan. You may not have cared for the damp weather here in Beatrice, but I think it saved a mob scene.

It is great stuff to have all the Weston boys around home again. Jeff and Col have played golf almost every daylight hour. Herb sticks close to his mother.

Am enclosing herewith a sheet which may rejoice you very much. Emma and I hope it does. Gawd knows few enough of these victorys perch upon your bridge banner!!

Love to all Burroughs from all Westons,

Yours,
[HTW]

Tarzana Ranch, Reseda, Calif.
June 17, 1929

Mr. H. T. Weston, Beatrice, Nebraska.

Dear Bert:

Was glad to have your letter of June 10th. Am sorry that I missed meeting Marion Sherwood. I shall certainly be glad to have a letter from her and you may rest assured that I shall answer it.

I was much interested in what the boys had to say about the Tarzan serial. They need not be afraid of offending me. I had nothing to do with the making of the picture; in fact, I have never seen it.

Did you happen to think to order me some Cine-Kodak films? If it is still perfectly convenient, I should like to have about a dozen.

Emma and the children join me in love to you all.

Yours,
Ed

Mr. H. T. Weston, Beatrice, Nebraska.

Dear Bert:

The enclosed, which Ralph mailed to me while I was East, was just returned and I thought that I would forward it to you for your information.

In the matter of escrowing the stock as mentioned in the sixth paragraph of Ralph's letter, I may say that there are 37,500 shares outstanding and that I told them that I would escrow mine provided they would guarantee that a total of 30,000 shares be escrowed, and this they have agreed to do. In other words, if 30,000 shares are not put in escrow, the escrow does not hold for any of the stock.[65]

In return for placing our stock in escrow, we are permitted to purchase an additional amount of stock equivalent to ten percent. of our present holdings at $12.50 at the time that the stock goes on the market. We can buy this for twenty-five percent. cash, the balance in six months. I am quoting these terms from memory, but I think they are correct. If you and Margaret want to put your stock in escrow with the others, send it on to me.

To be perfectly candid, I do not know enough about these matters to make an intelligent decision. I am simply going to put mine in if the others do, because I have reasonable confidence in Heffron, McCray and St. John.

Kindly return the enclosed. Best regards.

Yours,

Ed

6/21/29

Dear Ed;

I forgot to order the films for you, or rather never thought about em when I was in the store, BUT I have ordered them today, and you should have them within a week anyway.

I have also got a Route No3 Nebraska Highway sign for you, and that will be along before many days.

Pleant strenuous around here with the younger generation around, but very very pleasant.

Had a hellofa blow just west of here night before last. Not a twister, but it just flattened things on a 20 mile strip. A hellofa climate, but I cant help but like it.

All the kids are home from school, and no one has pulled out for the summer, and the gang at the C Club dance last night was a joy to behold. They certainly raise fine crops of youths here in this corn belt. Wish you and Emma could have happened along about now and seen the younger generation. Youth is sure wonderful!

Margt has got herself so damned thin she looks like my daughter; that, and your irritating example, worried me so I sent and got one of these damned rubber suits. Wore it while I shot 18 holes (temperature 99!) the other day. Buckets of H_2O leaked off me, and I was pleanty pleased. However, next morning I had lost but a simple 16 oz!!! Guess I am eternally slated for the fat grand-pa class, and may as well just accept it.

Have emmitted this in much of a hurry—Love to all

Yrs

[HTW]

June 25th, 1929

Dear Ed;

Have yours of the 18th in re Mtro Field.

Had a telegram from them, asking what our subscription would be, etc.etc.

We do not want any more of this stock, good as it may be. When we fly, we fly, and our flier in this is over, except to sit back and see how she comes out, which I think will be ok.

Am sending you the certificates, and ask you to please escrow them. Also, if you want our allowance of new stock, I will send, or wire you a certificate of "Rights" so you can buy what we are entitled to.

We are in no way displeased with this flier, it is simply that we do not speculate, except in small lots, and feel that we have staked enough on this particular venture, aces though it may well be.

This issue of more stock, is ofcourse, no surprise. It was very probable when we bought ours.

We are glad to have your opinion on this. We hold you not remotely responsible, either for the original investment, nor for anything which occurs later. The only point is, we want you to give us what dope you pick up, as you are on the ground, and we rely upon you to sort of keep us posted, so we can continue to take an interest in this flier. I will be obliged if you slip me any gossip you pick up from time to time, as to new buildings, new lines, etc.etc..

I am having the time of my young life with all three Weston Boys caving around!

Love,

Yours,

[HTW]

Reseda, Calif.

July 3, 1929/br

Mr. H. T. Weston, Beatrice, Nebraska.

Dear Bert:

The films came the other day. Please accept my sincere thanks for your kindness.

I also received the stock, which I should have acknowledged sooner, but I have not been at the office much lately and neglected it. I turned your stock in at the Metropolitan office together with mine and they made out a receipt, a copy of which I am enclosing. If you wish a separate receipt for yours, let me know and I will have it made. I will also attend to placing this stock in escrow and will send you the necessary receipts when this is accomplished.

I am wondering if they sent you a copy of "The Future of Aviation," and on chance that they did not I am enclosing one herewith.

I have not been over to the airport recently, but I understand that it is developing rapidly. The company built a hangar which was rented immediately for two hundred dollars a month and I understand that they are building another one which has been rented in advance. Everything seems to be working out just as they had hoped and I am still confident that the outcome will be profitable.

The engine company expects to have two of their engines in the air this month and it is their plan to fly them back to Washington for the fifty hour test on the block. They will then fly back here and let the publicity story break, after they have received their permit from the Department of Commerce.

There is a persistent rumor that General Motors is trying to get control of Metropolitan Airport and I understand that the company is willing that they should take stock, but not controlling interest. As I see it, they will almost be forced to come in with us in order to have adequate facilities for competing with Curtis and Boeing, both of whom have fields here, though neither as good a field as ours.

I am also informed that the Government has bought a dirigible base near Zelzah, which lies about five miles north of Tarzana. Whether this is in addition to the army flying field that they were reported to have purchased some time ago or is the same proposition, I do not know.

Anything of interest that turns up I will advise you about. Emma and the children join me in best to you all.

Yours,

Ed

July 9th 1929

Dear Edgar Rice;
Thanks for yours of the 3d, in re air-ports, etc. They seem to be coming along!

I get more or less communications from the promotors — that booklet you sent me for instance — so I guess they are not neglecting us.

The Genl Motors rumor is good news. Also the Government developements in the SanFrenando Valley. I should think you would hang around the air-port a lot. I know I had a good time the twice I did. Or are you getting over your air-mindedness?

Glad you got the fil-umms all right.

Margt is selling her portion of the Owl to Harper on an amortization plan. It is the only way he can ever get on his feet, and I doubt if he makes it even with the break she is giving him, and I suspect we will have the store on our hands in a year or two more, tho I hope to God NOT!

Margt, on the 30th of June pulled the following; Played golf all pm (it was hot as the 7-hinges too) with Herb. In the pm, Jeff dated her, and they, with three of his pals drove to a public dance 15 miles from here, where she danced all evening with these kids; THEN she came home and took one of those red hot Lesser Baths! Result, she was floored next morning and has been pretty sick ever since.

She took off over 20 pounds from May 12th till June 30th. Too much, and also over-did in activity.

She is getting along ok, and will be all right in a few days. I had her out driving yesterday and again today, but she is pretty darned weak. She says Never Again for her; not if she weighs two hundred!! And she is right. After the ole 45 mark, it is easy to be too d——d strenuous.

Am today sending you the No3 Nebraska Road Marker. Hope it looks as well in your drawing-room as you thought it did on the road through the rain.

Hope your business matters in re Tarzana are breaking your way.

Love to all,

Yours,
[HTW]

Did you buy a flock of Yo-Yos?[66]
Hope the recent quake did not topple your chimney! The first one they ever had in LongBeach. That is because I have a lot there, and I suppose now L B will become the quake center of the Pacific Coast.

Margt just bought a 4d convertible coupe. Just like my Lincoln but dark blue and smaller.

Mr. H. T. Weston, Beatrice, Nebraska.

Dear Bert:

The road sign arrived in perfect condition and I certainly appreciate your kindness in getting it for me and also the courtesy extended by Mr. Cochran. It will have a place of honor in my "studio".

We hope that Margaret has entirely recovered from her over-exertion. We cannot do those things all at once, though we are still young enough to work up to them slowly.

Hulbert and I have just about completed a sleeping trailer for his Buick and we expect to take a trip in the near future.

Jack is on his way home from Michigan, driving his grandmother, his aunt and one of his cousins. We think they must be somewhere in New Mexico by this time.

Things are progressing nicely at the airport and Whiting tells me that those most intimately conversant with such matters believe that the stock will go to forty. He tells me that they are keeping you posted on all developments and I am sure that they will, because they were very glad to have you folks come in and they are positive that they are going to make a lot of money for you.

Emma and the children join me in best to you all.

Yours,

Ed

Reseda, Calif.

October 7, 1929/br

Mr. H. T. Weston, Beatrice, Nebraska.

Dear Bert:

We were glad to have your interesting postal from Hot Springs, marked by a cross where body was found. It is a good thing that they labeled the photograph, which otherwise I should have immediately identified as the picture of a Federal penitentiary.

Nothing very exciting is happening here. Jack is a senior in the Van Nuys High School; Hulbert is a freshman at Pomona College and Joan is waiting with more or less patience for the big event in December.

The Metropolitan Airport stock went on the market just about the time that the big slump occurred. I have not talked with Heffron or Whiting about it, but I am inclined to think that owing to the publicity the airport is getting and its steady growth that the stock will eventually make a good showing, though not as rapidly as it would have had it not been for the general slump that has occurred.

The engine stock is, I think, a different proposition and I believe that after the Department of Commerce test and the actual start of manufacture that we will be able to show sufficient orders to make the stock extremely attractive.

Emma and the children join me in best to you all.

Yours,

Ed

10/10/29

Dear Ed;

When Margt and I got in from our recent trip, I found your last book here, and have observed it with much interest. It looks good to me, a good get-up, I should say. I know nothing whatever about books or how they should look, but this one would attract me as a properly produced volume.

One thing I do know, is that your newspaper strip is certainly drawing a whole lot of attention to Tarzan and his Creator. I see them reading it everywhere, and hear them talk about it. I'll bet that strip has boosted your sales a great deal.

Here in town a number have borrowed your books from us, knowing we have them, and I asked at the library the other day, and they said your books have always been in demand, but recently they are never in.

Hope everything is going over big with you with these new publishers. Also that things have been breaking better on that land matter.

It is a matter of history that Maggie Collins and Bertie Weston officially met-up at the Evans Hotel, in Hot Springs, SoDak, in July 1893.

Dr Lee and I took a motor trip up that way last year about this time, and I liked it so well I conceived the brilliant idea of taking Margt up to that country this fall. At this time of year the weather in the Black Hills is always God's best variety; they got the word Indian Summer from up there.

Margt and I never saw the sun or a patch of blue sky for 5 days. We hit gumbo roads.[67] Did not see hardly a d——d thing, on account of clouds, mists, fog and rain. Caught one 4 $1/4$ inch cloud burst. Etc.Etc.

It was sure onehellofa pleasure trip. We did get a decent day at Hot Springs, and we did see and eat at the same table in the same dining room in the same hotel where we met.

We beat it for home over 160 miles of gravel-less gumbo road to start with, and with rain on our baggage rack all the way. We got home at 4:55 pm, and at 5:05 it started to pour, and has rained here ever since. Some outing!! I think I will never plan anything again; I think my middle name is Jonah.

Have I written you that Sally and Simmy are now here? They shook the dust of LosA county from their feet about a month ago, and are now holed up here—I hope for life. Sim is working for this Ford outfit. They are growing so fast they had to had some guy like him, and when I wired him he came on. I am very fond of both of them, and I am extremely glad to have them back here.

Margaret and I are going to Culver and Chicago for about a week. I hope to see JB play two games of foot ball. He did right well his first game, according to the school paper report, busting through and throwing em for a loss several times. Gawd knows if a lineman gets any mention he has to be good.

Poor Jeff aint no stoodunt, but he may be a footballer. You know he tutored most all summer and went back to try to pass off four subjects; well, he made it on three but flunked 1, so now he is trying to carry five subjects and play football. I am none too hopeful of the net result. As an academic shiner, JB, to date, is a total loss.

Am glad to hear the motor company is a comer. We had some dope from the promoters on it, which seemed favorable. My information is that with the numerous air-ship factories which have sprung up, there is an over production in cheap planes, that is, the ones up to about $3500, but that the makers of the larger planes are booked up for some time. I know that some pretty good little planes have been offered around here at way under "list" price.

I do not know how good realestate is going in LosA County, but I do know the guy who has our Long Beach property leased cant pay his rent, and we have to collect on his bond. The truth is that everyone with any spare money is speculating with it. It is sure a crazy world as far as finances go. None of the old, tried and true rules have applied for the last two years, and where the eventual get-off is going to be Gawd only knows. I dont see how anyone actively in the market would ever dare go to sleep, or even take a short nap. And the real he-fortunes which have been made recently by guys who have long records of being close idiots!!

Hope all you Burroughses are going strong. Our love to you all, and thanks for the last Tarzan book,

Yours,

[HTW]

Reseda, Calif.

November 11, 1929/br

Mr. H. T. Weston, Beatrice, Nebraska.

Dear Bert:

It was mighty nice of Margaret to send the "doo-dad" to Joan and I suppose Joan has acknowledged it before this. It will be but a few weeks now and Joan can scarcely wait, but I guess she will have to.

I have one of those noiseless typewriters, but as far as I am concerned it is a total loss. I want to hear them go.

I envy you your trip on your cousin's yacht and I can certainly give you some pointers on the uniform you should wear. In fact, you should have several. The hat is the principal item. This should be of the well-known cocked variety with a white plume. The hat should be done in blue or green to match the sea. In addition to this I suggest large epaulets and a red sash. What else you wear will be a matter for your own discretion, but if you like suntan and do not freckle the above will be all that you will require.

It will be nice if Collins can go with you. I fully agree with you that a trip of that kind is worth just as much, if not more, than an equal length of time in college.

I hope Jeff and his team come out here to play, and if he does tell him to be sure and let me know.

I believe that you are perfectly right about the real estate conditions here. We all feel this way, only we expect the good times to come next year. It has always been next year ever since the last boom expired five years ago.

I was just trying to recall whether you and Margaret met the Corwins while you were out here. If not, you certainly heard us speak of them as they were two of our best friends. Mrs. Corwin died the last of October and we have been trying to see as much of Bill as we can and keep him cheered up.

Emma joins me in best to you all.

Yours,

Ed

Tarzana Ranch, Reseda, Calif.

November 15, 1929

Mr. H. T. Weston, Beatrice, Nebraska.

Dear Bert:

We received the photographs of the boys today and do not wonder that you are proud of them. They are certainly fine looking boys and I know that they are just as fine as they look.

We are both fortunate in our children and I guess we both appreciate the fact.

Emma joins me in best to you all.

Yours,

Ed

Dear Ed;

Please note enclosed tax receipts.

These so bs did not send us a notice this year and only today I discovered that the '28 taxes on these hot lots had not been paid.

Will you have your secretary phone the collector's office, find what the tax is, and then send them a check for it, and I will remit you pronto, when I hear from you.

Sorry to bother a literary man on a business proposition, but you are all that is left of our gang in Southern California, the Holberts, Simmons and Scotts all having pulled out.

If I wrote the collector, it would be two weeks before I got the d——d thing paid, and think of that old 10% penalty you will save me!! And, by-the-way, pay the d——d thing in full, as I don't want to bothered with the April payment.

THANKS!!!

Zero here! too d——d cold for this time of year!

Love to all,

Hastily yours,

[HTW]

Reseda, Calif.

December 4, 1929/br

Mr. H. T. Weston, Beatrice, Nebraska.

Dear Bert:

We are getting busy immediately on the tax bill, but I am positive that nothing can be done to avoid payment of the ten percent. penalty on the first installment. They are terribly hard boiled at the Collector's Office, but we will do what we can.

I am enclosing two letters from Hugh Thomason which I thought would interest you. Please return them when you have read them.

Yours,

Ed

Mr. Robert Dominquez, City Clerk,
Los Angeles, Calif.

Dear Sir:

Will you kindly make the necessary notation on your records in such a way that Mr. H. T. Weston of Beatrice, Nebraska, will receive all notices of any special assessments that may be levied by the city or county of Los Angeles against his real property located in Los Angeles and which is known as:

Lots #30 and #48, Tract #9546, as recorded in Book #134, Pages 56–59 of Maps, Records of Los Angeles County.

This is especially desired by Mr. Weston so that the assessments will not lapse without his knowledge and form liens against the property.

Thanking you for taking care of this matter, we remain

Very truly yours,
Edgar Rice Burroughs, Inc.
[Stamped]C. R. Rothmund

[Stamped on lower right corner of page:] We are unable to find any unpaid special assessments on the above described property this date. DEC 9–1929

Bureau of Assessments
By Harrison

Beetruce 12-9–29

Dear Edgar Rice;

I hate to send back Thomason's letters. A breath from the past — as it were!

That long-legged, big-footed, big-moustached soB NET!!

The last time I saw him, I was with some rah-rahs in NY for the week-end, and Buffalo Bill's Wild West was showing at the Madison Square Garden. Craving a whiff of the wide open spaces, I switched my gang from women, and such, to go see this show, which, by the way was a real he-show in them ole days! And who should be herding the US Cavalry but this same guy Thomason!

Well!!!!!! We foregathered a-plenty!!! This was just as that horrible affair, the S—A—War was breaking to the fore, and Long Hugh and I discussed matters plenty.

That windy guy told me, he was the black sheep of a rating Tennessee Family. That Tenn. had no national guard, that they would ofcourse fill their quota, and that he (being a real he-army man, tho a B.S.) was to go as colonel of one of the two regiments which this same Tennessee had to raise, and he looked me over very carefully, saw my chest expansion, and observed my youthful entheusiasm, and said: "Chemical, you come with me, and be my adjutant!!!!!!"

I had already applied to be numbered amongst the Ruff Riders, but was silly enough to wire my withdrawal.[68] (Indicently, the guy who had sat next to me in all my classes at N Haven was the first American Soldier wounded in Cuba), and (excuse blushes, he never got his letter) so I might have been wounded at least three times on rating!!!!!!! And well, anyway, I finally went out with the YYaallee Battery and had about as much chance (soon learned) of getting out of the USA with that bunch of multi-millionaires, as I did to be appointed Chief of Staff, or Stalf! But, after you were in, wot could you do??

I suspect that Hugh remains something of a bull-spreader and all that, but if I go to Cuba ever again, via NOrleans, I am going to look him up and hear his ear-ful. And I am very much oblidged to you your sending his letters on to me.

Needless to state, I have written to him.

Of course they will soak us somewhat on the 10% on taxes, but think how much less it will be, than as though I had gone through the usual channels!

Love to you all, especially Joan, who is doubtless going through plenty right now,

Yours,

[HTW]

Dear Ed;

The enclosed letter just came. It seems a silly letter to me.

The lots Margaret owns are the ones described on the tax receipts for last year, which I sent you.

Without looking up the deeds, which are in the safty deposit box, I cant give full descriptions, but the last years tax receipts checked with the deeds.

When I sent you this matter, I thought all you would have to do, was to call up, get what the tax was, and send them your check, which I could refund to you pronto.

If there is any complication in this matter, as indicated by this d——d fool letter, please wire, me, and I will get a hold of Sim, and have him wire his bank to handle the matter, and you can turn the papers over to them. I am sorry to have bothered you with this.

I had expected that Simmy would be in LosA, and that he would handle such matters for us. I am inclined to think that one is a d——d fool to have anything to do with realestae ever, unless it ones sole business. Too many opportunities to be jipped, and a-plenty, at every turn of the road. I just bought a Gage County farm last week too. I think I need a guardian.

Collins has decided NOT to go to Cuba with us. Says he is plenty sick of going to school and wants to get it over. Good sense on his part, but a real personal disappointment to his dad, who likes very much having Col around.

Jeff and Herb are due here day after tomorrow for three weeks. They certainly will change the phase of things around 910 N 7th!!

We are having and have had simply rotten weather all Fall and so far this Winter. This is certainly onehellofa climate, and I envy you your SanFrenando Valley.

Much love to you all,

Yours,
[HTW]

Mr. H. T. Weston, Beatrice, Nebraska.

Dear Bert:

I have your letters of the 12th and 13th. You give me a new line on Thomason. I judge that a considerable proportion of his conversation may be taken with a grain of salt.

In the matter of the taxes. We are glad to be of any help we can in this matter, so do not worry on that score. The trouble is that this tax office, like every other tax office I have ever done business with, is operated by a bunch of pin heads who have no conception of their proper relationship toward the taxpayer. It is impossible to do anything with them other than suffer and cuss. We shall try to get the business straightened out for you and the tax bills paid, but you are stuck for the penalty.

Sorry you are having rotten weather. I chanced a glance at the thermometer Saturday afternoon as I was starting out for a ride. It was one hundred in the shade. We have had magnificent tourist weather, but rotten for us. What we need is rain, although conditions are not so serious now since they have had a series of heavy storms in northern California, which is the source of our water supply. If these storms have resulted in a heavy snow fall in the High Sierras, we are safe. However, we should like a little rain here.

Yours,

Ed

Tarzana Ranch, Reseda, Calif.

Jan 3 1930

Dear Bert—

If you are asked to sign an extension of Met. Airport stock escrow will you please send the signed extension to me, together with an order for the return of the stock to you, provided you have not already decided what you wish to do.

I will then do with your stock whatever I decide to do with my own, but I want a little time to investigate.

Yours

Ed

Beatrice, Neb.

Jan.6th,1930.

Dear Ed;

Had just taken my t-writer in hand, and was going to write you in re our speculations north of Hollywood, when I received yours of the 3d.

Will do as you say, and send the extension of escrows to you; also an order to deliver the stock to you, if you conclude this is the better thing to do.

Another thing; all we have ever received, or rather, all that Margt has ever received on that Apache Engine deal, is a receipt from the Metropolitan Development Syndicate, for $10,000.00, as full payment for ¹/₂₀ syndicate interest. This of the date of April 10th, 1929.

So far as I recall, we have not had another word from these birds in re this Met Dev Syn, and we certainly have received no stock certificates; no report of progress or whatinhell they are doing.

I do not like the idea of Margt being on record as owning this ¹/₂₀ interest, as it might make her a partner, and Gawd knows, that might be plenty bad.

Why dont this outfit incorporate? Why dont they give us some news of what is being done? I am not going to have Margt as a partner on any outfit like this, and my advice to you, is to view the thing from the same angle. It is a plenty liability to be a partner anyway, even with your brother, and the lack of interest this Heffron gang show in their "interest" holders, is far from brotherly.

Since I get little word from the Heffron outfit, would you take your pen in hand, and briefly tell me something of the present set-up of the METROPOLITAN DEVELOPMENT SYNDICATE and LOS ANGELES METROPOLITAN AIRPORT.

I am writing Heffron today, and telling him we are sending the escrow extensions to you; that we have heard little from him; that we know nothing of the Development Syndicate, and how-come all around.

I know, that since the Street went blah, "times are hard", but all the more reason that Heffron should keep the guys who kicked in with the cash, fully informed as to what, if anything, they are doing with said cash.

The boys all pulled out yesterday, and a last years bird-nest looks like a night club in full blast, compared to this lonely house.

This Jeff was just 6′2″ Jan 12th '29. In June '29, he hadn't grown any. Sept '29, he measured 6′2¼″. I measured him yesterday, and he showed 6′3″!! Now that is ¾ inch growth, in three months time, and at the age of nearly nineteen and he carried and past 5 subjects, and football as well. Also, football at Culver is a hard game, for they have to grab the time, as at West Point, and get the all the worst of it from all angles. It makes me pause to think.

Margaret just brought me in the announcement of the arrival of Joan Burroughs Pierce. She and Santa Claus must have just missed connections! We want to congratulate you Grandpas and Grandmas, and incidently the parents. How does it feel to be in the Grandfather Class? But then, I know a man named George Randall who was a great-grandfather at 52.7!!![69]

Please tell Joan and Jim that we are certainly glad to have the glad news, and wish them every joy that Olive Branches bring proud young papas and mammas.

We had one streak of luck; most of the time the Boys were home, we had regular Indiana Summer weather. Then, six hours after JB & HT headed east, the dere ole thermo dropped 45 degrees, and a pleasant little 40 mile wind slipped in from the north. It is a great climate, if you dont weaken!

I hear that you are desparately short of water around LosA. Hope this is one of the usual knocks, and not a fact.

I think that Margt and I will head south about the 20th. I have got all my stuff in shape for the alluring task of making out our income tax schedules, and am only waiting for our auditor to put in a couple of days, and then, as far as I am concerned, we can beat it any day. And, incidently, this is the first time I have ever had the years business right up, and ready to close Jan. 10th, and I am not a few proud of myself, as an active punctilious old manager!

Our good maid, Minnie, leaves tomorrow; object; Matrimony!! And the worst of it is, she is practically forced into this venture by her parents. I certainly will miss Minnie. She is all-around the nicest one we have ever had.

You know that Margt and I plan, if all is well in Gage County, Culver, and Lincoln, to go from Cuba to SanFrancisco by boat, so we should hit LosA the first ½ of March, or thereabouts. Get the chiken coop ready!! Those plans may easily all be knocked in the head ofcourse, but we would like to carry them out, as, as Margt says; "We will never be any younger."

Much love to you all, in which Friend Margaret joins me,

Yours,

[HTW]

[The following is presumably a telegram draft. — Ed.]

Western Union Night Letter, Beatrice Nebraska
Jan 13th 1930

Edgar Rice Burroughs, Tarzana Ranch, Reseda, California.

Letters of eight received. Thanks for the full information. Agree entirely with you in regard to escrow etc. and handle ours as you own. Dont send us Burroughs Feature Film, as we leave for Cuba the eighteenth, and would nt get it. Will see it at Reseda! Love.

H T Weston

charge to H T Weston

Dear Edgar Rice;

Damnedif I can find your last letters. Margt must have them, and she is asleep, and has been for 2 hrs, as I am slaving (as usual) and trying to get cleaned up for the get-away Saturday.

Anyway, I was mighty glad to have you give me the dope on the Metro-LosA, and the Metro-Syndicate. Also I am much obliged to your secretary for giving me the entire low-down on that d——d Miramar lot business.

I have a note to get into the ole Navy Strong Box tomorrow and send you the accurate description of just whatinhell the deed on these lots calls for.

We will be out there before April whatever it-is when the next tax is due, and possibly, by that time, your highly efficient California system will find what we owe for taxes.

When Margt (not I!) purchased these fine (?) lots, Simmy (whom you dislike) said; "Do you want us to handle your taxes, et cetera?" I told him something to the effect Oh Hell No, I have it all arranged to have us notified, and all that sort of thing. Seze he; OH ALLRIGHT!!

Little did I suspect the iniquity of LosA County!

You may note an occasional Type-a-graphical error in this letter, but the plain fact is that I had a quart of Bacardi Rum, which I had paid a great price for, and as Friend Margt was a little low tonight, I suggested that I mix, as nearly as I could, a fruit jar of Presidentes, to which she agreed. But she did not like them any too much, and I, being a thrifty soul, consumed same to save same!!!

We have 8 inches of snow on the ground. It hung around 10 above all day, and a 40 mile wynde from N-W. I think we are getting away just about right!

We will be at the following; c/o Dayton Hedges, Esq., Cayo la Rosa, Hoyo Colorado, CUBA. None of this sounds remotely Christian to me, but anyway, it is very pleasant. I may get home sick, and you might just as well write me there as at Beatrice, and besides, your file is the largest individual file in my letter drawer. Also, unless our luck fails, which it likely wont, being ½ of us Irish, we will be along the first week in

March, or thereabouts, and further you <u>must</u> have that chicken coop ready for us!

You must be working your imagination extra hard on your Tarzan stuff, for you have not told me one word about how it seems to be a Grandpa!! And, incidently, I glanced at a Blue Book today, and saw some pictures of Tarzan with some sort of lizard-men, which curled my remaining three hairs so tight, that they (3 of em!) look like a hi class permanent wave.

I sent you a nite-letter because I did not want you to send me that Burroughs Feature Fil-umm. Too bad to have that out of circulation! I am looking forward to that. If it is as indecent as those kodacs of you in Emma's shimmey, with a rose in your hair, I am amazed that the Ciné people developed them at all.

Please dont think that is any fake address I gave you for Cuba. It sounds that way, but is not.

Also, dont forget about having the chicken coop cleaned and deloused! Quick lime is the best, I understand.

Love to all of you,

Yours,
[HTW]

PS: You will be getting Old Spanish Custom postal cards from us in a week or ten days. And please get plenty envious when you think of the Real Bacardis, et cetera.

PS agin; Ofcourse, we told you, and you know, that that Airport and the Apache motor was a pure speculation on our part, and just like shooting craps; if we win Fine, and if we lose, also Fine! That sort of a thing is a Game and not an investment, and we know it!

[Telegram]

Western Union
Received at 74WM CD 13 NM
NORTHLOSANGELES CALIF JAN 14 1930

H T WESTON

BEATRICE NEBR

THANKS FOR TELEGRAM EMMA JOINS ME IN WISHING YOU A MOST

ENJOYABLE TRIP

ED
640P

[Telegram]

Western Union
Received at 33WM DA 19DL
NORTHLOSANGELES CALIF 1040AM JAN 15 1930

H T WESTON

BEATRICE NEBR

ENDEAVORING TO GET APACHE STOCK IF YOU WILL MAIL ME ORDER ON

METRO-POLITAN DEVELOPMENT SYNDICATE WILL GET YOURS ALSO

ED
129P

Jan 16th 1930

Dear Edgar Rice;

I return here-with the stuff on that d——d Miramar tax matter. I am certainly obliged for all the trouble you have taken, and I wish you would thank Mr. Rothmund for me, as he has certainly accumulated a real he-file on this matter.

If we get to California at all, it will be before April 28th, and if we do n't get there, thrash the d——d thing out, and we will be even more grateful.

I am enclosing herewith Margaret's order on the Metro Dev outfit to deliver her stock to you (if any!). They may not do it on the telegram.

I an close to nutty, getting ready to leave, and having dozens of tail-end things to tail up, and incidently having too many stop in, and phone.

Margt is all packed. I have nt touched a thing! She would be and I would nt!!

Our mail address is;

c/o Dayton Hedges,

Cayo la Rosa,

Hoyo Colorado, Cuba.

Our cable address (in Cuba) is DAYHEG.

15 below when I got up this a.m. Never got above zero all day. 8 below when I looked at her a few minutes ago; also snowing. Col and his gal motored (in my car, bytheway!) back to Lincoln at 10 pm tonight. We are a hardy folk!!

Must hurry on.

Hastily,

[HTW]

Reseda, Calif.

January 21, 1930/br

Mr. H. T. Weston, c/o Dayton Hedges,

Cayo la Rosa, Hoyo Colorado, Cuba.

Dear Bert:

Yesterday I got the Metropolitan Airport stock belonging to you and Margaret out of escrow and placed it with mine in my safety deposit box. When the Apache Motor stock is issued and delivered to me, I will put that in the same place.

I think we are going to have a great year here. Our week of rain with heavy snows in the High Sierras has practically assured us a most prosperous 1930. It has relieved the tension that we all felt because of the drought, which, incidentally, was not at all unusual. Bill Corwin told me that his company, the Los Angeles Investment Company, has already felt the effects of the better feeling. They sold five houses last week.

The All-Year Club is as usual taking a daily check of all automobiles entering the state on all the main highways, the number of people in each car, where they are from and whether they are visitors or expect to remain permanently. The information thus gained indicates that thousands of people are entering the state weekly with the expectation of remaining permanently. More large concerns are building or planning to build plants here; the latest, I believe, is the Proctor & Gamble Soap Company, who offered the Los Angeles Soap Company ten million dollars for their business, but were turned down. They are now coming in to build a large plant here. The head of the Goodrich Rubber Company told Corwin the other day that every tire manufacturer in the United States is planning and hoping to come to Los Angeles because they realize that this is the center of distribution for the world. In addition to which is the fact that 99.44% of all the people in the United States want to live in Southern California. I have lived in Idaho, Utah, Arizona, Illinois, Michigan and have made fleeting visits to other parts of the U.S. and, with the possible exception of Arizona or New Mexico, I have never seen any place where I would rather live than here, and, of course, for most people there is no comparison even between Arizona or New Mexico and Southern California, their principal appeal to me being that there are fewer people there.

Furthermore, my profession is such that I can live anywhere I please; yet I choose to live in Southern California and I am only one of a hundred and thirty odd million people who would like to do the same thing if they could.

All of which leads to the conclusion that Margaret made a good buy when she bought the two lots at Miramar.

I envy you your trip to Cuba. If I live long enough and am fortunate enough to become a plutocrat, I hope to make that trip myself some day on my own yacht.

I am still looking at yachts, principally through the classified section of the Los Angeles Times, which is about as near as I ever get to the ocean. Yet I may say that there is nothing in the world that I have ever wanted very much that I have not eventually secured, so some day I expect to have a yacht. It may be only twenty feet long and propelled with oars, but still I can call it a yacht.

I cannot see that being a grandfather makes much difference. For years I have been the oldest living human being, so that when at my own great age I become a grandfather it makes me feel quite youthful.

You cannot raise my temperature even one-tenth of one degree by your recurring references to Bacardi. Insofar as I am concerned, there are only three drinks—Scotch, Bourbon and beer. All of this other stuff is poison. I had some famous cocktails last night mixed by some bird from New Orleans that Bill brought up from Mexico Sunday. He raved so about them that I had to be polite, but as a matter of fact they tasted like medicine, and bum medicine at that. It seemed almost criminal to spoil good whiskey in this way. However, I would not care if I never had a drink again as long as I live.

Bill had a wonderful trip down into Baja California. He went with a party of seven or eight of his personal friends in the private car of the Assistant Something-or-other of the Southern Pacific Railway. Having toured the East and Canada in the private car of the general manager of a railway, I know precisely what a marvellous and luxurious way to travel this is.

We are looking forward to seeing you early in March. I have told the chickens that about that time they will have to move over and make room on the perches for you and Margaret.

Emma joins me in love to you both.

Yours,

Ed

Reseda, Calif.
January 23, 1930/br

Mr. H. T. Weston, c/o Dayton Hedges, Esq.,
Cayo la Rosa, Hoyo Colorado, Cuba.

Dear Bert:
    I never did this thing before,
    Nor shall I do it ever more.

Forgive my first!
Of all the goddam pests there be,
Chain letter writers seem to me
    By far the worst;
But when the Prince of Wales I see
And others of celebrity,
    I almost burst
With pride and with avidity
I seize my pen and send to thee
    This thing accurst.

Mail it to nine other victims, whether you wish to or not, and tell them to pass on this epoch making slogan:

"Cross Crossings Cautiously,"

whether you know what it's all about or not.

                                        Yours,
                                        Ed

                            [Chain letter, on separate page:]
                This is that part of the chain of which you are a link.
                Your nine letters should go out within nine days,
                        or may God have mercy on your soul.

Senator Heflin to	Bernard Shaw
Bernard Shaw	Arthur Train
Arthur Train	C. G. Dawes
C. G. Dawes	Henry Ford
Henry Ford	Col. Lindberg
Col. Lindberg	Carl Ekener
Carl Ekener	Dorothy Dix
Dorothy Dix	Lady Hay
Lady Hay	Artistide Briand
Artistide Briand	Ramsey McDonald
Ramsey McDonald	David Windsor
David Windsor	John Willys
John Willys	John Barrymore

John Barrymore	Andrew Mellon
Andrew Mellon	R. K. Weber
R. K. Weber	Walter Scott
Walter Scott	E. M. Adams
E. M. Adams	A. C. Castle
A. C. Castle	Rae F. Bell
Rae F. Bell	Hugh M. Randall
Hugh M. Randall	H. F. Hoffman
H. F. Hoffman	Oscar Greenwald
Oscar Greenwald	Carl F. Geilfuss
Carl F. Geilfuss	James B. Blake
James B. Blake	Charles B. Blake
Charles B. Blake	A. A. Hilton
A. A. Hilton	S. A. Perking
S. A. Perking	C. L. Hufferd
C. L. Hufferd	F. E. Jeffires
F. E. Jeffires	J. W. Towne
J. W. Towne	Earle B. Bertz
Earle B. Bertz	Martin Stelling Jr.
Martin Stelling Jr.	Louis Weidenmuller
Louis Weidenmuller	Dr. T. E. Bailly
Dr. T. E. Bailly	Allan Hancock
Allan Hancock	P. N. Morgan
P. N. Morgan	T. E. Ivey Jr.
T. E. Ivey Jr.	I. H. Malin
I. H. Malin	Edgar Rice Burroughs
Edgar Rice Burroughs	H. T. Weston

Reseda, Calif.
January 30, 1930/br

Mr. H. T. Weston, c/o Dayton Hedges, Esq.,
Cayo la Rosa, Hoyo Colorado, Cuba.

Dear Bert:
I am in receipt of the enclosed check from the Title Insurance and Trust Company for refund of overpayment of 1928 taxes on Lot #48, Tract #9546, amount $10.85.

I had a letter from Woodruff Ball the other day in which he asked if I ever saw anything of you folks. He is still in Salt Lake.

I also heard from Bob Lay. He said he has not been to Los Angeles for four or five years.

We drove down to San Diego with the Rosenbergers Monday, intending to go to Julian to look at some ranch property, but on account of heavy rains all the way and flooded roads we were delayed so that we could not reach Julian before dark and, therefore, went on to Agua Caliente and spent the night. I have forgotten whether you and Margaret went there or not. It was our first trip. It was interesting, but my God what a way to look for enjoyment.

Five more chickens were hatched yesterday, but I am going to train them to sleep on the ground so that there will still be room on the perches when you and Margaret arrive.

Emma joins me in love to you both.

Yours,

Ed

Reseda, Calif.

February 10, 1930/br

Mr. H. T. Weston, c/o Dayton Hedges, Esq.,
Cayo la Rosa, Hoyo Colorado, Cuba.

Dear Bert:

It will certainly be fine for you and Margaret to have Collins with you and we shall be glad to see him here.

In relation to the roosts in the hen house. You know that we would like to have you all with us and that no one would be more welcome, but the fact remains that in our measly little dump I am afraid that we could not make you comfortable and I want you to feel perfectly free to go elsewhere without fear that you will offend us. If we were back in the larger house on the hill, we should insist on having you stop there, but as it is the disappointment is ours and we shall have to put up with it.

Hulbert came home unexpectedly about one o'clock Sunday morning, after having driven fifty miles through a dense fog the greater part of the way from Claremont. Much to his surprise, he passed his examinations at the end of the last semester with what we consider a most creditable card. He received an A in English, which is really the subject that they bear down the hardest on at Claremont and he tells me that it is very difficult to get an A. I think he had something like ten more credits than he required for passing. He had two C's and the rest were A's and B's, while D is passing. Naturally, we were all very much pleased.

With American cigarettes at sixty-five cents per pack in Cuba, I should think you would be glad to get back to the U.S. At Agua Caliente the other day we found Bourbon at one hundred twenty dollars a case, which is almost twice what you can get good stuff for in the U.S. under prohibition, so I guess America is a fairly good place to be after all.

Emma joins me in love to you both.

Yours,
Ed

Reseda, Calif.
February 18, 1930/br

Mr. H. T. Weston, c/o Dayton Hedges, Esq.,
Cayo la Rosa, Hoyo Colorado, Cuba.

Dear Bert:
There is going to be a meeting of the stockholders of Metropolitan Airport the third of March. I understand that one of the important matters to come before this meeting is the changing of the by-laws, or charter, or whatever it is that it is necessary to change, to permit them to assess the stockholders. I am against this. I believe that we have risked all the money that we should in this venture and that they are already sufficiently involved so that they will find some other way of financing, if they are compelled to.

I am enclosing proxies so that if you and Margaret agree with me you can sign them and return them to me, leaving the name of the proxy blank, as I am undecided now as to whether to attend the meeting myself or have Mr. Rothmund attend it. I think, however, that I shall do the latter, as they might be able to talk me out of voting against the amendment whereas they could not talk Mr. Rothmund out of it.

I am sending two proxies because I have not your stock here and I cannot recall whether it is all in your name, or all in Margaret's or part in each.

I may say in closing that recently the State Legislature passed a bill which forbids stock assessments by corporations whose charter or by-laws do not specifically authorize such assessments.

I am sure sorry that I was in any way responsible for getting you people into this thing. I think that it will come out all right eventually, but just at present it is a damned nuisance.

Yours,

Ed

Tarzana Ranch, Reseda, Calif.

3/4/30

Dear Bert—
Welcome! Hope you and Margaret and Collins had a good trip and that you did not monopolize the bar to the exclusion of all other passengers.

Expected to meet you at San Pedro Saturday and may do so, but am laid up with bad cold that may keep me in the house to ward off something worse.

Looking forward to seeing you all

Yours,

Ed

Hotel Del Mar, Del Mar, Calif

April 17th, 1930

Dear Edgar Rice:
I suppose you just could nt bear to tear yourself away from gophering around in your new plaything, and so could nt take the time to come down here. Also, if you hung around DelMar for a day or two, you would

shoot the SanFrenando Vally, and move Lakes Emma and Ed, and settle here for life. Also, Margt says you were scared, and thought your luck would cease to hold in bridge.

Anyway, we were sorry and disappointed that you did not come. We had looked forward to having a lot of fun with you both, and also to seeing you once more before we pull out for the more or less effete east.

Collins left today. Got hold of Fred Wertz at Yuma, and Fred joined him at noon today in LosA. They will take in the Canon en route home, but that will be the least of it. We are glad that Collins will not have that long trip alone. He and Fred get along great, tho there is more than 40 years difference in age!

We leave on "The Chief" Tuesday night, the 22d. Were lucky to get a stateroom clear through to Chicago without any trouble, which is unusual this time of year with so many "tourists" beating it homeward. Will be under our own vine and fig tree on May 1st, we think, after some days in Chicago & Culver.

Bytheway, both Jeff and Herb won their last boxing matches, which gives Mamma & papa considerable of a kick!!

Please note the enclosed, which came today, forwarded from Nebraska. Margaret Collins Weston took 5000 and HT Weston took 5000. My recollection is that it was a subscription to a syndicate first and later we got stock. Anyway, it was doubtless the same as your original subscription. I have nt my records on this with me, and so will you fill this out and mail it in? Please!! And thanks!!!

I spent my birthday (the 15th) with Collins and a classmate (one Lin Sherwood) at Caliente. Again I was right successful, and came home with considerable money (for me!) True, I had rather too much to drink, but suffered no ill effects.

Margt and I drove down again today; to trade a present I had brought to her, which she did not specially want. (I would buy that kind, would nt I?) I gambled a little while she shopped and lost. Oh, but not nearly as much as I have won! So now I'll go home with this Mexican money and buy a yatch or something—probably something.

Were interested in Palm Springs, but not just nutts about it. I can show you acres and acres of just as good young desert, and at much less that 50 bucks per day for 3!!

Mighty sorry not to have seen you again. Mighty glad to have seen you as much as we did. I realize that you, Ed, made a great concession leaving that aviary for those long periods, but dont think it was nt appreciated.

If one feels he is too old to go in for aviition, I presume he takes up aviariation! /?/ I would go misspell that d——d word just when I was being extra cute![70]

Emma; those two lovely cakes made a perfect desert for the whole croud at the Havey eating house at SanBernadino en route to Palm Springs. That was a most welcome present. What cooks you have got!! I fear Edgar will lose his figger.

Much love to you all from Margaret and me, and Col would join us, but he is doubtless playing rummy with Fred about Needles,

Yours,

[HTW]

Reseda, Calif.

April 19, 1930/br

Mr. H. T. Weston, Beatrice, Nebraska.

Dear Bert:

I have your letter from Del Mar. You wronged me grievously. No aviary could keep me away from you, but I will tell you what I could not tell you in the telegram. I was afraid to attempt the long drive, feeling as I have recently. I think you will understand.

Am enclosing Jack's enlargements from your films and am sending the roll under separate cover.

Hope you have a good trip back to Beatrice.

Ralph will attend to the statement of stock ownership which you enclosed.

Emma joins me in love to you all.

Yours,

Ed

Dear Jack;

You were more than kind to enlarge my poor efforts on that little 35mm Leitz film. As a still photographer, I am a good movie camering man. You will never believe this, but I took about a peck of 16 mm movies on our trip; 3250 feet to be exact, and there is not 1% but what would make deMille's ace camera man hang his head in shame.[71]

I am very much obliged to you for your enlargements. I am sorry I gave you such poor material to work upon. I think, though, that it was my fault. I believe the camera is strictly ok. I have taken movies for five years, and movies and stills are as different as can be. Your enlargements have educated me a whole lot, and I hope to do better from here in.

Ask your Dad if he remembers when I shot Lake Emma; a frog sitting, a-a g-fish swimming up to take a look at him? In colors, and it is Good. Incidently, this Eastman Kodacolor is not so hot. It is far from perfected, and everything has to be JUST right to get a true picture, and even then it is blind to true green and any purple, both of which colors occur plenty in dere ole Nature. I would never buy a Kodacolor camera if I had it to do over.

We were down to see the Culver Kadets, and found them getting along ok. Herb has grown a good deal, and has developed a deep base voice and a creditable hand grip. I think this Jeff has grown even some more, but he is making a strong finish in academics, and so he can hit the ceiling, if that is necessary.

Herb boxed creditably in the class bouts, and Jeff finsihed again the boxing champ, which Gawd knows he should, with arms longer, bigger, and stronger than my legs!

We sure had one streak of luck while at Culver. They have a hotel there which handles about 150 to 200, in a very primitive way. Commencement Week about a thousand Mammas & Papas and what have you, descend upon the place. I never put in a tougher week than when Col graduated. No food, a poor place to try to sleep, and not a Chinaman's chance to take a bath! This year we had had sense enough to rent a cottage, but it was a poor sort of a place, and we were going to have a strange cook, etc. I was talking to the football coach, and he was asking if we were coming down for Commencement, and to make a long story longer, he offered us his house and COOK, complete for Commencement Week. I'll bet that means that I'll live at least ten years more!!

There was a good deal of conversation in regard to you and Hulbert, or one of you, or both of you were going to chauff your Grandmother and aunt back to the middle west. Now, we want you and Hulbert, one or both, to join us before you return. We motor from here to Culver, leaving the 4th of June, and hitting there the pm of the 6th. JB graduates the 11th, and we pull out that day, and will be home either the 13th, or 14th. Now, listen carefully; your and Hulbert, one or both, can join us at Culver from the 6th to the 11th, and if not that, we will be here from the 13–14th till around the Glorious Fouth of July. You will be welcome as the Flowers in May at either Culver or Beatrice, and we will all be a whole lot peeved if you, one or both, do not show up one place or the other. And further than this, we would all be delighted to have you and Hulbert, one or both, trail along with us wherever we go this summer. And at that, I dont know but what it would be a mighty good thing for you young Californians to see something besides the SanFrenandanow Valley or the Hi Serrias. Please keep the above in mind.

Thanks again, and a lot for the enlargements,

Yours,

[HTW]

Reseda, Calif.

May 12, 1930/rr

Mr. H. T. Weston, Beatrice, Nebraska.

Dear Mr. Weston:

As Mr. Burroughs has been confined to his home for the past week on account of illness, he has asked me to write you relative to your letter, which he received today.

Regarding the Metropolitan Airport assessment. We received such a notice several days ago and immediately wrote the Airport asking for the names and number of shares of the stockholders who gave them written assent to levy such an assessment (written assent of ²/₃ of the subscribed stock being necessary) and a reply thereto was received by us this morning. I am attaching a copy of their reply for your information. Mr. Burroughs intends to determine the legality of the assessment and stated to me that if it is legal he will pay it, as he believes the property is valuable and that it has all the essentials of eventual success. As soon as we determine whether or not the assessment is legal, we will advise you.

Regarding your Los Angeles County taxes. This corporation paid your taxes on April 28th, which was the deliquency date of the second installment. The amount paid was $232.89, made up as follows:

Lot #30, total 1929 tax	$142.80
10% penalty on 1st installment	7.14
Part of Lot #48, total 1929 tax	79.00
10% penalty on 1st installment	3.95
	$232.89

We are sending you herewith the 1929 tax receipts for your files; also the 1928 receipts which you sent us some months ago.

Trusting that this is the information you desire and with kindest personal regards, I am

Yours very truly,
C. R. Rothmund
Secretary to Edgar Rice Burroughs

[Enclosure: letter and roster of shareholders consenting to assessment modification.]

Reseda, Calif.
May 16, 1930/br

Mr. H. T. Weston, Beatrice, Nebraska.

Dear Bert:

This is in answer to your letter of May 9th, which Mr. Rothmund acknowledged.

If anything new turns up in the matter of the Airport, I will let you know.

Jack got a good letter from you and appreciated it very much. Being a boy and consequently hating to write letters, I very much fear that he may not answer it.

We are sorry to learn that Collins and Jeff will not be out here this summer. I hope Hulbert is able to stop off at Beatrice after he drives his grandmother and aunt back to Coldwater, but it may be that he will want to come directly home if he has any particular plans made for the vacation period.

We were glad to hear about the boys' success at Culver. Tell Jeff, if he comes out here, we will get him a match at the Reseda Post of the American Legion, where they have a card of fights every Wednesday evening, and he can ascertain the Mexican technique, most of our scrappers being of that nationality.

Emma joins me in best to you all.

Yours,
Ed

May 17th, 1930.

Dear Ed;

I find Rathmund's letter of the 12th, with tax receipts, etc., and herewith Margaret's check for $232.89, which seems to be the amount of the taxes, but which in no remote way expresses our thanks to you for handling this matter for her.

We are mighty sorry to learn that you have been laid up. I can imagine about how well being confined to your house must set with one of your plenty active inclinations, and I sincerely hope you have been turned loose on the range again, long before this letter reaches you.

We are having a wet Fall!! It has rained most of the time recently. We have had to heat the house daily, and it seems to me we are heading into a long cold winter rather than a longer hot summer.

Tonight Margaret & I, past 50 and supposedly in our right minds, are driving more than 100 miles to attend an opening of a large handsome Shriner country club, all because we do not want to "hurt" those who invited us!! I am inclined to think we are g d fools.

Rathmund gave me some dope on the Metro. We will doubtless do as you do. That is not worrying us any. We made one turn while gone, closing out before this recent break, which paid for our trip and will take care of the Metro & Apache too. Now, if I could make another so we could write off those d——d Mirimar lots, we would have escaped clean!! And, by the way, this present market look like a buyers market to me.

Everything is fine with us. I hope to hear soon from you and that you are digging lakes and things again. How would you like a Nebraska shypoke to put in your bird cell? [72]

Much love to you all from us,

Yours,
[HTW]

Reseda, Calif.
May 23, 1930/br

Mr. H. T. Weston, Beatrice, Nebraska.

Dear Bert:

Thanks for yours of the 17th and for check enclosed. I can assure you that it was a great pleasure to be of any service whatsoever to you, however slight this was.

We got a kick out of the Mark Anthony story.

Am enclosing article that Emma clipped from the Los Angeles Examiner showing the fire at the Chapman Park Hotel. You got out just in time.

Best regards.

Yours,
Ed

July 3d, 1930.

Dear Edgar Rice;

Please note the enclosed copy of hot epistle addressed to one StJohn. I do not anticipate anything from this. [73]

Received recently a notice that the assessment had been postponed till the 31st of this month.

Was talking to Margt tonight in re to it. This is the way I stand; 5000 is a hellofa loss for me personally, but 5500 is a hellofa lot more. Also, I am a gambler by nature, and I shot the 5000 on a bad bet, and I personally will forget it, but I would become peeved at 500 assessments, and pretty soon 500 more, or possibly 1000s here and there, and also I cant afford to throw good money after bad. You and Margt can, but my sum-total and income are not sufficient.

Also, I do not see one thing today that will indicate that there is any hope for relief from the present business deperession for some time to come. There are at least 40 securities on the NY market that I would be tickled to death to own at present prices, but I would not buy now, for I feel sure that they will sell much lower before they go higher. I made a bet three days ago that before the Jan 1st 1931, the average would be lower than any average to date, and no less than three wise guys offered to split my end with me! 1930 averages are referred to, ofcourse.

That Beoling Field is what I thought the Metro would be today. With their millions, they sure did put in one real he-field. They are going to grab much revenue from Metro. Doubtless there is room for many a field in the SanFrenando Valley, and there will be, in time, many a prosperous one there, but Air planes, like every other industry, is sagging and will sag for some time. The Metro was financed like a kids pop stand. They may lose clear out. In any event, it is sure going to mean that the present stock holders are going to have to meet deficits, and plenty, for some time to come.

So far as I am PERSONALLY concerned, I am inclined to sell my stock, if possible, or to give it to you or Margaret, or to anyone who may happen to want it. It is like a poker game to me. I had it and I apparently lost it, and I can forget that just like having a full house beat by a bigger one, but I (again PERSONALLY!) have no desire to stand these 500 and probably 1000 assessments, which the legal number of stock holders seem to think great stuff.

Granting that I am correct in thinking that business in general, will not start on the up for, say, 12 months, what possible reason is there for believing that Metro is nt going to have much need for further assessments?

How can they pay their interest, taxes, etc. et al? How much additional revenue can they possibly expect from a depleted industry? And then, when General Business does start on the ups (which, ofcourse, it surely will eventually) how long before the effects of "good times" is going to reach dere ole Metro?

Again Personally, I am through, and I dont care a doggone. I never did lose that much in poker or on the Black Jack table, but I have lost plenty here and there, and am used to it, and really care mighty little. I am much more concerned about you and Margaret, than about my shot.

I admit I know just close to 0 about it, but I am inclined to think if you plutes pay assessments, that you are just going to keep right on paying same, and I really do not see, where, during any reasonable time, you are even going to have a chance to get your sous back. Why not just charge it off, like the wrong ticket at most any horse race? If you have real reasons as to [text missing] . . . would admire to have same!!

Please, Ed, dont think that this is any Big Thing to either of us. It is NOT. It is just like a party to Caliente, and we happened to get on the evens instead of the odds. There is no remote sign of grief in this household on account of Metro, and all I am doing, and genl mgr, is to try to get out from under as lightly as possible.

I was right, there is no grief at 910 right now. We are having a big time with them all home and around. True, it is hotashell, and the wind blows most of the time; the market is going down and down, my golf game is the worst in 7 years, and every little thing like that utterly wrong, but we are having so good a time that I sort of shudder sometimes, and wonder; "Who am I, to have so very much in my over-middle age?"

We are breaking for Bemidji before long. About the middle of the month, I think. Herb pulls out the 5th, in his 4d, with a buddy, and they are going to investigate Minnesota thoroughly, all the 1000 Lakes of Sky Blue Water, and finally round up at Birchmont. Col is delaying to play in the State Tournament, when he and his Best Beloved will join us. Col is a d——d good golfer, playing against me, but he just has not the ole tournament temperment. Example; for 10 days had not been over 2 over par, and then we had what they call an open day, and he shot himself a 47!! Col is so much like his dad that I sometimes weep for him.

I think it would be a mighty good thing for you thin-blooded SoCalif Burroughes to summer in Northern Minnesota. You are just like the whites trying to beat the tropics. If you think that the good ole Minnesota cold lakes and northern woods would not put the old blood and iron into you semi-tropicals, you are crazy.

Also, I want to call your attention that we have not seen one doggoned Burroughs to date. What about Hulbert chauffing his relatives to Chicago? What about him at least giving us the once over?

Jimmie Hedges went to Canada on some sort of a convention of western hemisphere lithographers, other than those of the USA, and promised faithfully to come see us. Then his mother, who was in NY, broke her wrist, and had to have her tonsils out and we missed out on Jimmie!! In some ways we just have no luck at all.

Three days ago, I bet more than I should, that we would see a lower average on the NY market than any 1930 average to date. Three wise guys offered to split my end with me. If you have surplus to invest, don't do it yet! Put in orders from 5 to 10 below the market and you'll likely get them all.

Probably you thing I am rapidly getting to be a nutt on business in general, markets, and whatnot. Well, you know a manager has to let his mind, or what passes for it, on such matters. At that the Firm and I have seriously discussed just putting the whole smear into governments and municipals, and letting her ride!!!

How's the aviary?

Yours,
[HTW]

Reseda, Calif.
July 14, 1930/br

Mr. H. T. Weston, Beatrice, Nebraska.

Dear Bert:

No matter what you say, I feel like hell about the airport and engine company investments, which you certainly would not have made had I not brought them to your attention. I have paid my assessments this year, being willing to take that much more of a gamble, but if things look no better next year than they do now, I shall drop the whole business at that time, and I am frank to say that they do not look very good now, though probably conditions are no worse at the Metropolitan than at other airports.

Jim and his father were over at Boeing Field Friday and Jim told me that it was dead as a door nail.

I have been working to finish another story, which accounts for my delay in answering your letter. It looks now as though we were going back up on the hill to live and I have been very busy in connection with that matter also and expect to be for several months, as we have a tremendous amount of work to do in and about the house before we can occupy it again.

Please tell Margaret that I was mighty glad to have the lovely letter from Jeanne Warfield, and if Margaret is busy you can kiss Jeanne for me the next time you see her.

Let me know how Collins came out in the State Tournament. Hulbert is going to try to qualify in the Los Angeles City Tournament. He is getting real interested in golf again as he expects to make the Pomona team this Fall.

I know that you will have a wonderful time at Bemidji and if there was not going to be anyone there but your family, I think we might come, but the thought of going to a summer resort and being high-hatted by a lot of strangers leaves me cold.

Hulbert did not drive back from Chicago which accounts for his not stopping to see you. He got ritzy and flew back. He left Coldwater, Michigan, one morning and arrived in Los Angeles the next evening.

Jack is in charge of a cabin full of kids at some mountain camp for the YMCA for a week. We hope that he will be home tomorrow. All the rest of us here send love to you and yours.

Yours,

Ed

Mr. H. T. Weston, Birchmont Beach Hotel,
Bemidji, Minnesota.

Dear Bert:

Was glad to have your letter of July 26th, to which I should have replied earlier had I not been trailing Hulbert around the Pasadena Municipal Golf Course most of this week. He qualified for the third flight with an 87, won his first match 4 and 3 with a 79, the next match 4 and 3 with a 78, and today he won the final 6 and 4 with an 81. He brought home a nice cup, which is a good thing since Emma discovered last night that two other cups that he won several years ago seem to have been stolen.

The new deal under which we expect to get back our old home is in escrow and everything seems to be moving along satisfactorily. In the meantime there is not much to do as I hesitate to start alterations until we are safely out of escrow, as I may have anywhere from five to fifteen thousand dollars to spend on the hill right away.

Know you are all having a good time at Bemidji, but when you talk about fires morning and night you find me uninterested, having spent most of my life where it was necessary to keep the home fires burning from six to nine months of the year.

I don't know whether I wrote you or not, but Hulbert did not qualify in the Los Angeles city tournament. I have forgotten now what the trouble was, but I guess he was just playing bum golf that day.

Emma and the children join me in love to you all.

Yours,

Ed

Mr. H. T. Weston, Beatrice, Nebraska.

Dear Bert:

I have this morning received a copy of Mr. Martineau's letter to you of September 3rd together with a copy of the agreement, and before leaving for town to keep an appointment I wanted to drop you this note.

After studying the matter carefully I have decided to execute the agreement, as I believe this is the best way out. There is little likelihood of anything materializing in a remunerative way for us until the motors can pass the test, which, of course, cannot be accomplished until all, or at least the major part, of the present indebtedness is wiped out and this would mean an additional outlay on the stockholders' part, something which I am not prepared to do.

Am glad to hear that you are all home again and well.

Emma and the children join me in love to you all.

Yours,

Ed

Reseda, Calif.
September 13, 1930/br

Mr. H. T. Weston, Beatrice, Nebraska.

Dear Bert:

I am returning Martineau's letter herewith for your files as you requested.

It may be that they are taking this means of squeezing everyone out, but right now I am perfectly willing to be squeezed rather than stand a chance of putting up any more money.

I sure am sorry about this whole affair, because I feel that had it not been for my interest in it you and Margaret would not have come in and I still think that we would have made some money had the Wall Street slump not taken place.

Emma, Hulbert, Jack and I just returned from a trip up the Redwood

Highway to Grant's Pass in Oregon and back down the Pacific Highway, which follows the Sacramento and San Joaquin Valleys. We made the trip in two Aerocars, which will give you a great laugh when you see them, if you have not already been so fortunate.

They are trailers that hook on behind a car, with a special hitch. The big one, which is called a Pullman and is twenty feet long, was hauled by my old 1921 Packard Roadster. This car contains two lower berths, two upper berths, long divan, lavatory, toilet, refrigerator, clothes press and various drawers and compartments for clothing or what have you. The other trailer, which we used as a commissary car, was hauled by a Ford Pick-up car that I bought for the purpose. It was our dining room and kitchen. We took the cook and his wife, who slept in the commissary car.

It makes a very easy way of camping out and the whole outfit worked out very nicely. I think one of these cars would be a great thing for you and Margaret, who are always tearing around the country.

Jack left for college yesterday and Hulbert leaves Monday, so that Emma and I will be very much alone.

All join me in love to you and yours.

Yours,
Ed

Beetrice
9/17/30

Dear Ed;

Have yours of the 13th today. Not that it matters at all, but it does make me d——d mad to see you pay 5¢ for an Air stamp, and then the letter get here slower than the regular mail. I have had a number of such experiences, and especially to Calif. The Air Mail Service is sure going to lose me. 4 days for a letter to come here! Heck, I can leave LosA at 10 a.m. Tuesday and be here at 9 p.m. on Thursday. Your 2¢ letters come in 3 days.

In re you feeling any personal regretfullness about this Apache-Metro stuff, that is pure rot, as I have already explained, and at some length. Forget it.

I know just how you and Emma feel to have Jack, the last one, go off to school. But Gosh, Ed, think of the break you have had by keeping them around as long as you have! Monday, when we put ole Herbo on the train for Culver, was the third year we have been without off-spring.

Truth to tell, this year is nt going to be so bad, for both Collins and JB will be within 40 miles, and we are feeling quite cocky about that.

Jeff went Phi Psi too. The same outfit Collins is in. I don't know as this means anything, but I am glad they sort of like to buddy around together.

Your Land Yacht is fine. Yeah, I have seen them, and they certainly are wonderful. Your suggestion that Margt and I get one, might be ok, if it were nt for three things; towit; we have few servants and no chauffs: we frequently go over seas: and last, and most unimportant, I anyway, like people more than I do places, and someway I do not feel that any Land Yacht would be very chummy. (To be honest about this over-seas stuff, as you know we have been to Cuba twice, which same aint really "frequently", but at that, we might go again!!)

I could not but think of the difference in you & tribe batting over cement roads in your Aerocars, and the trek you took when second heading for Calif. Hope you kept a log of this last trip and the comparison will be mighty interesting.[74] If you had the same Man & Wiff you had when we last dined with you, this last trip was plenty de lux as far as provinder was concerned.

You do not mention the House on The Hill? Have you moved, or what? I should think you would sure hate to leave Lakes Ed & Emma, to say nothing whatthesoever about the new bath-rooms and the aviary, tho, ofcourse you might possibly move the last.

You may have read in the papers aboit the big bank robbery at Lincoln today. Margt arrived right there an hour after it happened. This is sure getting to be a hellofa country, when the law hounds are so busy trying to round up a $1/4$ of 1% bootlegger, that they just have nt time for the real thugs.

Much love to you all,

Yours,

[HTW]

Mr. H. T. Weston, Beatrice, Nebraska.

Dear Bert:

Notwithstanding yours of the 17th inst., the air mail is perfectly all right if used with intelligence.

Air mail to points at which the ships ground to discharge and receive mail cuts down the time tremendously, but where a transfer is necessary, as in the case of mail to Beatrice and other points off the direct air route, except possibly to points in the far East, there is no saving in time.

Our mail to and from Chicago and New York comes through several days sooner by air mail than by train. Hereafter, we will not waste air mail stamps on Beatrice mail.

The matter of the house on the hill is still in escrow and there is a possibility that the entire deal will fall through because of their inability to raise the necessary cash.

Everything has been very quiet here and with the children all away the house seems rather dead.

Emma wanted me to ask you when you and Margaret expect to be on here again. You certainly should come and take a look at some of your remarkable investments in Southern California. At least no one can gyp Margaret out of her lots.

With love to all, I am

Yours,

Ed

Dear Ed;

It seems to me it has been plenty long since we have had a word from [*f* and *r* on top of each other] the San Frenando Valley. (You will note that this d——d step-on-a-cat-in-the-dark t-writer piles up on the Fs, under my too fast two finger touch, but it is easily deciphered) I would like to learn of the Burroughs Tribe, of its comings and goings and general state of being?

After years of waiting, we have had a regular He-Fall. Never any place is there lovlier weather than Nebraska when Fall Weather is normal. When I was a youth, we wore flannels (whatever they are?) till the Happy New Year, but since Herb appeared, Fall has been a horror, with 60 degree changes, rain, snow, heat, and what have you. We certainly have been lapping up stuff which would make the best Calif climate (which is doubtless DelMar) hang its head and blush hotly.

As per usual, we have followed the so-called Corn Huskers hither and yon.[75] I am still nutts on this F ball, and this year have had an unusual kick and thrill (vicarious tho it mayviciously be!) to see a real he-coach take a bum squad, without a trace of a star on it, and through brains and strength of character, get these lads together, get them to clicking, and make a real team out of just so many youths, and have them get in there and play all the time way over their heads.

Win or lose in football means nothing the wahtsoever to me, but the team I like to see, and what gives me the big Kick, is to see these kids, under sane strong leadership get right in there and do a little more than their best just because of this One for All, All for One stuff, which, after all, is mostly football's excuse for being.!

Last Saturday, Lee and I motored 400 miles to see Nebraska trim the highly salaried Kansas team. Next Sat. we see em take Missouri. The next week end we go to Iowa City and see two hot-shot defensive teams battle, and incidently glimpse some of our Bemidji friends, the least one of which is not Margt's buddy, Burt Ingwersen, the Boy Coach of Iowa. The next is Thanksgiving, when Nebr cleans the Kansas Farmers, and then there is a long wait till October 1931. Doubtless all this seems footless to you, but to me it is the (again) vicarious renewal of Youth. When I know personally a number of the team, there is nothing which gives me the real ole chills and thrills like a first class football battle.

I think I have written you that Collins is in the Law College now. Apparently that boy has found himself. He is crazy about it to date, which is to the mid-semester. We had a heart-to-heart over a bottle of beer recently, and he said that he had done actually more real he-work since September, than he had ever done all the rest of the time [text missing] . . . I hope his interest holds. I do [text missing] . . . has had some right distinguished ones slipped in on her side.

This Jeff, as you have heard, was in all-same convent for 5 long years. He is just lapping this university stuff up. Everything is a fine adventure to him (as Gawd knows it might well be after five terms in Kulver!).

Your boys may be interested to know that he is a Phi Psi pledge, which happens to be Collins' croud too.

JB leaves tomorrow night to go to Culver. You know; the ole grad going back to Homecoming!! Both he and Herb will get the big time out of that.

Margt and I saw Hot Shot Herb two weeks ago. He was at that time "Acting 1st Sergt" of A Company, and I will state loving it, himself and everything plenty. Herb has not outgrown Culver. He is doing well there, fits in, and is getting a whole lot out of a really remarkable school.

Incidently, Culver played St Johns in Soldiers Field last Saturday, beating them 19–0. The two Corps were there, and paraded before 40,000, and two Governers, et al. Mebbeso you thing that Herb did not lap that up!!

I cant help but think of the difference when the MMA team played in Chi in our meek day!!

They knocked me and my gang cold this last election. We did carry this village for Hitchcock against Norris; but we were nt a drop in the bucket against the German vote which swept him back in office. I have nothing against this guy personally; but he is just as valuable to us here in Nebraska as is the King of Spain, and cares just as much. We are 80 per cent farmers out here; Norris was <u>Chairman</u> of the Farm Relief, or whatever it is, committe in the senate and what did the SOB do?? By letting this chairmanship go, he had a chance to get on some damned committe which might possibly be against the POWER Trust!!! Wotell do we care about the Power Trust? We mostly make our own power out here in the short grass country, if any. We dont care any more about the Muscles Sholes, or the Hoover Dam than just exactly nothing. Ofcourse we know we have to pay and pay and pay, but we expect that, and yet this SOB NET quits the definite farmer committee, and grabs something where he can strut and be against something and somebody. Certainly I am not for the purely destructive type. If we are, as a race, or a clan, or whatnot, are to continue, we have just got to be constructive, or if not that, at least creative. This miss-carriage Norris voted against the war because he knew there was going to be war anyway, and he knew that Nebraska was largely German farmers. He sure got his reward this last election, and by a type of support that a decent man would not think of for more reward than I can even conceive.

Margt's mother is like a lovely child of eight months. This arrangement which we have is perfect. Margt frets a good deal, but she cant help but know, every time she sees her mother, that she is having the best possible care, and is sitated the best she possibly could be.

We get a whole lt out of having both Col and Jeff where we see them often. It has been a long time since we have had two available.

We play almost no bridge. I continue to refuse to attempt Contract.

At least six of my contempories are on the verge of going completely broke. Pitiful! Not especially their fault either. The depression!! To assist them would simply mean to greatly help their creditors, and in no way them. A hellofa situation. It is plenty tough to have to try to start all over after the ole 50 mark! This winter is going to be Hell!

I am busier than for a long time. A matter of just trying to protect ourselves. Recently some considerable cash, for us, came in. I admit freely I dont know whatinhell to do with it.

I have so fallen from grace that I am about to apply for a pension for my extremely valuable services in the S-A War. We pay never less than 1000 a year to protect ourselves from the income tax low-grades who hound us from time to time, even tho we are perfectly and gladly willing to pay what the law says we should. If I can get part of this back, why is nt it reasonable? A horse did fall on me, and I still walk toed in, as you know, with the left hind leg. I have been so irked and irritated for the past ten years by these income tax vultures, and have been put to so much expense purely as protection, that I am going to grab what I can and as much as possible. This may be low, and I may lose caste, but I personally stand all right with myself in so doing. If I could get a 100,000 as "back pension", which ofcourse I cant, I'd lick my chops and feel just as good as the dere ole cat who had just swallowed the canary.

We are so well pleased with having Col and JB available that we do not think we are going to leave home much. Margt declares herself to the effect that we are NOT going to Calif this winter (or spring). This is not for publication or discussion, but I sort of think, that when things get deep with thawing snow, and all that kind of thing, that we possibly might get in my roadster and drift westward over the southern route, sojourn in Calif for a week or so, and then motor slowly homeward. We just have to go to NY [text missing] . . . thereabouts, but a little after that we [end of letter missing].

Reseda, Calif.

November 17, 1930/br

Mr. H. T. Weston, Beatrice, Nebraska.

Dear Bert:

We enjoyed your long and interesting letter of recent date and I am rather conscience stricken to think that I have not written you recently, but the truth of the matter is I have nothing either interesting or pleasant to write.

I fully appreciate your interest in football, an interest which I share with you, though I take most of my football via radio, not having the courage or energy to combat the traffic conditions surrounding our big games here.

Emma and I recently drove to Tucson, Arizona to see Pomona defeated by the University of Arizona. We made the trip down in one day, five hundred and thirty five miles, which is some feat for me. This we did on a Friday, spent Saturday at Tucson and drove home Sunday. Our actual running time going was twelve hours and twenty minutes and returning twelve hours and thirty-nine minutes. This would be slow time for some drivers, but it was like racing to me and was only made possible due to the wonderful driving qualities of the Cord.

I know what it must mean to you to have two of the boys within easy motoring distance. We are situated similarly, and the boys ordinarily come home weekends.

I feel sorry for your friends who have to start all over again at fifty. Perhaps, however, they can find some satisfaction in the fact that they are not the only ones.

It may interest you to know that the old place on The Hill was turned over to me yesterday, though the deal is not yet out of escrow. My attorney, whom I talked with this morning on the 'phone, expects it will be within a day or two. This will give me back three hundred and forty five acres, including the improvements, entirely clear, but the fly in the ointment is caused by the question as to whether it is not going to be too much of a burden for me to carry, in addition to which I can see anywhere from fifteen to twenty-five thousand dollars expense in rehabilitating the property, which was permitted to run down badly.

Although conditions are not particularly good here at present for liquidating, I think I shall start in unloading, even if I have to take considerably less for the property than I know it to be worth.

We hope that you and Margaret will change your minds and decide to come out here for a visit this Spring, as I am sure you will want to when winter finally closes down on Nebraska.

Emma joins me in best to you both.

Yours,

Ed

November 19th, 1930

Dear Edgar Rice;
The time is near when we pay our real estate taxes here. I am wondering howinhell about those hill-side lots in Miramar?

Let me know so I can send you a check when it is time to add to the total charges against those super-fines!!

I have a confession to make. I today applied for a pension for my extremely important service to the US. Army in the fateful year of 1898. I hope to Gawd to get $50 per month.

Nearly all the S-A vets of whom I have any knowledge are getting pensions under this last law. We pay just a retainer of $1000 per year for protection against the low grade tax auditors. We have never had a tax matter, which, if taken to the higher-ups, has not been immediately ruled in our favor, and in some cases have received refunds. I therefore feel, if I can get anything back from the USA to somewhat recompense for the money we spend to head off low grade employees, I am entitled to all I can get up to and including what we are forced to pay tax experts.

JB returned early Monday from dere ole HomeComing at Culver. Reports a big time, Herb going strong. We get a very large kick out of seeing both Jeff and Col once or twice a week. Collins is still entirely pleased with his law school. He was home for two hours tonight, and talked just 100 minutes about law cases.

Hope all Burroughses are as well as all this tribe. Love to you all,

Yours,

[HTW]

Reseda, Calif.
November 24, 1930/br

Mr. H. T. Weston, Beatrice, Nebraska.

Dear Bert:

Mr. Rothmund was talking to me Saturday about your tax bills and he was going to write you today, so I will leave that in his hands. Of course, we can't do anything, you understand, without the bills.

As a taxpayer I am delighted to know that you are going to get fifty dollars per month pension. When the next war looms I am going to suggest that they pay everybody in the United States a thousand dollars cash not to enlist, so that we will not have to spend all the rest of our national existence paying pensions. However, I see no reason why you should not get yours as long as the rest of them are.

There is nothing very thrilling to report from Tarzana, except that we believe that we shall have an independent postoffice here by the first of the year, which is quite thrilling to the Burroughs family at least. We are hoping that our future address will be Tarzana Ranch, Tarzana Drive, Tarzana, California, which ought to be the height of something or other.

With best to you all, I am

Yours,

Ed

Mr. H. T. Weston, Beatrice, Nebraska.

My dear Mr. Weston:

About a month ago, when the local tax bills were in the mails, I in-tended to write you relative to your Miramar property, to remind you far enough in advance to avoid paying another penalty. It slipped my mind, however, and only last Saturday did I again think of it.

Did you receive the 1930 bills on your two Miramar lots and if so, I presume you will pay from there. The first installment becomes delin-quent December 5, 1930. Please write and let me know if you are going to handle the matter this year.

I am today writing for duplicate copies of your 1930 bills so that in the event you did not receive them, we will be in a position to pay them for you, if you will drop me a note to that effect.

With kindest regards, I am

Yours very truly,
C. R. Rothmund
Secretary to Edgar Rice Burroughs

Beatrice, Nebraska.
November 29th, 1930.

Dear Ed;

Have yours and Mr. Rothmond's letters of the 24th in regard to the taxes on the Miramar lots.

I have requested three times, the last time through you, I believe that the amount of taxes due on these lots be sent me; just the usual tax notices, which are sent out most everywhere, and only once did I ever receive anything of the kind, and that was the first year.

Needless to state we have had no notices, and neither will we receive them.

I will be very much obliged if you will have Mr. Rothmond pay these d——d taxes, and will be most please to remit promptly. If you dont we will be cracked for non-payment again as we were last year.

Margaret had not gone to sleep, so I got her up to give you a check for the same amount as last year, $232.89, which I enclose. The amount may be a little more or a little less, but we can balance that later on. And also, she prefers to pay all in one payment, thus saving trouble, if not a very little money (as 2% on cash balances does not about to ahellofa lot on 116 bucks for 6 mos.)

Am sending this by your favorite, the Air Mail, and trust it gets to you before the fatal day.

Our team sort of fizzled toward the last. A good enough team, but a line cant score. We had about nine backs, but they were all just fair, and about a tie in ability. One thing, these little guys shot way over their head and beat h——l out of Kansas, but they could not be pepped up to super-human stuff more than once in a season.

We are now awaiting Herb's return, which will be along about Dec. the 17th. Margaret has also invited her God-child and Name-sake and the Lord-knows-what-not, Margaret Cook, of New York City, to spend the Holidays with us. 18 years old, and two years ago a very attractive sort of a female cub. We all hope that she will come. She has never been west of the dere ole Hudson River; she has never met up with the Weston Boys since she was ten. Her reactions ought to be good!

I see you had quite a wind storm the other day. Must have been along your neighborhood, from the looks of the pictures of the Mack Sennet outfit. Hope it did you no damage at Tarzana. I did not know they had em quite that strong out there.

Your own P.O. sounds like almost too much Class to be. That is allsame as being an American Dook, aint it?

I was glad to read of your trip to see the Arizona game. To my grief, last spring, you did not come down to mere DelMar to see us, and I am mighty glad to know you are agin up to these more than 500 mile treks. That is Fine.

Here is an item, which I should have the pen, or t-writer of one ERB in order to do justice thereto.

Dr Lee, MD, a rough neck friend from a little town eight miles north, was dropping in one morning. I had to go hide some likker, leaving Margt and him gossiping. When I got back Margt had been called to the phone, and Lee said; "She certainly cut that solicitor mighty short, and got rid of him plenty." Just then Margt returned, full of conversation, and this is about what she emitted: "The NERVE of that man to take my time, or try to!! Why, he tried to get me to help Mussolini and the Italians!" With this Lee goes off into a lot of merriment, and this is what had actually occurred;

A presentable highly trained young salesman appeared, and said to Margaret: "Can I have a few minutes of your time? I want to interest you in our mausoleum." Sez Margt: "NO, I have no time, and besides I am not remotely interested in Italy." Seze: "But Mrs. Weston, we all come to it some time, we all must be interested." Sez Margt: "Not I! I'll never come to it, and I am NOT interested in any Italian. Good morning!!" — and slammed the inside door.

This incident is certainly a bright spot in my life right now!

I do hope that gale did not damage you around Tarzana any.

Much love to you all, and good luck,

Yours,
[HTW]

Reseda, Calif.
December 2, 1930/rr

Mr. H. T. Weston, Beatrice, Nebraska.

Dear Mr. Weston:

Your letter containing tax check arrived in yesterday's mail.

The 1930 taxes are somewhat lower than last year's and, therefore, your check for $232.89 was just $31.36 too much and I am enclosing Mr. Burroughs' check for that amount. As the signature on your check was "Margaret Collins Weston," I have made our check payable to her, which I presume is correct.

For your information, the 1930 taxes on your two lots here are:

Lot #30, Tract #9546,	$129.87
Lot #48, " "	71.66
	$201.53

As soon as the receipted bills are returned to us we shall forward them to you.

The writer will be more than glad to take care of your yearly tax matters and hereafter will secure the bills sufficiently in advance to avoid any last minute hurry.

Yours very truly,
C. R. Rothmund
Secretary to Edgar Rice Burroughs

12/18/30

Dear Edgar Rice;

Have been in Lincoln today, on a considerable of a business sweat, and driving home, I thought of the undoubted nearness of the Happy ole Yule Tide, and that I was about due to slip you and Emma, and a few others, a drop or two of the merry old Cheer—of value, only because I had known you folks so d——d long and was still on speaking terms with you, and, as matter of fact had quite a hi opinion of you, and e'en somewhat of a feeling of affection for you.

And whatinhell did I find in the mail? A letter from this poor benighted blighter, Sue Ball! And he tells me that you have been ill, and in a hospital, and gawd-knows-what. Which makes me feel like helland hi water, and especially the fact that you have seen fit, and best, to conceal same carefully from me.

Speaking of this same Sue (Emma's and Margt's Boy Favorite!) he wrote me he was to be in Lincoln, a few weeks ago, and that we were to get-to-gether. The day I got our letter from friend Sue, we were leaving for Chicago, Culver, and points east, and so that was one real break I have had in 1931!

Being a creator, and not a trader, as I seem to be attempting, you are doubtless not interested in matters commercial, but I want to state that this year has been Some Year. I have been right up to my neck recently. We have had direct losses, and Gawd-awful shrinks, but I think we are better off than most, and that in from 3 to 5 years we will be able to look back with some calmness!

Herb is home. He got a sergeancy. I think he should have been first sergt, but that is doubtless papa prejudice, as Herb is feeling perfectly ok about it. Herb has gone through the Big Change the past 3 mo. 75%

of his adult friends and associates here do not know him when he first bursts upon their vision. An amazing change in so short a time.

Col, JB and Margt Cook, Margt's god-daughter, from NY, will be here soon. This looks to me like somewhat strenuous doings for the next 2 to 3 weeks.

I am terribly sorry to know you have not been feeling so good recently. I hope you are ok from here in. Much love to you all, and a Fine Holidays,

Yours,
[HTW]

2/3/32

Dear Ed:

MMA '95 received today.

Whether you did, or not, I got quite a real kick out of same, and thank you for same!

Am having it copied, and will return original to you soon.

It has not been above plus 15 here this year, and I am beginning to believe that this is no place for oldsters, like Maggie and me, after the Holidays.

This is practically certain; Margt, her second Son, JJ, which stands for Joyful Jeff, and their janitor, HTW, will be heading westward about March 1st, so you had better start cleaning out the ole chicken coop, and getting the mould off your Beach House!

(I think we will mostly round-up at Coronado, as that seems the most normal place in SoCalif., also the closest decent place to the gambling and booze of Ole Mex!!)

Ka-bitchee-ka-ba-hooie!

Also very much thanks for dere ole '95 MMA !

Yrs,
Bert

[ERB Collection]

Mr. H. T. Weston, Beatrice, Nebraska.

Dear Bert:

I tucked your letter of February 3rd into one of those little catouchers for unanswered mail, where it has remained buried until today.

Also, today, we received the announcement of Collins' marriage, which, of course, was quite a surprise to us. I suppose you and Margaret were in Chicago for the wedding. We all wish Collins and his bride every happiness.

The chicken coop has not been occupied for over a year, so you folks can move right in when you arrive.

I had a letter from Moreland the other day saying that he had sent you a copy of the class picture. I told him that you had had a picture made, but I think he must have misunderstood me.

We are looking forward to seeing you, Margaret and Jeff in the near future.

Yours,

[ERB]

[ERB Collection]

Hotel Del Coronado, Coronado Beach, Calif.

3/15/32

Dear Ed—

Have been here since Thursday.

We are missing real winter at home, and are having a big time lapping up this perfect climate—playing some golf and fooling around. Jeff evidently is getting a real thrill out of the S.W.

Thanks for your well wishing for Col + Bride. This was a sudden thing but am inclined to think a very good thing. Margaret will have to tell you about it when we meet up. Too long to write—especially long hand!

Am glad your chicken coop is not occupied—as we will be heading north in 2 or 3 weeks.

We want Jeff to see all of So Calif possible. We will be in LosA a few days and then go up the Coast. We came in through Yuma + will return via Barstow, the Canon etc.

Wonder what you will spring on us this time—I do not think anything could be more amazing than the land yacht!

Love to you all

Yrs
Bert

[ERB Collection]

Tarzana, Calif.
March 16, 1932/br

Mr. H. T. Weston, Hotel Del Coronado,
Coronado Beach, Calif.

Dear Bert:
Was glad to have your letter of the 15th. We are looking forward to seeing you when you come north. Please let us know beforehand, if you can, so that we won't be tied up, as I imagine you are only going to be here a day or two from what you say and we want to have you out for dinner while you are here.

Emma joins me in love to you all.

Yours,
[ERB]

[ERB Collection]

Tarzana, Calif.
March 18, 1932/br

Mr. H. T. Weston, Hotel Del Coronado,
Coronado Beach, Calif.

Dear Bert:
I have yours of the seventeenth saying that you expect to leave Coronado in about a week.

Can you arrange to be with us Sunday afternoon and evening, March 27? If so, we will spend the afternoon at the beach and drive back to Tarzana for dinner. I think, Joan, Jim, the baby, and the boys will be with us at that time.

We can call for you right after lunch Sunday, and if this idea works in with your plans drop me a line.

We are looking forward to seeing you all.

Yours,
[ERB]

[ERB Collection]

4/20/32 @ 11ᵘ in the midst of much intensive packing!

Dear Ed—

Note the map and the part marked. If one were seeking seclusion, why not in that area?

Now I am going to get somewhat sloppy and perhaps sentimental, but am going to risk it, and even if it shows I am doddering, am going to state flatly that I am so damned glad to see you so infinitely better than when we were here last year, that the depression is canned! As our boys say, it was sure "slick" for Margt and me to see you had come out of your physical depression of a year or two ago.

I may state further that the only thing wrong with our '32 sojourn in So Calif was that we did not flock more with the Burroughs.

Also, I hope your children liked Jeff as well as he did all three of yours!

Yours
H T Weston

[ERB Collection]

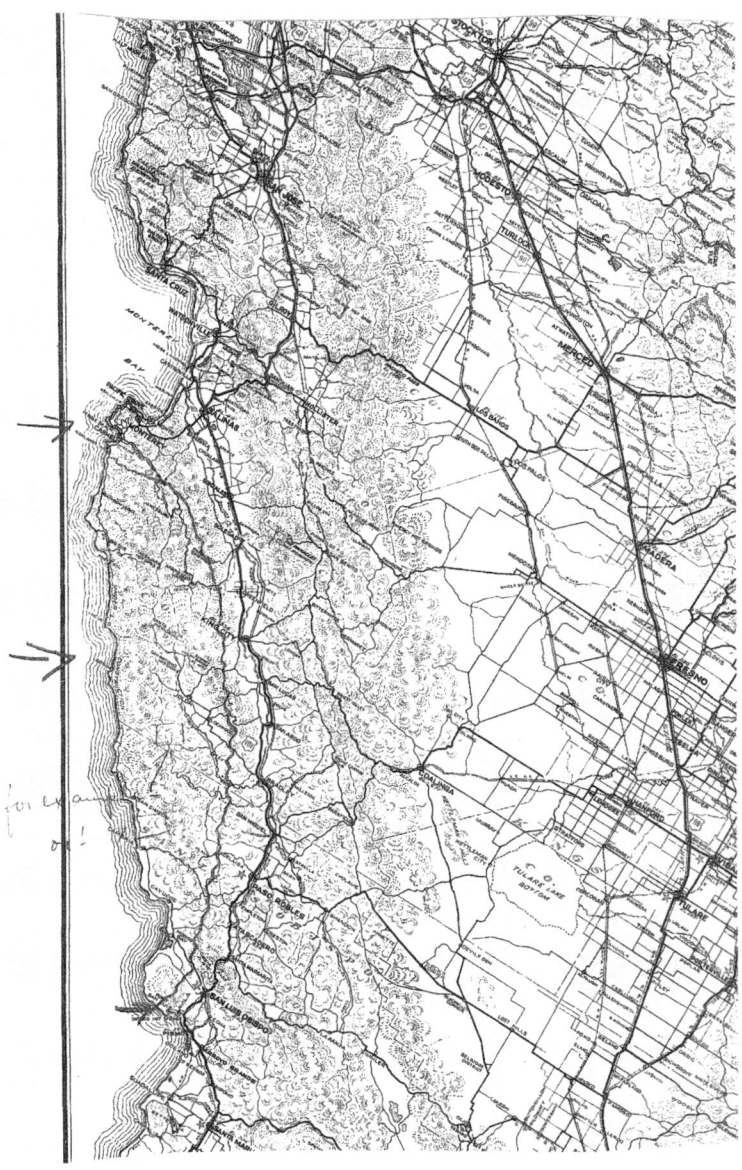

16. Map of California coastline included in Herbert T. Weston to Edgar Rice
Burroughs, 20 April 1932. *Courtesy Edgar Rice Burroughs, Inc.*

Tarzana, Calif.

April 23, 1932/br

Mr. H. T. Weston, Beatrice, Nebraska.

Dear Bert:

Thanks for your note and the map. I imagine the district you indicate is more or less of a wilderness. I have never been through it and know nothing whatever about it. However, I am inclined to believe that that stretch of the Coast is subject to a great deal of fog, which naturally makes it unpleasant.

I appreciate your reference to my health, and return the compliment. I never saw you looking any better. And speaking of health, a friend of mine called me up yesterday and said he heard I had died. Possibly he meant from the ears up.

Hope you have a pleasant trip north and that you enjoy the beautiful country above the Tehachapi.

We were all crazy about Jeff. The boys think he is a peach.

They are home today and, with Emma, join me in sending best to all of you.

Yours,

[ERB]

[ERB Collection]

Antlers Hotel, Colorado Springs, Colo.

May 5th 1932

My dear Ed!

I'm cutting out a part of a letter I had from "Irish" Yates—she is Jack Yates wife and was as you'll deduct one of the couples at our house— he's head of Swifts in our town—also territory and has had chances to go to Chi—but strange as it seems prefers Beatrice—We arrived here last night and our pals the Dempsters came at 8 and we were with them till 11—and they came for lunch to-day and we play around then dinner + more play—We used to see an awful lot of the Dempsters when we were having children and they were too—they have 3 daughters—

all married now—Jeff got a big thrill out of Yosemite, Grand Canyon—
etc—so far as that goes Jeff is the sort that enjoys almost everything
and we are so glad Hully + Jack like him—You should hear how he has
been for them—"Keen Guys"—no more praise could be put forth, for
that means the best ever—We start home to-morrow—will be there Sat
P.M—Love to you, Emma + the rest—

Yours

M.C.W.

[Attached clipping, typescript:]
Oh Boy! Did Edgar Rice Burroughs let his imaginative brain child go on a
spree? We went to see the picture Tarzan on the third night it was shown
here—it played to a packed house all 4 nights, by the second show they were
always lined up out in the street. We thought it was 2 hours of good entertainment and of course was doubly interesting as we had met Mr. Burroughs at
your house. Certainly was a diversion from all the sex and gangster pictures
of late.

[ERB Collection]

Tarzana, Calif.

May 9, 1932/br

Mrs. H. T. Weston, Beatrice, Nebraska.

My dear Margaret:
Thanks for your letter of May 5 and the clipping from Mrs. Yates' letter.
    I am glad to know that Tarzan is doing so well back there. It opened
Saturday at Lowe's State here, and according to their advertisements is
breaking all records. The rush was so great Saturday and Sunday that
they advertised in this morning's paper that they are forced to put on
seven shows a day starting at about nine in the morning.
    Tonight, Mr. Van Dyke, the director, Miss Maureen O'Sullivan and I
have to make a personal appearance on the stage, and I am darn glad
that you and Bert are not here to witness my embarrassment. I'll bet
that stage will look forty miles wide when I start out to reach the center
of it.

Hope you had a nice trip, but fear that you ran into some cold weather in the northern part of the state.

We all speak of your visit here often, and the boys mention Jeff and their liking for him.

Emma joins me in best to you all.

Yours,

[ERB]

[ERB Collection]

Tarzana Ranch, Tarzana, Calif.

May 18, 1932

Dear Bert,

No telling where you folks are. I should think you'd get get dizzy running around so much. However, I'll address this to the old home town.

Have nothing to say so that is why I am writing. Thought the enclosed clippings might interest you.

The golf course is open and we are losing only about three grand per month. But everyone is having a good time.

Emma joins me in best to you all

Yours,

Ed

Beatrice National Bank

H. T. Weston, Vice President

May 25th, 1932

Dear Ed:

We just missed the Tarzan picture all the way home. It had been here the week or two before we arrived. I think I had heard described every sequence in the film.

Last week, it was shown in a small town 14 miles south of here. Our friends, the Youlls had us down for dinner and the show.

I was thrilled! I give it to the Metro folks for the way they got your ideas over. Margaret & I went to bed when we got home and soon JB blew in. He too had gone to Wymore and seen Tarzan. He came into my bed-room (You Know? The one with the ropes, things all over the floor, and a lot of funny things!) and we talked about two hours about this picture.

We disagreed about but one thing; this O'Sullivan gal; I wondered why she was picked, and Jeff said she just fitted. He finally talked me into agreeing that she was There in the place where she & Tarzan were sort of foolin' around in the swimming pool. We agreed that that little real monkey, Chee-chee, or whatever his name is, stole the picture. He was the comic relief, and he was the best filler of this hard role we ever have seen.

In spite of us both knowing more about this picture than any we have ever seen, we were both regularly thrilled.

I think that you and Metro have done a fine job, and I congratulate you both.

Incidently, I think you took too little for the next three Tarzans.

Also, where did Metro get the Tar-zan pronounciation? I have been around a whole lot with Tarzan's papa, and know all you Tarzan folk fairly well, even to being well acquainted with two Tarzans of the canine species, and I have never noted any accent on the zan!

Also, did nt Metro pull a boner when they did not give Tarzan a real he-permier, let C Gay do his stuff, and just knock em cold with a new idea, and the surprise of their lives, with the pull that Tarzan has, properly produced!

Needless to state, if we had known that you were going to make none-other than a personal appearance, Margt, Jeff, and I, not only would have staid over for it, but we would sent for Collins & wiff, and Herb! I'll bet you held this out on us; you dirty crook!!

I infer that Margt has been writing to you more or less since our return. She says she has been sort of pinch-hitting for me. This I do not believe even remotely. Margt is something of a crook herself!!

Anyway, I have been somewhat swamped, since getting home. Company for a full week, and more, and then trying to beat the accumulation of a two months absence. We got home the 7th, I think, and this is the first other than business letter I have picked and poked out.

You gave me the double cross again. The first time we ventured into

LosA County, was largely because we thought you were somewhat of "a sick woman". You were not so red-hot last year. So we wobbled out again, and we found you back, just about as you were in 1900! I ask you? Is this any way to fool-hell-out-of your friends?

I do not know whether it is the climate, or what, but you certainly have shaken off at least ten years since '31. I hate to see you guys, who are my seniors, looking a good ten years younger than I do, but, someway, all the rest of the family seem to like it, and even go so far as to twit me about it!

But, to verge upon the detestable sentimental, I certainly got a whole lot of joy from seeing you looking so damned fit this year.

I suppose that Margt has written you all this and more, but, daring to repeat; we had the finest sort of a trip home, and "educated" JB a-plenty all the way. He just lapped it up.

Mother's Day occured soon after our arrival. Collins thought his bride should see her mother on this date, and taking advantage of reduced rr fares, sent her to Lincoln.

She was with us for two days. The first real look I have had at this gal, and I am pleased with her. Unless she fooled me plenty, she is much better than any "of the others", I am crazy, and she seems the type that does not want to fool anyone. I flocked with her for five hours straight, and never changed my mind! I am much inclined to be much for this Mabel, the latest addition to our family.

Item: This Collins, our First Born, has concluded that he is not cut out to be a rating attorney. Showing amazing intelligence, he says he wants to just get a job. The sad thing is that he does not even know what job, or what kind of a job he would like to have!

So, it is up to papa to get Collins a job! There is just one thing that I now know about this job; to-wit; it is going to be the type of chore where, from morning to night he will never sit down, and, if I can help it, will never have both feet on the ground at the same time. I am very much hoping that Collins will get a little real education, along lines that he little dreams of, in the next few years.

We leave next week for Culver; my last stand! I am what they call, an Eight Striper there, meaning, I have put in eight years (on and off) at Culver.

There are so damned many things I have on my mind to write, that I do not where to begin.

As I, anyway, get older, I am inclined to value the opinions of my juniors. We have now brought all three of the Weston Boys to Tarzana, and they have seen the Tars in their natural habitat; and it makes me feel good to have them all strongly endorse Margt and my picking as to friends. Everyone of our Boys think there are no better anywhere than the Tarzans.

This free-mouthed Jeff, expressed it. He said: "Are nt they a wonderful family? Why, they even have the nicest dog I ever saw!" And, you know that Jeff and Tarzan put in some time together, and he is qualified to form an intelligent opinion!

We were sorry not to have seen more of Jack, this last trip. Heretofore we have seen a good deal of Jack, and we sort of missed him. But, this trip, this Hulbert certainly made the Big Hit with this family.

You have written that Jeff rated all right with you folks, and with your boys. There is nothing I would rather hear.

Item: After he has got to going, JB is shooting from 72 to 78 golf all the time. The most consistent game he has ever played. He and I agree that he learned a whole lot from playing with Hully. Hulbert is a real golfer, if I ever saw one. He has got whatever a golfer has to have. That little final wiggle, before he starts his swing, is just the sort of thing that all rating golfers have, in some form or another. That is just a warning that here goes a long one straight down the center!.

You have pulled some inovations upon us poor Corn-belters. In fact, every time we have hit California, you have sprung something upon us. Some fine, and some mostly just surprising—like that damned land-yacht! But the best, the most pleasing, was your beach house! I have even been invited by you, to occupy your chicken-house at Tarzana for a nice visit. This is a warning, dont put any chicken house in your new additions to your beach house, or you will find the Weston Tribe crouding the chickens! Of all of SoCalif that we have seen, we like your beach house best, and you gave us a lot of pleasure by letting us use it.

If we had up-rooted sooner, as you did, and pulled out from this Indian country, I cannot imagine being better situated than you are, with your ranch-house in the SanFranando, and that fine beach location.

Tell Hully, who was just no help at all! that I have some fine colored movies of your small female neighbor to the north, in her yellow bathing suit.

If you were not so damned tight, and had a Kodacolor attachment to your projector, I would send you a batch of films, and give you a real treat, seeing yourselves, and your yellow clad neighbor. The beach is certainly the place for a mere amateur to take colored pictures!

Before I go on to something else, I want to return thanks for returning to us the very valuable Gage County clippings, which Margt, carelessly left around, when we were plenty enjoying your beach house. You see; we also have a clipping bureau! Yeah?

Next week is Herb's week to howl, and plenty! Age for weight, he is the rating guy in this Tribe, and that includes Collins, Jefferson, and their father. We will flock down there to urge him on. But this Herb will not let out even one small Yip! He will just take it in his stride, and go on to the next job, which happens to be the Plattsburg ROTC. For his age, this Herb certainly out-rates the rest of us. If he can hold up for the next seventeen years, this Tribe has hopes for the future.

I have my mind upon Herb's Commencement. I will never cease to regret that you and Joan did not come down to Culver, and flock around with us when Collins was strutting his First Class stuff. You were in Chicago, and we got in communication, and you just poohed-out on us! You would have seen a lot of things and people that would have interested you, and I know that Joan would not have had one dull moment. I have often wondered just whyinhell you and Joan turned us flat down.

Margaret says my letters are always much too long. I see that this one certainly is!

Love to you all,

Yours,
[HTW]

[ERB Collection]

Mr. H. T. Weston, Beatrice, Nebraska.

Dear Bert:

Am glad that the Weston tribe approve the Tarzan picture. I fully agree with Jeff in the matter of Maurine O'Sullivan. I thought she added quite a bit to the picture. As a matter of fact, she is far more attractive off the screen than she is on, which is unusual for motion picture actresses.

Their pronunciation of Tarzan was their own. I don't give a damn what they call him as long as their checks come regularly.

One reason they did not premier Tarzan and roadshow the picture is because they all underestimated its value. One of their publicity men told me yesterday that it was their biggest money maker so far this year. As a matter of fact, it just swept them off their feet.

Woodrough Ball's father was buried last Wednesday. Woodrough was on here when his father died and has promised to come out and see us before he goes back to Salt Lake City.

Thanks for your reference to my health. You are no doddering old fossil yourself; yet I suppose we are kidding ourselves and that we appear at least a million years old to the kids.

We are delighted to know that the entire Weston family feels the same way about us as we feel about them, and we are looking forward to seeing more of them in the near future.

Hulbert and Jack finish school on the ninth of June, following which Hulbert goes to Monterey to the ROTC training camp for six weeks, and Jack up somewhere around Big Bear to attend the summer art school, so that we will not have them with us all of the summer.

We have started the addition to the beach house and hope to have it completed in a couple of months.

Emma and the boys join me in love to you all.

Yours,

[ERB]

[ERB Collection]

Dear Ed & Emma:

Last night we had Ed Austin in for dinner and he & I played contract against Margt and her twin JB, till 1 pm. Ed held no less than 4 ¼ honors each hand and either made 700 rubbers or set them. It reminded me of the cards I held at Tarzana, and thereabouts. Also, I thought you would like to know that I have invested the money earned in Calif this year, where it is paying me about 23%, and two more trips and I can retire! And, incidently Ed would not have been here, only his wife is away!

Will have been home a week tomorrow from seeing Herb do his stuff. I am free to admit that I think mighty well of this same Herb. If he can hold up the next 17 years as he has the past seventeen, Margt and I need not fear for our later years.

Herb is now doing his six weeks ROTC. At Plattsburg. He drove east from Chicago, where we all were for five days, picking up three sidekicks en route. I have been told by Army officers that Plattsburg is a plenty good place to train, but both Jeff & Coll say that Herb and his buddies picked it because it is an hour by motor from Canada!

Jeff goes to a cavalry camp the last of August; at Fort Meade, SD.

While at Culver had the jolt that Seth Thomas had dropped dead. This was a real jolt, as, tho only ¼ year younger than I, he looked a good ten years younger the last time I saw him. You know how fond I was of him. I am surely going to miss him.

Did you buy a 12 Lincoln, and 2 Auburns? I got the Auburn for Herb, and drove it 100 miles to Culver, and liked it very much. It seemed to have everything.

You know about Col's car being stolen, and wrecked. He got 420 from the insurance company, which was ok. I gave him a Plymouth, and he and I both think that is the most car for the money either of us ever saw.

Business here is so damned rotten that we have even stopped talking about it. I see no immediate cheer in prospect.

Margaret is about to go into active business for herself. She is about to build three six room houses (one for Col & Mabel).

Coll is to work for the contractor, just as a 30¢ per hour man. We hope he will take an intelligent interest in this sort of thing, like it, and want to stick to it.

My information is that the one thing that the USA today, is short on, is small homes that can be bought for 5000 or less. If Col takes an interest in this game, and shows ability enough to be able to be a useful factor in it, it is a big field, or will be within the next ten years, and might well prove to be just his meat.

Anyway, working on these three houses; he will get a chance at two (to him) priceless things. To-wit: find out just how well he can stand a ten hour per day drag against just any body, and second, to find out if a largely outside job is what he thinks it is, as opposed to Law, which is sure under cover work.

She cant lose on these three. They will give Collins a whole lot of experience, also doubtless considerable surprise and amazement. They may also give him a chance to go into something which he will really take to.

I know I could put Col into a dozen places in this village where they would pay him a living salary. He has no attraction for any of these. Also, with them, he would have a "position" and not a "job". Also, any of these concerns would be at low ebb, due to the hard times, and would already have more help than they needed, and the Fifth Wheel Collins, would be idle much of the time, which I know from my own experience, is a terrible and most discouraging thing on ones first "job".

Unless Margt's contractor misunderstood my talk with him, Col will never have both feet on the ground at any one time so long as this three-house job lasts!

I have a lecture at least three yards long, and single spaced! on the present political situation in the USA. I would be due right now to shoot this in to Seth Thomas. Seth would give me much to think about in one page; then I would use pages and pages on him, and finally wear him down, and he would admit I was right, more from pure exhaustion than anything else.

I know that politics interests you just about as much as Art does me, but with Seth not on the mailing list, I am likely to be forced to shoot at you!

I cant help but wonder if Tarzana saw Sue Ball?

When it sizzles here, doubtless Margt, JB and I will depart of Bemidji again; the place with the plenty queer name, but much charm! Col & Mabel will hold the fort here at 910 No 7 and try to keep them from stealing our rugs, and Col will work on said three houses. Herb will join us early in August, when he has completed his 6 wks stretch. When I think of the 615 mile trek to Bemidji from Beetrice, and your 16 mile trek to your lovely beach house, I somewhat feel that we made an error a few years ago!

It is a strange thing for this immediate tribe to have a girl around the house, but we have had a week with Mabel now, and Margt, JB and I, in a huddle tonight, admitted that she wears mighty well. I am much inclined to think that this Mabel is a real break, not only for Collins, but for us all!

Love to you all,

Yours,
Bert

[ERB Collection]

[Clipping from Beatrice newspaper attached; see fig. 17.]

Tarzana, Calif.
August 26, 1932/br

Mr. H. T. Weston, c/o Birchmont Beach Hotel,
Bemidji, Minnesota.

Dear Bert:
Thanks for your letter and postcard. Am glad that you liked the Tarzan picture on second viewing. Hope you will like the radio broadcast also, which starts September 12.

I imagine the St. Paul station might reach you. It will be broadcast over KSTP, but I do not know the hour.

Joan comes in at the third episode and Jim after the twentieth, when he is supposed to have learned to speak English.[76]

The addition to the beach house is finally completed and we are far

:some Mon-

contract bridge
.y.
oursome Thurs-

Weston dinner
ιy evening in hon-
Curry.
ρellman contract
lay afternoon.
**

as given at Chau-
ednesday morning
Griffin of Kansas
ughter, Mrs. Ald-
Kathryn Griffin
who are guests
ι home. Besides
ts those in the
ιnd Mrs. Fred
Klein, Mr. and
ett and Mary
rs. Dean Sackett

Scen; at graduation exercises of Culv Military academy when
diplomas were presented to 171 cabets at the final formation i:
front of the historic Main Barracks. In this picture Cabet H. T:
Weston, Beatrice, is receiving the congratulations of Brig. Gen. L,
R. Gignilliat, supertendent of the Academy. Cabet Weston was
vice president of the Hi-Y club, a member of the Hop club and
Cabet club. He held the rank of captain in the Corps. Over a
thousand visitors from 36 states witnessed the award.

Charles Beuthner
buffet supper at
ιy evening in hon-
· relatives from
F. Beuthner,
and Mrs.
Γrs. David
ιlma Na-
Ɔr. Char-

ɔntertain-
in honor
and also
ɣ. After a
was serv-
ɔly birth-
served.

Celebrates 80th Birthday

Frank C. LaSelle of this city
celebrated his eightieth birthday
on Wednesday, June 22, being hon-
or guest at a dinner given at the
home of Mrs. J. A. Reuling at Wymore. There were 15 at the large
dinner table which was decorated
with delphinians and larkspur.
Those attending from Beatrice
were Mr. and Mrs. E. M. Carrith-
ers, Mrs. Leroy LaSelle and daughter, Beatrice, Mr. and Mrs. J ·'
C. Fisher, Mrs. T. O. Wa
with Jeanne and Janet, ρ
and Mrs. A. D. Spencer ·
ton.

Mr. LaSelle rec·
gratulations w·'

an announcement by Chancellor E.
A. Burnett. He plans to enter the
college of Arts and Sciences.
These scholarships, with an estimated value of $70 each, were
awarded to the winners in an
academic contest held in the various schools last May.

All of the 470 full-
high schools in Nebr
vided into three ·
each group cor
'·-' of the

𝕿𝖍𝖊

T'

Mat

17. Beatrice newspaper clipping announcing graduation of
Herbert T. Weston Jr., from Culver Military Academy, included in
Herbert T. Weston to Edgar Rice Burroughs, 20 June 1932.
Courtesy Edgar Rice Burroughs, Inc.

more comfortable than we were before. We are looking forward to seeing some of the Westons there this winter.

Emma joins me in love to you all.

Yours,
[ERB]

[ERB Collection]

Birchmont Beach Hotel, Bemidji, Minn.
8/29

Dear Edgar Rice—

This ought to about hit you on the merry ole birthday—I hope your tribe remembered it and celebrated the glad occasion properly! Gawd knows that Margt gave me <u>one</u> Birthday Surprise Poker Party—where I won 200$^{\underline{00}}$ and the poor suckers gave me a 69$^{\underline{00}}$ bag!—and that is my idea of a proper Happy B-Day! Hope yours was even happier!

Also I congratulate you, and am certain your years on earth—since '93—have been a great joy to me anyway!

With love and kisses
Bert

[ERB Collection]

Tarzana, Calif.
September 6, 1932/br

Mr. H. T. Weston, c/o Birchmont Beach Hotel,
Bemidji, Minnesota.

Dear Bert:

Thank you for your birthday letter.

I had a bully birthday at the beach with all the children present at dinner time.

I am glad that Emma did not arrange a poker party for me, as my birthday would have cost me plenty had she. I am the world's worst gambler.

Emma joins me in love to you all.

Yours,

[ERB]

[ERB Collection]

Tarzana, Calif.

September 16, 1932/br

Mr. H. T. Weston, Beatrice, Nebraska.

Dear Bert:

Am glad that you are home again. I don't see why people with such a nice home leave it so often. Just think how we stick to our measly little dump. If we had a regular home we probably would not even go out doors.

From your remarks, I take it that you and Margaret will be out again this winter. You will find us at 90 Malibu LaCosta, I think, as we are going to stay there anyway until after the Christmas holidays and I have a sneaking idea that we may just remain on. The addition gives us a much more comfortable home than we have at Tarzana, and Ralph just told me today that some lady with a lot of jack wants to buy the Tarzana dump.

Speaking of voting, I don't know who the hell to vote for. I wish to God we had a king so that we would not have to have any presidential elections, and if the king got snotty we could bump him off. I cannot get excited about Hoover, and I never could get up much enthusiasm about the Democratic party. Anyway, it makes little difference which side is in; they are all a bunch of grafters.

Yours for repeal and free bourbon,

[ERB]

[ERB Collection]

Tarzana, Calif.
November 12, 1932/br

Mrs. H. T. Weston, Beatrice, Nebraska.

Dear Margaret:

I was very much interested in the page from the Beatrice Sun and the two clippings.

The house must be dandy and I can well imagine that it aroused a great deal of interest in Beatrice and the surrounding country.

I wish you and Collins every success in the venture, which I am sure is going to be very successful. Evidently the whole thing has been done efficiently and completely and if anything will sell these days, this exploitation should sell your houses for you.

Emma will be very much interested in this when I show it to her.

With love to you all in which Emma would join were she here, I am

Yours,
[ERB]

[ERB Collection]

Malibu, Calif.
December 31, 1932/br

Mr. H. T. Weston, Beatrice, Nebraska.

Dear Bert:

Just a line to wish you all a Happy and Prosperous New Year and the hope that you had a very happy Christmas, which, of course, we know you did.

Sue Ball is in town and we have asked him to come out to dinner Wednesday.

I thought you and Margaret would like to see the picture of Malibu LaCosta Beach which was recently taken by an itinerant photographer. The second house on the beach is the new addition which we have built since you were here and which completely hides the old house, which stands just beyond it. The gables projecting above our house are those of Hunter's place. The Hunters are still there and we get together evenings occasionally.

With love to you all in which Emma and the children join, I am

Yours,

[ERB]

[ERB Collection]

Beatrice, Nebr.
Jan. 15th, 1933.

Dear Edgar:

It has been a long time since I have had anything personal from you. It may well be that it has been just this long since you have had any long-winded screed from me.

I have been somewhat cramped in my style, for the past few months, due to the fact that I am a sort of Gawd-d——d Trustee to the Chester Worthing Collins Estate, and have been doing my damndest to hold same together. I have to read ALL the commercial news, I have to get this one's and that's ideas. This my chore.

Even in these Dire Times, I have still to report, that I have been a fair sort of a Trustee. I feel reasonably sure that Margaret will be able to feed her immediate tribe, three squares per diem, so long as anything holds together.

As for me! I made an honest statement, the first of the year, and, my so-called assets, just equaled my liabilies, which is onehellofa fix for a 56-year-old to be in.

The answer is; I am a much better Trustee, than I am out on my cock-eyed own!

Margt and I, have put close to $100,000.00 cash, into dere ole California. We blame only ourselves. Margt's loss means little to her, but my loss means a lot to me, in my small way.

But, tohell with it!

We are not going to California this winter.

I will tell you why; almost everyone we know in SoCalif, <u>except you,</u> is flat busted. Margt has everything she ever owned, and also some cash surplus, thanks to her far-seeing Father. If we went to SoCalif, as we would like to, I know d——d well, that Margt's soft heart, and my none too sound trustee-ship, would weaken, and it would cost her plenty, to help our poor busted friends in SoCalif.! It may be just plenty cowardly on my part, but as a trustee, I do not know why we should hear the Hard Luck Stories of SoCal., in addition to those, here in our own home town. I am busted, or close to. I cant do much. Margt is not busted, and she does a whole, lot for this and that deserving one. Why should she, even in a minor way, take on So.Calif.?

This will not interest you at all, <u>personally</u>. It will not interest you because you have a real-he-Gift! You, out of millions, have something, which you can put out, which, busted, or not, is in demand. Who am I to say what it is that you possess? You know, and I well know, that you have something which make a tremdous popular appeal. You have the ability to create something which makes a great appeal to most of the folks now on this earth. You have had many immitators, as I well know, and not one of them has got to even First Base. There is some g-d——d spark which you possess which just bars competition.

At 56 I get no greater kick, and satisfaction out of reading anything, than I do out of the original Tarzan, and Tales of Tarzan, which last, I think is your very best, especially the Tale where he works out this God idea.

This seems a hard thing to say; but what about your Sons? How do you know that either of them are going to inherit your "Spark"?

Ed: I am no preacher, as well you know, but I am trying desperately to make my three sons KNOW that nothing is an asset, till Same is hard-cashed in! I am trying hard to make them realize that a liability NEVER gets any less, and, as recently, a liability may increase amazingly.

If I ever get out of this present mess, I am never going to owe another dollar.

Since I have been on my own, I have always been perfectly willing to go in to debt. The past three years have taught me, if they have taught me anything at all, that the most idiotic thing in the whole world, is to go into debt. If you owe no one, even though you are flat busted, you can tell the whole world to go plumbtohell! If you owe money, your creditors are telling you what you can, or cannot do! And HOW!!

***** This is being finished after a three day interim. There has nothing happened in the last 72 hours, which has changed my ideas any in regard to Ever owing Anyone Anything!

I may add, that, even after this interval, I still do not have the courage to go to SoCalif., where we both like to go, and face our actually hungry friends. You and the Scotts are the only prosperous folk we know in the vicinity of LA![77]

I have not written anyone a personal letter for so d——d long, that I do not know as I have given you the local gossip?

As to-wit; Margaret has hi hopes of becoming a grand-mother some time in June![78]

That Collins is now selling Plymouth cars, and is making a very good effort, but howinhell can he sell many, when it takes 6,000 bushels of corn to buy any "Low Priced" car?

That JB is working with a Farm Loan company. He works out with the best farm-loan may in So-Eastern Nebraska, likes it plenty, is learning a whole lot.

That Herb is around home about ½ the time, but so far has got slick marks at this small, but scholastically rating Doane College. Needless to state that he is mighty welcome around 910, after his recent 4 years at Culver.

That Margt and I are fine! A little fatter, a little greyer all the time. But; "Age has it's compensations!" And I may admit that we are getting a lot out of having all three Weston Boys around most of the time, which same, has not happened, since Coll kicked into Culver in '23.

That we have all had the Flu, but we are all out from under.

That one of the reasons I would most like to hit SoCal. would be to renew my relationship with Hulbert. I have not seen much of your Olive Branches, but saw something of Hulbert last year, and I know of no youngster who has made the hit with me, that he did. ³/sths of this tribe had the opportunity to learn to think a lot of Hulbert last Spring.

I see that I have run over two sheets, and Margt says, and she Knows! that one sheet is likely to be too much!

One more item: We have a married old maid in this village who has seriously taken this so-called Contract, in the last two years. And this barren matron has learned it!

I have had just one seance with her, and she opened up a vision to me that I did not know even existed before!

I will not go into details. She not only knows the current rules, but she knows Why!

She eased into me, not that she had any idea of what these things are, that Modern Contract, is simply a matter of Combinations and Permutations, just simple mathematics!

I checked this natural born school-teacher, and, after five hours of various hands, I found she was never off more than one (1) trick, and that her well-learned Combinations and Permutations were right, to a gnat's eye brow. I have since heard that this Contract, was got up in the very first place, by a first class navigator in the Navy. That he had much idle time on his hands, on cruises, etc., and so he mathematically figured out thousands of Auction Hands, and suggested a better game; Contract!

I think that my elder old age, I am going to get much out of playing this Combination & Permutation game.

Wish we were going to see you soon.

Love to you all,

Yours,
[HTW]

3/11/33

Dear Edgar Rice:
Was damned glad to get your wire. Sent at 9:22 a.m. and received by me at 7:02 pm, which gives you and idea of the wire congestion around LA.

I know little of earth quake, or "tremors"(?). I had read of tidal waves; I thought of you folks in your beach house, and after listening to the radio, got panicy, and sent that wire early this morning.[79]

These are indeed strenuous times! It got my goat, and seemed to me a little too damned much that you SoCal guys should also have Nature against you.

I am not going to dwell on your recent "Tremor" for I know you Native

Sons are someaht toughy[80] on said subject, but I state freely this whole and entire Tribe is <u>most glad</u> to know that it did not touch any of you Borroughes, in any way.

I will slip to personal stuff: to-wit: Jeff, at last has fallen; he has a girl, AND HOW! Being a Twin to his Mother, there is no remote doubt how he feels on the subject. (Note: JB has never brought any girl around that Margt and I did not take to, and this Jean rates high, with us, amongst these numerous young females; which certainly helps Margt and me along a whole lot!)

Item: the Beatrice National Bank could have, at any and all times paid off every damned depositor, just as fast as they could have passed through and been paid. As a bank, we have had nothing whatever to ever worry about. We could have paid off on our own resources, with no recourse to the Federal Reserve. So long as we run any bank, it will be just this way. So this "Holiday(?)" has meant just nothing in our banking life, tho we have worried a good deal over our immediate community.

Item: As I have told you, we retain a very superior Income Tax auditor. The entire tax that this Tribe pays this year pays amounts to $417.17. I think this is most smart on the part of said auditor, and a little credit to me, on account of distributation. I suppose you will smack me down and tell me you paid <u>no</u> income tax for 1932!! Please don't, even if true, for I am proud of this income chore, if I am proud of nothing else, in these times.

Item: Margt had the yearn for SoCal, and we planned to motor out, incognito, as you suggested! I got a gawddamned cyst on my neck right where the collar most bound, and had to have it removed; then the bank Holiday! Sub-item: If we had gone, as planned, we would have been just about at Needles when the Holiday hit us; and we would have had two check books with us, and possibly 15 bucks in currency between us! Also, we certainly would have been in LA County yesterday when the "Tremor" occured!! The next above is proof positive that it is a fine thing to me wed to a Lucky Irish Wife, even tho the cyst was mine own! Neither of us, at our age, crave any even "Slight Tremors"!!!

I see that FD Roosevelt is most apt to cancel my veteran pension. Hard luck, but, Oh Well, we Vets are used to a tough break!

Certainly am glad to know you all came out of the "Tremor" with no harm. Much love,

Yours,

[HTW]

5/8/33

Dear Ed:

Have you ever had a gun shy dog in your family?

We have one, to-wit; Morning View Julliete; she will be fourteen next November, and she is crouding my left hind leg as I write this, as her sense of hearing is still too d——d keen, and she hears a thunder-storm 100 miles away, and whichwill never come this way, for I, in my Youth, cant hear any sign of any storm of any kind!

We left dere ole H-wood on the a.m. of the 30th, as per schedule. Stopped at The Apache. Put in ½ a day at the Boulder Dam!

Personally, I think that said dam in the worst graft on the tax payer's money ever put over in these none to up-right United States.

I freely admit that said dam is going to be the First Wonder of the Whole World, when completed. But it is also going to be the best known wonder as a graft and dirty steal that even the USA, used to such things, has ever known.

As a sort of a ½-ass engineer I marvel at it; as a tax payer, And How! I am inclined to throw-up at the thought of all this money wasted!

We had the very worst possible weather en route home. From Cedar City east, rain, snow, or blizzards. We never saw more that 100 yards from where we were. Fine paved roads to the Nebraska Line, and then just no roads at all. Gently slid into the ditch once, and had to hire a house-moving outfit with block and tackle to get that little Plymouth out of the quick-sand. Once it took us 4 ½ hours to get over 74 miles. I would have gladly gone to the sage brush, but I could not get through the damned fences.

Margt took this rotten trip, ditch and all, right on the chin, and never turned a hair! In fact, while we were sitting in the ditch, waiting for first aid, she read aloud to me! I am quite sure that this Margt gets better and better the older she is!

Everything seems ok here. No actual riots during our five week absence. Have never had a better time than flocking around with the Westons the time since we got home. Whatinhell have these folk who have no children? We were sorry not to have seen Joan, Hulbert, and Jack, but were mighty glad to foregather with you and Emma. Folks, people, are my chief interest. The Burroughs Clan rates high with me.

Much love to you all, and all the breaks!

Yours,

[HTW]

Beatrice, Nebr.

6/9/33

Dear Edgar Rice:

We accept your congratulations, gracefully, and believe that we deserve them. I have glimpsed Margaret-Collins only once, but she looked like Some Baby to me. She has fur, instead of hair! Not much, but even all over her head like a baby seal.

The production was put on in Lincoln, as Mabel's mother lives there and Mabel knew some medico, who she thought was hot stuff, and I guess he is, as both Mabel and Margaret-Collins are doing all right. They are paving between here and Lincoln, and the detours make it 55 miles instead of the normal 40 miles, also the dust is not only choking, but dangerous, as you cant see a d——d thing ahead, any more than in a fog, and it has been over 100 for sometime. So Grandma & Grandpaw have not ventured over this road but once.

I used to be considered an expert on babys in the early party of this century. Ofcourse, I was no champion on baby-girls, but I think I still know a Real Baby when I see one, and I rate this one AAA!

In my baby expert days, I could pick the sex of a coming baby with amazing accuracy. I picked 29 times and was wrong only once, and that woman had a tumor and not a baby. Ofcourse, I have not been working at this for some years, but I thought it was like swimming, if you know how, you always could, so as I used to do, I gave 2–1 I could pick the sex. Herb and JB joined me in this business vernture. I was wrong!

Well, even though we have lost our knack at picking 'em, we are all so

226

damned glad to have another female in the family that we do not mind the financial loss!

Gawd, how I would welcome some of your Malibu fog and cold! This is the hottest June ever recorded in these Parts, and 105 the other day is the hottest we have had anytime in several years! I have forgotten what fog and chill means!

I like your report on how Joan takes charge of Sunday-school! Doubtless she has something on her mind, and will eventually change the whole trend of thought regarding S-schools, and like matters.

Glad to have heard from you. Thanks for your congratulations. Love to you all,

Yours,
[HTW]

Please take careful note of this:
Northgate Star Route #2, Bemidji, Minn.
8.24/33

Dear Edgar Rice:

Yeah, you owed me anyway one letter and probably several postal cards and I was getting to feel as the recruit did the second day when the Colonel did not return his salute, that the Colonel was probably mad at him!

We are all glad to get news from the Burroughses. The younger generation seem to be having very fine adventures, and it would seem that you and Emma were getting around some too.

You mention the boy Brugh, from Beetrice.[81] I know his father but not the son. I think he must have happened along about the time that the Weston Boys were going to Culver, as they know him but little, but I have heard good things about him from several other sources.

We had the hottest June that even the Nebraska Indians have any tradition. We pulled north July 2d, and July 1st and June 30th both hit 111 in Beatrice. Desert heat, and in a supposed agricultural section!

Have been here ever since, that is, Margt, Herb and I. Jeff had things to do, and followed in ten days. Col and Mabel got here last Sunday, for his two weeks vacation off from his particular marts of trade.

Gawd, but this is a lovely summer climate and country!

I think I have mentioned to you, that for five years, I aided by our sons, have battled Margt off from buying a place up here. Reason; the Birchmont was a d——d good hotel, and she had nothing on her mind there except her hair and hat; just no responsibility of running a house; feeding the animals, or anything like that!

But she got us down this year; wore us completely out! She burst forth and bought 300 ft lake front; 2 acres; a log house 26 paces one way and 14 paces the other, and an artesian-well! She took another burst, and bought a 24 ft cruiser, and named it Margaret Jr. after her grand-daughter.

Truth to tell, after eight years of Bemidji, we are reasonably certain that it suits us as a tribe. Also, she stole the place, from a widow-woman, who had been poison-ivied. Said widow-woman last summer had cash in the bank for $^9/_{16}$ths more than Margt paid her this year. I am certain that within the next two years, with the New Deal, Inflation, and what-not upon us, Margt can sell the place without a loss. Also, Margt, as she probably has often stated to you and Emma, always wanted a boat big enough to hold a rocking chair in which she could sit. This Margaret Jr supplies that want, and I am certain that this type boat will cost 50% more next summer. So I think Margt has not been throwing her money away, and I also think that she rates what she wants anyway, and also that all this is a much better buy than those Mirimar Lots!!!!!

Moved in the Third. Were lucky and caught a good plain hard working km the 3d day, after Margt had done the house work for the intervening time.[82] We are all crazy about it.

It has so happened th[text missing] . . . have a name, why isn't this North Gate logical? Ofcourse I was all set to christen it Numa, or Kala, or some such, but after thinking it carefully over, this North Gate suits me, and I am a good deal swelled up to be dwelling in a dwelling with a name![83] Ofcourse, this is old stuff to you, but, believe me! it aint to me!

Now to get to this Star Route stuff. I asked the pm what our new address was; seze; star route No 2! Sezi: Oh yes, rfd #2. Seze: no! Then he told me that there was rfd #2 running out of Bemidji, and also sr #2. There is a difference! A rfd runs out and comes back to the same starting place. A Star Route is one that carries mail to some outlying town, and drops letters en route!

Hence this mouth-filling summer address!

Jeff's Jean arrived three weeks ago. The second day she was here, it was very rough. Herb was going to take her out in the speed boat to bump the waves; she slipped on the wet fore-deck, and crashed the glass wind-shield. Result; a terrible gash where she sits down. We have a AAA MD here; got him in 23 minutes! 26 clamps! She is young. She came out of it just fine, and a few days ago was swiming and playing around as usual. She is a great child! Never turned a hair, just all guts. This whole family, and especially Jeff, is getting a Big Break to annex this fine Jean.

Her mother and cousins took her home today. Unamious tears on the part of the Westons! I know little of modern girls. I do not get along with any of them much. But Jean and I talk just the same way. I know it is always going to be a wonderful thing for me that Jean & Jeff happened to meet up.

Herb will go home about the 8th of Sept. JB has to get on the job some earlier. Margt and I hope to stay here till the 15th to 25th.

Jeff & Jean are to be married in November. They aim to motor to Calif on their trip, so you will give them your once over, and I know will tell me how right I am about Jean.

It it were not for Bemidji, I think I would most like to dig around where our early settlers once abided. That So-West Indian country fascinates me. But I think I would work out of Santa Fe, which berg I like better than any place I know, next to Beatrice and Bemidji.

Much love to you all, and I would like to hear from you more often than just seasonally!

Yours,
[HTW]

Have recently had word that my very good friend Henry Porter died last Friday. Do you remember, long ago, when you and Bob Lay came to the train to see me off, and Henry's coach-man and foot-man, and gawd-knows-what delivered me? Ever since New Haven, Henry and I have been mighty close. Henry broke in June '32 because he was trustee for too many. I have not seen him since. He was almost my age. His family looked on me as a sort of a freak, and for that reason I saw Henry often, but not much. Next to Wallace Robertson, Henry was the wisest, soundest, kindest man I ever knew in a financial way. Also, he and I have spoken the same language i[text missing]

Dear Emma:

I do not know that the enclosed will especially interest you. They dont me; not any! You will see Jean, as they are in California, and before long, will drop in on you.

I think you all will find Jean much more youthful and charming than this awful newspaper picture shows her.

The burden of this recent wedding was, in only a small part, on us. We wonder howinhell the Wilhelmeys stood all the fuss?

We are now offering Herb a cash bonus if he will just elope!

Ofcourse, you and Ed were some younger, but we wonder how you and Ed stood up under the Joan wedding?

I think weddings are awful: necessary, but why fuss around?

We think you Burroughses sent a very grand present. You did wonderfully by these two.

For the first time in years, Margt has not made up our mind what we are going to do after the First of the Year. So I do not know whether we are going to make our usual sojourn to California, or not.

We feel badly that you passed through Lincoln, only 40 miles from here, over a new concrete slab, and did not want to at least have dinner with us, and spend the night.

Yours,

[HTW]

This is written at 12:22 a.m.
Christmas Morning in the Year of Our Lord 1932![84]

Dear Ed & Emma:

Very glad to have letters from you both, since you met-up with Jean & Jeff.

They pulled out for Lincoln this afternoon. The Wilhelmys have a strange habit of having their Big Christmas Time, at 5 A.M December 25th! That does not seem possible!!

But J & J will be there, and with bells on! Then they will come back to

910 N 7, have dinner with the Tribe at 1 pm (a very decent hour, I think!), and the Westons will have their Christmas following this dinner.

Little did I know that, when Jeff wed into the Wilhelmy Tribe, that it was the Time Honored Custom for this Tribe to put on their Real Christmas Stuff at any 5 A.M.! I had checked these Wilhelmys in many ways, in the short time that I had, but I never thought to check up on their wierd Christmas Customs. They seemed very normal to me, and to rate way above average.

I was a lot amazed to learn of this tribal 5 A.M. habit, on Christmas, of all days!

But, after all, Dec. 25th happens but once in any year! There are 364 other days in most years! What difference does one cockeyed day make in any group of 365 days? Answer: Close to nothing at all!

You gave them a very fine time. They got home last Monday. I have had a good deal of conversation with them. They had a grand time. No small part of this "Grand Time", was being with the Burroughs Tribe!

Much love to you all, and I hope that all your hopes will be fulfilled in '34.

Yours
[HTW]

Tarzana, Calif.
March 14, 1934/br

Mr. H. T. Weston, c/o La Playa Hotel,
Carmel, California.

Dear Bert:
I am sorry that your letter of the fifth has gone so long unacknowledged. In the first place, I did not get it until two days ago, it having been held at the house for several days before being sent to the office.

Hulbert was badly shaken up, but not seriously injured. The plane was a mess. It was a new one that I had bought for us to take our training in. I had the pleasure of flying it for five minutes.

The fault was not Hulbert's; it might have happened to anyone. He made a bad landing, tried to correct it by taking off again, got ten or fifteen feet in the air and crashed into some trees on a golf course. It was a wonder he was not killed. We were so glad that his injuries were not serious that none of us gave a damn about the ship. I am getting it repaired and will have it again in a couple of weeks.

Am glad to hear that Jeff is doing so well on his job. Like all the Weston boys, he is a great guy.

I doubt very much that Emma and I will drive up to see you. I suppose you have got to know it some time, so I might as well tell you that we are not living together. Emma is still at the beach, and my address is Tarzana.[85]

I should certainly like awfully well to see you and Margaret. Give her my love, and with best to yourself, I am

Yours,

Ed

Tarzana, Calif.

March 26, 1934/br

Mr. H. T. Weston, Hotel Del Coronado,
Coronado, Calif.

Dear Bert:

I was sorry that I did not see you and Margaret when you came through a week ago as I certainly should have liked to have had a visit with you.

I doubt very much that I shall be able to get down to Coronado. I have never flown alone far from the home airport, and am not ready to undertake a cross-country flight at present. Furthermore, I am unusually busy here, as we are about to start the production of our own Tarzan radio program.

Hope we shall have better luck next time you are out this way.
With love to you both.

Yours,

Ed

[HTW to Charles Rosenberger; in ERB's hand, in pencil; copy date unknown; letter date presumably August 1934:]

Aug—

What I write, Margaret and I agree upon. She has known Ed and Emma only 10 less years than I have, and I think there has not been a day when we have not discussed them.

I note in your letter, you do not suggest any action on my part, or on our part. I agree with this, for the reason that in all these years, Ed has never asked my ideas on any subject, even on matters about which I was much more experienced than he could be. Also, there have been times I, sort of off my guard, have offered him suggestions, and these received no consideration whatever from him. So we feel, that of recent years anyway, I have been just a sort of habit with Ed and not a very welcome one. We feel, if I should go to see Ed, or write him, that it would do no good, and would probably make him more determined to go ahead with his present plans.

I have known Ed since the fall of '95. He has always been unusual and erratic. I have told Margaret many times, when Ed has done or said anything which seemed sort of queer, that as long as I had known him he had always done or said just such things.

I suppose looking back, that the fact that Ed always has been unusual, erratic, and perhaps queer, has been his great charm and attraction for me. I have known Emma only a few less years than I have known Ed. About the last time I saw Hulbert, I told him how Margaret and I felt about Emma: how high she rated with us, the way she had stood by Ed, and the fine children she had raised—After matrimony Ed had some lean years, and they were damned lean! And there were a lot of them! So far as I know, Emma staid right in there. Item! I knew Ed's father as well as a youngster could. He was a grand man. He scared most youngsters, but I used to stand attention, and Say: Sir, to him, and we got along. As long as he lived I never failed to call on him when I went through Chicago. His office was only a step from the Union Station. I was Ed's good friend and admirer, and during those worthless years in Ed's career, I battled Mr Burroughs in Ed's behalf. He said Ed was no good. I told him that Ed was plenty good. That he had not happened to Hit yet. I wonder what Ed's father would think of him now? I think the fine old gentleman has won his arguement with me! You and I have lived long enough to know, if we know anything, that no man of our age can get along with any woman, around half our age, even tho this woman is a very fine person as I get it. Ed's Elder Year Light O'Love is anything but a fine person—

If Ed goes on with this, he is doing a terrible injustice to Emma, he is doing an awful thing to his children, and he is letting himself in for such real trouble as even he has never known! If Ed goes on with his present program he will too soon be busted, broke and just a tramp. The combination he has in mind, just does not work out. You know this; I know this; and if Ed wasnt crazy he would know it too. I suppose that Emma has a tender feeling for Ed, even yet! She would have, for she is a grand person—

If Ed insists upon going on with this Young Bride program, the damned old mis-lead fool! Emma should think of Ed as one she loved, but who is dead, and gone—

Through you I suggest to Emma, that she employ the best attorney in L.A. to take her case, on a percentage basis, and to sue, and lay Ed to the limit. If this silly old man, insists on going on with his present ideas, Emma should forget Ed: she should look on him as dead, and she should get from this stranger all that she possibly can for herself and her children. For certainly this new younger female is going to wreck Ed, and quickly, and utterly.

I do not know for whom I am the sorrier, Emma or Ed. This is tough on Emma, and undeserved, but if Ed goes on through with his absurd program, he is going to experience hell and repeat, and there is no doubt of that!

You state in your letter that Ed says he has always wanted to get rid of Emma. That is just a damned lie. That is a statement of a person who is not sane—

Charming, unusual, erratic personality that Ed is, there is no woman on earth that would have lived with him, and put up with him, except Emma; and do not be fooled! Emma suited Ed plenty, until this insane streak hit him. Why, if your wife, or mine, had happened through some sad mis-chance to have married Ed, they would not have lived with this nut for a month, and Emma has stood by him and wonderfully, through all these years.

I had no right to ask you to write me about the Burroughs' affairs, and my only excuse is that we have great interest in them. I am very grateful to you for the fine letter you wrote me—That was a fine thing for you to do—What you wrote is of course confidential in every way—

The Burroughs situation seems to us to be a hopeless sad affair for both Ed and for Emma, unless Ed makes a return to Sanity.

I am sure I could not have any influence with Ed. I never have had, and in his present mood, he would not listen to me—

[One line erased. It seems unlikely that the letter ended here; perhaps there was more, or at least a farewell with signature, that ERB did not copy. The handwriting is loose, often corrected, and looks hurriedly executed.—Ed.]

[ERB Collection]

Tarzana, Calif.

May 13 1939

Dear Bert:

I can't tell you how much I have missed hearing from you. I think of you very often, and am always running across things that remind me of you. Just the other day I came across a snap shot you took of me on the steps of the QM Building at Orchard Lake forty-five years ago.[86] I was Officer of the Day. I had a 23″ waist. Them days is gone forever—at least in this incarnation—and so is my waist line.

I never hear from Bob. Saw him in Chicago a couple of years ago. We went to the races at Arlington with them. I heard the other day that he had divorced and was remarried, but it may be only idle rumor.

If you feel like it, and have the time, I'd like awfully well to hear from you. I have hundreds of acquaintances and some friends, but none who mean as much to me as you and Bob.

Please give my best to Margaret and the boys.

Yours,

Ed

Dear Ed:

Ofcourse I am glad to have your recent letter. I am quite sure that men of our age cannot change enough so a fine relationship that has continued for forty years can be just forgotten.

I do not know why you have not written to me for five years. I thought the letter I wrote after you told me that you and Emma had separated was friendly and understanding, and I have wondered why you did not reply to it.

And now, what about you and me?

You have made for yourself a new "incarnation"—I borrow this word from your letter. Will I fit into it?

I think this is for you to determine, as I, in the same "incarnation" I have been for the last ⅓d century, and have changed little, except to have slowed up and become much fatter and balder.

There must have been something sort of fundamental that kept us interested in each other for forty years. It was not propinqinty, for gawd knows we have never lived anywhere near each other.

I dont knowwhat it was and dont care. It may still exist. What do you think?

Much love and good luck,

Yours,

[HTW]

Tarzana, Calif.
May 25 1939

Dear Bert:

I was sure glad to have your letter of the 20th; and to know that our old friendship was not broken, as I feared. It was that fear that kept me from writing—that and the unjust and abominable treatment I received from others whom I thought were my friends. Perhaps they felt that they were justified, for they only heard one side of the story and that garbled and slanderous. Under the circumstances I could not tell my side even when I had the opportunity. I just had to keep my mouth shut and take it. The fact that some have since acknowledged their error and apologized did little to lessen the hurt.

My family all understand, and acknowledge that my action was warranted. My two brothers, my neice, and my nephew, who have met Florence since our marriage, all love her and appreciate the fact that she is a very fine woman. You can have no idea what we went through, though—bombarded with filthy anonomous letters for years.

While some of my "friends" would not accept Florence, she has always accepted my friends; and without exception they have all liked her. She has done nothing to alienate my affection for my children, even though Emma has forbidden them coming to my home. On the contrary, she is always urging me to see them; and when any of them do come to our home, she is very sweet to them.

I am writing you thus, as I have never written anyone else, because I value your friendship; and because I hope that some day you will meet Florence.

Had a letter from Bob Lay the other day. Hadn't heard from him nor seen him for about two years. Florence and I went to dinner with them and to the races at Arlington at that time.

My new picture, TARZAN FINDS A SON, is being previewed here tomorrow night. Florence and I saw it about two weeks ago at the studio. It is an MGM picture. If it comes to Beatrice, I hope you will see it. It is the best Tarzan picture yet.

Lots of the best,

Yours,

Ed

Beatrice, Nebr.
June 25, 1939.

Dear Ed:

I have much interested in the rite-up that Life gave the Tarzan Family in the current number. I note that your picture is one of a series that Hulbert had in Life some months ago. Some where in my files I have the letter you wrote me telling of selling the original Tarzan of the Apes.

I will run across that some time hwen digging through my old records in order to keep the Tax Bureau from setting up now claims, and will send it to you.

Recently while going through an 1934 file I ran on to some Burroughs letters. One stated that you had recently passed through Lincoln, 40 miles from here, and had not let us know, which I recall peeved me likehell.

Another expressed your entire approval of the Wilhelmy Tribe starting their Christmases at 5 a.m., with the singing of Carols—which also peeved me!

I was glad to have your letter of the 25th of May. It is true, as you state in your letter that I heard "only one side". I have never taken "sides" in matters like this. My experience makes me believe that one's marital affairs are very much one's own business, and for that reason, what inhell could I do when you just quit writing to me?

But we will just forget that part. If you come this way, hope you will let us know, and I'll see you next time we are in California.

I might add that we have seen Emma, and are on good terms with her. We have also seen Hulbert and Joan, but have not seen Jack or Jim. We also saw Charlie and Chris once.

Herb and Marian live in Father's house.[87] No children. Jeff and Jean are across the alley from us. 2 girls. Collins across the street, 2 girls. The grand daughters run from 6 years to 17 months, and no more en route so far as we know.[88]

The New Deal has shifted the Collins Estate around a lot. We now have all three boys working for it. Jeff is sort of Front Man, because he is big enough to meet the public, and besides seems to be the only one of us four males who has what might be called, "the commercial instinct", and a decided sense of responsibility as well. We have the following corporations; Fidelity Finance Company, a loan company: Weston Real Estate Company, a number of farms and income town property, and that damned furniture store. I continue to run the listed securities. We have a board of directors, sort of, consisting of the four Weston males. We pass on everything of importance, then Margt either oKs us, or vetos us. This system has been going about two years and has worked out very well, besides relieving Margt of much burdensome detail.

Margt still has her place, North Gate, on Lake Bemidji. But now the boys are working, they can spend very little time there. They can take vacations in the winter better. She and I are going there July 5th, and will stay till September.

This Spring two men have wanted to buy North Gate, and it may be Margt will sell it if she can get her price for it.

I do not know whether these Local Items will interest you, but they are about what I would have written you five years ago.

Jeff dug up the enclosed somewhere and brought it to us. It is amazing how much Jack looks like you did at his age. I hope they may be as successful as their Father at this new venture.

Incidently, Arlington Brugh, or Robert Taylor has certainly made a wonderful success. He visited the old home town two years ago, and made a hit with every one, man woman and child. I happen to be about the only inhabitant of this village who [did] not know him as a boy, so did not meet him while here, but all his old pals and friends said he was an un-spoiled grand boy.

Love and good luck,

Yours,
[HTW]

Our Minnesota address is:
RFD No5,
Bemidji, Minnesota.

Tarzana, Calif.
July 6 1939

Dear Bert:

I was glad to have your letter of June 25th and learn about the Weston Family. You are fortunate in having the boys and their families near you. Jack and Jane live in one of my houses here at Tarzana, and I see Jack often.[89] Hulbert gets out here occasionally; but I do not often see Joan, though we often visit over the telephone. Hulbert recently returned from a magazine assignment in Nevada where he made photographs and obtained data for an article on ancient Indian culture. He damn near killed himself climbing a mountain under a broiling sun, and when he reached the top would have been struck by a rattle snake had his companion not saved him. He has always been bugs on climbing, and I hope this experience has gotten it out of his system. I never could climb anything over four feet high without getting the jitters. Even when I see pictures of people climbing mountains I fold like an umbrella.

I should certainly like to have the letter you mention—the one I wrote telling of selling the original Tarzan of the Apes. The old boy has become quite a character since then. Original first editions of Tarzan of the Apes are now collectors' items. Scribner's had one in 1936 which it quoted at $25. It is practically impossible to get one now. I didn't have one; and it took me nearly two years to get one, circularizing my fan list and advertising in one of my novels.

I take it you don't care much for your furniture store. Do you still have the drug store? I was 100% for the drug store on account of the nice discount you gave me on films. I must have overlooked the furniture store, or perhaps I didn't need any chairs at the time.

You mention Charlie Rosenberger. I suppose you know that he died some time ago. I haven't seen any of them for over five years.

We got through the 4th without any casualties. I superintended the detonation of firecrackers and radio bombs for three hours in the morning and took them to the American Legion Circus and Fireworks Display at the Coliseum in the evening. There were more than 72,000 people there, but with my chauffeur dragging one of the kids by the wrist and I the other we managed to wriggle in and out without losing either of them.[90]

Hope you and Margaret have a swell time at Bemidji. My secretary comes from Minnesota, and likes to go back there for his vacations. He is familiar with Bemidji, but the lake he goes to is about fifty miles away.

Yours,

Ed

Dear Ed:

On July 6th, Margt and I tooled our '36 Air-Flow up here. It was loaded to the guards with baggage and two dogs. We made the 637 miles in less than 15 hours, which, without bragging, we think fair time for two whose total age in 124 years, and total weight 205¼ lbs.

The most exciting thing that has happened to me since leaving home, was the Saturday Evening Post with you very much occupying the front pages.

For a good many years the Post has been sort of a weekly bible to me, and I suppose you have no idea how much I enjoyed reading that article on you. I have too much to say about it to write; will have to talk it with you when I next see you.

Collins, wife and daughter have been here part of the time. Herb and Marian for three weeks. So we have had plenty of company. Jeff, being the "front man" of our businesses in Beatrice, was unable to come this summer.

We do damned little up here. Play golf in the morning. Lay around in the pm, till swimming time comes, when Margt does her daily ¼ mile. Fish some, but the pike have been on a vacation mostly this summer. In the evening go to a movie and have one or two drinks in a very fine Municipal Bar; or shoot a little contract. Life is indeed simple here at Bemidji! Ofcourse, early in the season I spend a good part of my time pulling wood-ticks off the dogs.

It is now 5:35 pm, and I do not know whether Hitler has slopped over into Poland, or not. Too much iron deposits around for radio to work well. It is a very terrifying prospect. Gawd knows what would follow another World War.[91]

Herb and Marian leave next week and I suppose that we will follow in about a week later. They have had a lot of rain in Nebraska the past month, and the weather is cool for that part of the USA.

I recall some years ago you had Tarzan raising hell with some Huns in some jungle. I wonder if Mr. Hitler has barred you from his Nazi Realm? If so that is going to be a lot of territory soon unless some one steps on him.

Have not seen your last Tazan picture. It was in Beatrice after we left, and has not been shown here. Hope to see it some place on our various travels.

Much love and good luck,

Yours,
[HTW]

Tarzana, Calif.
September 2, 1939

Mr. Herbert T. Weston, Northgate,
Bemidji, Minnesota.

Dear Bert:

I am glad that you enjoyed the Saturday Evening Post article. They certainly played it up for far more than the subject was worth.

Your account of your life at Bemidji sounds very interesting. I am sure that it must be a swell place to loaf and play. It must be great to be one of the idle rich and not have to work hard like the rest of us poor boobs. However, it may not be so nice when comes the Revolution.

Yes, I was barred from Germany for a great many years and, as far as I know, I still am. I know Metro-Goldwyn-Mayer's Tarzan pictures are barred there. However, I do consider it a compliment to be barred from anything Nazi.[92] I am only hoping that we are not going to be dragged into Hitler's private war. It would mean a lot to you and me with the number of sons we have.

With love and best wishes, I am,

Very sincerely yours,
Ed

September 23d, 1939

Dear Ed:

We have been amazed at the contunued heat reports coming from Southern California. Sorry too, for we have felt that we could go there and be sure of at least an even break as to weather, which same we never get here, as you know, being somewhat familiar with the Middle West.

Two years ago we were in Coronado during the flood period. It did not bother us much as the weather there was not bad. However, we had no mail for five days, and the telephone and telegraph wires were engaged 24 hours ahead. We came north on the first Santa Fe train out of SanDiego. I sat on the rear platform and saw more oranges scattered around than I thought were in the whole world.

Ofcourse, I, in common with 98% of those in the USA hate and detest Hitler. I listened to his Danzig speech the other day, and it irritated me greatly to think his foul gutturals could come into our peaceful home. Ofcourse, I would have turned the raido off, but did not. From the nazi point of view, it covered about everything, and must have been written by their best brains to be recorded in history.

All our sons are in the Reserve, just 2d lts, as they have not worked at it since getting their first commissions. I suppose they are just in the Army, when the reserve is called out. Perhaps that is a good thing. I agree with Lindenberg that we want no part of European politics. I do feel, tho, that the USA should mobolize plenty of troops just as a matter of defense and protection.

We have ofcourse talked the situation over and over. Jeff said today: "There does not seem to be much we can do, except to do the best we can at our own small jobs." And I guess that is about it.

Yours for no possible war, except for defense,

[HTW]

Tarzana, Calif.

September 30 1939

Dear Bert:

If you were amazed by the continuous heat reports coming from Southern California, what do you suppose we were by the continued heat? Amazement isn't the word for it. Perhaps the French have one; but if they have, Prof. McCurdy failed to enlighten me. I have always been able to stand a lot of heat, but this came near getting me. It was 120 in the shade in downtown Los Angeles and the business section of Hollywood; and the humidity was terrific; or, as we say in Hollywood, colossal. And there was no relief even at the beaches. Since the "warm spell", as the C[hamber] of C[ommerce] describes it, we have had the tail end of a hurricane; as you have probably read. Some of our friends returned from Catalina in a cabin cruiser through 45 foot seas. Thirty-five ton rocks were washed from the breakwater where they had reposed in serene security for thirty years. Many beach houses were washed into the ocean. Some storm! When we do things in Southern California, we do 'em a little bit bigger and better.

The Pacific Southwest Tennis Tournament is on. This is our one dissipation of the year. We go every day.[93] It is fun, as we know many of the players and officials personally; and as a considerable proportion of our friends are tennis minded it is much like Old Home Week. Then, too, we see a lot of funny hats.

The situation in Europe (and Asia) looks bad. About the only bright spot is the fact that Germany, Russia, Italy, and Japan each fear and hate the others. All are liars, cheats, and murderers. I do not believe that such a coalition can endure. (My disparaging remarks and insults are intended to apply to the leaders, not to the people.) Another gleam of hope lies in the fact that none of the masses of these countries wish war, and that most of them are under-fed, under-clothed, over-worked, and dissatisfied. Again, how many Italians, do you suppose, are honing to die for Germany? They hate the Germans from goose-step to guttural.

We shouldn't get into this war unless we are invaded or the Monroe Doctrine violated, but we should prepare for both these eventualities. I believe this to be Roosevelts policy. I hope so. But we should sell to all belligerents on a cash and carry basis. If the warring powers wish to embroil us they will find an excuse whether we revise the neutrality act or not, and we might as well be making a little money in the mean time.

Having successfully disposed of most World problems which seem to be confusing all statesmen and other lesser minds, I now approach one of our own—the insidious boring from within by Communists, Fascists, and Nazis in this country. I should proclaim membership in any of these organizations high treason. I'd kick out all alien members by deportation without trial. I'd exile all American members who would not renounce their allegiance to these organizations and swear renewed allegiance to the United States, and I'd finger-print every one of them and put them on ten years probation, requiring them to report to some authority periodically. And I'd start in on the Reds in the Administration. I understand that there are over two thousand of them in key positions.

Have you ever read Pitkin's A Short Introduction to the History of Human Stupidity? I've probably asked you that before. The one trouble with that book is that while it conclusively demonstrates the stupidity of every one else, it also convinces you of your own stupidity, which leaves you in something of a mental mess after expounding such gems of wisdom as this letter contains. However, you feel that you are not alone. Take for example the fact that our most brilliant minds are divided on the neutrality question. There is a wise side and a stupid side to that question, as there must be to all questions; so many of our most brilliant minds must be stupid minds. It is all very confusing and depressing.

Now I have to go to the tennis tournament, which must be a relief to you.

Always,
Ed

Beatrice, Nebr.
October 22d, 1939.

Dear Ed:
I got a real kick out of your last letter. You gave your general idea of how things, in general, looked to you, and I feel that you wrote about all there was to be said on the general subject.

I have never read, nor even heard of Pitkin's History of Human Stupidity. I have ordered it. From the little you said of this book, I can see that I will agree with much it says, and perhaps become much more confused than I am now.

I use the radio just as I use a telephone. Margt is only a little more of a radio fan than I am. She falls for various radio music, which is just so much noise to me. But the other night, I turned her on, thinking, and hoping I might stumble on to some war news, and some program was announcing that Edgar Rice Burroughs was to be their Guest Artist!! That was duck-soup for us.

We staid on this program.

I must say as a radio performer you are a damned good writer. We were terribly disappointed. The only thing that sounded to us like you, was when the announcer called you Mrs. Burroughs. Then you really laughed, and it was the same laugh, that, to drop for a moment into perhaps the sort of sickly sentimental, that I have loved for more years than I like to think about.

Margt and I, following our habit of many years, are heeling the NU football team. I retain an insane, for one of my years and weight, interest in football. I guess I should have tried to be a coach, like ole man Stagg. And Margt too will sit in the rain and retain her interest. We have had a pretty good season this year. Our team is doing all right, and so this Fall is pretty swell for us. You tell of your tennis interest. Football is much the same to us, we follow the team around, and we too see many funny hats—and a lot of other funny and most interesting things.

The clipping enclosed reports another thing that has held our interest this Fall. This Sue looks like a boy and acts like one. She is the most perfectly co-ordinated infant I ever saw. She is a 16 cylinder wild cat![94]

Margt has spent most of this day, both a.m. and p.m., sitting on the porch, reading, knitting, or just sitting. This Nebraska climate is the most perfect on earth, for $1/4$% of the time. The rest of the time it blasts us with drouth and blow-torch hot winds, chokes us with dust storms, or floods us, or freezes us. We also have grass-hoppers which eat anything left out and upon which they can get their teeth. But, consider, spending a day on the porch in So E Nebraska on October 22d!

For more than a month, in fact, ever since we got back from Minnesota, we should have gone to New York. It is well for me to go there and spend a week with Margt's brokers, sort of getting their view point and letting the Corn Belt stink blow partially off of me. But NY is a sort of a horror to me. It is now mostly inhabited by the scum of Middle Europe. There used to be mostly Jews, Irish and Italians on the streets, but now there are hordes of mis-shapen, under-nurished queer folk, who look as tho they had crawled up out of filth, like unclean worms. Last time I was there, I went up on the tower of the Empire Building, as I always do.

It was a wonderful day and visibility was 100%. I looked for perhaps 40 miles in every direction. And I thought of the seething millions within one man's vision who had been transplanted from backward Middle Europe, and concentrated into this area, where none had a chance to know much about what it was all about.

It looked pretty hopeless and I was most glad to get back to close of the middle of the country. Drouth striken, hopper burdened, though it is, it is a place where, at least, most everyone eats.

I dont know just why I should have burdened you with the above, except I was thinking how much I disliked the idea of our proposed trip to New York.

In regard to the Embargo. Shamefully I confess on knowing too little about it to dare an opinion, but I was for keeping her on, because FDR wanted it off: reason enough for me! But when Al Smith came out flatly for the act to be amended, I switched to FDR's side. I am quite sure Mr. Smith dislikes and suspects Mr. Roosefelt fully as much as I do.

Am much amazed that a submarine could slip into a fully armed harbor and smack down an active British battle ship. Have discussed this with some ex-Navy men and they do not see how it was possible unless the Germans have prefected some device that will prevent sound detection—or that the British felt secure and were asleep.

Yours,

Bert

Tarzana, Calif.

October 30, 1939

Mr. Herbert T. Weston, Beatrice, Nebraska.

Dear Bert:

In the first place, let me remark that as a dramatic critic you are a damn good corn miller. From the far-flung suburbs of Tarzana, from Seattle to New York, I have received encomium from discriminating, discerning, intelligent admirers who were fortunate enough to listen in to my stupendous performance a couple of weeks ago.

Just to show you what a dub you are, I will quote from two of them, this one from Seattle from the President of the Evergreen Theatres Corporation:

> "Listened to your radio broadcast last week, and you were very good. As a matter of fact, you sounded as if you were part of the program and had been doing it every week."

And second, from New York City, from a letter from George Carlin, head of the United Feature Syndicate:

> "I just happened to tune in on the Texaco Radio program tonight (October 18) and found that Edgar Rice Burroughs was appearing on same. He certainly was good. He did his stuff in a quite professional manner with ease and poise and a winning way far superior to the average radio guest."

If I were you, I would go back to corn milling.

The pictures of Skating Sue are very cute. I can see from this clipping one very important reason why you like to live in Nebraska.

As I have been away from the office for the past week entertaining a friend from Honolulu, I am swamped with work; and so only this brief line, which I hope will put you in your place.

Yours,

Ed

Tarzana, Calif.
November 14, 1939

Mr. H. T. Weston, Beatrice, Nebraska.

Dear Bert:

The outcome of the recent election indicated that there are not quite a million screwballs in California. The great danger, however, lies in the fact that they will all get out and vote every time this Ham-and-Eggs business comes up, while many of those who oppose it may not go to the polls.

Thanks for the reminder of the inscription in your copy of TARZAN OF THE APES.[95] I think you must have an original edition and, if so, you may be interested to know that this is now a collector's item, almost unobtainable. When I was in New York two or three years ago, Scribner's had a couple which they quoted at $25.00 apiece. It took me a year or two to find one for myself; but I finally obtained a fairly good edition for $10.00 from some one who evidently didn't know what it was worth.

You say when you "next come to California"—does that mean that you are contemplating a trip in the near future? I hope so.

With best to you all, I am,

Yours,
Ed

Tarzana, Calif.
December 22 1939

Dear Bert:

Just a line to wish you, Margaret, and the children a very Merry Christmas and a Happy New Year.

Was in New York the last of November, and on the way home saw Bob in Chicago. He has leukemia, and looks very bad. I have read since I got home that no case has ever been cured. Bob was remarried about a year ago. They went to Honolulu on their honeymoon, and tried to find us while they were in L.A.; but because I'm not listed in the city telephone directory, we missed them. You see, we're listed in the county directory; or, rather, a special directory issued for the San Fernando Valley; so when you come on, please remember that.

Florence, the children, and I are driving to Yosemite for the holidays tomorrow. At The Ahwahnee, where we shall stop, they put on a special Christmas Eve party for the children; and many families go there regularly every year. It took us two years to get reservations, there is such a long waiting list.

Florence and the children are hoping for lots of snow, the particular thing that I came out here to escape; but, if there is plenty of snow, we should have a real Christmas, for it is very beautiful there in the winter.

Hope we'll be seeing you soon.

Yours,
Ed

Tarzana, Calif.

January 9, 1940

Mr. Herbert T. Weston, Beatrice, Nebraska.

Dear Bert:

I meant to write you a week ago to tell you of Bob Lay's death, but neglected to do so. It is possible, however, that you have already heard of it.

I had a wire from his wife on the morning of the second, saying that Bob had died the night before. I was not greatly surprised because of his appearance when I saw him in Chicago the first of December. His divorced wife called me up from Palm Springs that same evening to tell me of his death. It is too bad that Bob died for he certainly enjoyed life.

Florence, the children, and I spent the holiday week at Yosemite where we went to enjoy the snow, of which there was none; although it did snow the next day after we left.

I hope that you, Margaret, and the rest of the Weston tribe enjoy a Happy and Prosperous 1940.

Yours,

Ed

Beatrice, Nebr.

January 13th, 1940.

Dear Ed:

Thank you for telling me about Bob Lay.

When the boys were in Culver I used to drop in his office occasionally and we had lunch a few times together. Margt met him and liked him a lot, as I guess most women did. He was friendly and very interesting. He was very vivid, if that is the word, and seemed to be getting much out of every day and everything.

You have always been close to Bob and you have my real sympathy in your personal loss.

It is probable that Margt and I were in New York at least part of the time you were. Funny we did not meet!

I am sorry your outing in the Yosemite was snow-less, and there was a heavy snow the day after you left. You must be getting like me: my ideas are grand but my timing is lousey!

You may recall Jean, Jeff's small blond wife. She had her appendix out last Monday, which disturbed everyone but Jean, very much. She is getting along just fine and we are all glad that this is one more appendix that will never bother anyone.

Why dont you just write me your phone number and I will write it down in by black book in which I already have five phone numbers of yours recorded?

Right now we have 9 inches of even falling snow on the ground. This, doubtless, seems disgusting to you, but after seven lean years of abnormal weather, we Native Sons thankGod for shaking loose some real he-weather on this drouth striken country again!

Yours,

[HTW]

Tarzana, Calif.

January 18 1940

Dear Bert:

While I seldom saw Bob, I feel sort of lost knowing he is gone; but we'll be kicking off shortly. It has been a wonderful world we have lived in. In no other era could we have seen so many wonderful things come to pass. In no other country could we have found greater peace, security, and happiness. Even the New Dealers haven't been able to ruin it entirely.

Are you still playing bridge? Florence and I have been taking a course of lessons, and start a new course tonight. It has helped our game, especially mine, which is still nothing to write home about. Florence plays an excellent game.

Sorry that I missed you in New York, but I was there only a short time—Nov. 26th to the 29th.

Am glad that Jean came through her operation O.K. It must be a relief to know that that is out of the way permanently. When I had a double hernia operation in '38, Charlie Phillips opened me up on the right side for about a furlong to take out my appendix, just for luck; but he couldn't find any. He said that in some 2000 cases he's only seen a couple without an appendix. However, he took the joy out of it by saying that he might have overlooked mine.

Am glad you have snow, for I know you need it. I don't. I hope I never do.

Yours,

Ed

February 6th, 1940

Dear Ed:

We had four inches of snow last night. This makes close to two feet since December 23d, and makes all us dirt-farmers very happy. Tho I heard Margt say as she left for her card club that she could do with less snow.

There is never a dull moment around here. The latest to break is that Marion hopes for addition to the Herb Weston family between May 1st and 15th.[96]

Jean is entirely over her operation; drives her car, dances and everything. Either she had a hellofa good surgeon or she is a remarkable gal.

Incidently you were bragging about your operation and how you were so much further advanced than the mine run of folk, that you had no appendix. That is nothing. I have no wisdom teeth, and never did have!!

The last time we were in LosA County, as is our want, we drove around to see if Margt's two fine lots were still at Mirimar. Margt is always afraid they will have slipped off or something. This time we found one of them with a large handsome sign on them offering them at a real bargin, as the owner had to sell. I wrote the realator and mentioned that the lot had never been offered for sale. That was an error as he phoned many times, when I happened to be out. I presume that is a good ole Southern California custom to "contact" lot owners.

We find the Sat Eve Post a very interesting publication. Not long after they wrote you up, then are running a series of F.W. Woolworth the 10¢ King. Margt used to know him almost as well as I know you.

Thanks for sending your addresses and phone numbers. I am going to paste them in my black book before I forget it.

Yours,
Bert

Margt and I still play a good deal of contract, not as a science, however. Our games are largely conversational, and I think we have only seventeen rules many of which we forget from time to time. We must be gawd awful lucky however, as since we have been playing as a team we have done right well financially.

Tarzana, Calif.
February 20 1940

Dear Bert:

I can't recall whether or not I have written you since the death of my brother Harry on January 21st. That leaves only George and me of our generation.

Harry had been hospitalized for eight months with sclerosis of the spine. As he was practically blind, almost entirely helpless, and his case hopeless, we all felt that his death was a release from an intolerable condition which he must have hated, though he never once complained. He was one of the finest men I ever knew. No one could have deserved such an affliction less than he.

I recall that there was an old superstition in our home when I was a boy that if one friend or relative died there would be two more similar deaths following quite closely. Well, in this instance it was Harry, Bob Lay, and Joe Bray, former president of A.C. McClurg & Co., which published Tarzan of the Apes and many other books of mine and a friend for a quarter of a century. I hope this ends the thing for a while.

Speaking of Tarzan of the Apes, I saw a New York friend of mine at The Racquet Club in Palm Springs Sunday who is a collector of first and rare editions. He told me that firsts of Tarzan of the Apes were bringing $50 to $75 each according to the condition of the book; so if you have a first hang on to it. I didn't have one, but managed to buy one for $10 about a year ago. I doubt that the first printing was more than two or three thousand. I have the long-hand manuscript of the story, which should be worth something some day if there continue to be nuts who are interested in such things.

I know how Margaret gets to feel about the snow. Rain here means to us what snow does to you, but after a week or so of it one almost wishes it would never rain again. Right now we are having beautiful spring weather—some of the flowering fruits are blossoming and the plants are popping up in the garden like Jack-in-the-Boxes (or Jacks-in-the-Box, or Jacks-in-the-Boxes—take your choice); anyway, things are growing. Tomorrow may come the deluge.

Drop me a line when you have the time.

Yours,
Ed

Lanikai, Oahu, T.H.
May 13 1940

Dear Bert:

Am still enjoying the visit I had with you and Margaret. Hope you got home safely and found everything O.K.

I sailed April 24th, the day that Florence and the children arrived here, and landed on the 29th. Had a reasonably pleasant trip. Met some nice young people from the mainland and some Australians who were mighty good company. Won both nights that they played Keno and two nights at poker. Did very well for myself.

We have a comfortable house smack on the ocean, with a nice white, sandy beach and good swimming. We can wade out for a hundred yards or more and then not be in deep water. No coral nor seaweed. There is good surf fishing here, but I haven't a pole nor a hook. Duke Kahanamoku's brother told me that all I needed was a bamboo pole, a piece of string, a hook, and some fresh shrimp to catch more fish than we could use. I was especially warned by another Hawaiian not to have any bananas on the beach when I was going fishing; and that if Florence asked me where I was going, I should reply: "I am going for a walk up in the mountains." This is quite necessary, because the fish would hear me.

It has rained every day since we arrived; and some days, like today, all day. A native who came to see me today told me that in a storm like this it rains about an inch an hour. In a day, we get more than the entire annual rainfall of Los Angeles. It might be a good plan to bring Nebraska over here for a month.

Lanikai, the name of our postoffice, means Heavenly Sea; and Oahu, the name of the island, means Place of Assemblage, or seat of government, as it has been since King Kamehameha I conquered the islands.

God! You should hear it rain. I have my office in one of two small rooms in the garage. I'll bet Florence is going nuts in the house, with the two kids shut up there. She doesn't like a rain that never lets up— neither do I. If someone hadn't already done it, I could write "Rain". Am think of writing a play called Suicide on the Beach in the Rain, or somep'n.

Well, so-long! Drop me a line once in a while.

Best to you both, in which Florence joins if she hasn't gone out and drowned herself.

Ed

Lanikai, Oahu, T.H.
June 7 1940

Dear Bert:

Margaret's letter of the 20th May and yours of the 22nd arrived yesterday. I was delighted to hear from both of you. Tell Margaret I never gave the books another thought after I sent them. I have been too damn busy myself; so I can appreciate that others may have been busy, too.

Wrote you on May 17th. You probably received it shortly after writing me.

It was great seeing you and Margaret again. Florence is so sorry she was unable to be with us. She sends her best to you both.

Congratulations on the new grandchild. One nice thing about it is that she won't have to go to war when she grows up.

Am glad you said nothing about this war. I hear plenty about it here. These people are not so happy. An enemy from the West would probably try to mess up this island—the largest military and naval establishment belonging to the US. Worse still, the food problem would be terrible. They don't raise enough to feed the population I am told. We live between two heavily fortified Points which an enemy would certainly bomb. They might miss and hit us.

Am not so happy myself today. Went on a picnic yesterday with the Hallidays and Mitchells. Halliday is John Halliday the actor. I spent four hours on and in the water during the hottest part of the day, and although I tried to protect myself to some extent, I am badly burned and swelling. My hands and arms look like those of pithocanthropus erectus; and my head will, I fear, soon bear a startling resemblance to that of a man from some distant planet. We picnicked on Sand Island in Kaneohe Bay. I went over in Halliday's sampan and came back in Mitchells speed boat. It was lots of fun, but not so funny today. Sand Island is a spit of sand. When we arrived it was about a quarter of a mile long and a few yards wide. Not a tree or spear of grass on it—just white sand. Before we left the tide had come in and you could have covered the whole island with your front parlor rug. The swimming was fine, and so were the highballs on Mitchells boat—Kris Kraft (?) cabin job. A few days ago some swimmers reported seeing five sharks at the island. We didn't see any, but that was not because we didn't look for them.

Soo long! Aloha! Best of everything!

Ed

PS: Am enclosing clipping, though I don't know whether or not you knew Featherstone at Orchard Lake.

Beatrice, Nebr.
June 18th, 1940.

Dear Ed:
Have had two letters from you since you took off for Oahu. The fact that you got away from LA County soon after we did, indicates that you were able to rent your home, and I suppose to a satisfactory tenant and at your price. Migawd, imagine anyone feeling he was able to pay 900 per month for <u>any home</u> in these times!!

I guess Featherstone was one I missed at O Lake. If he was only 52 when he died, I missed him by more than a decade.

Margt and I have been surprisingly busy since our return. Our business matters always come in bunches. We will loaf along for weeks, then will wallow up to our necks for a month or so. Guess that is a good way to have it.

Your account of your day on Sand Island and your sun burn greatly interested me. I did not know that a handsome dark devil like you sun burned. With my skin I have burned my way along for more than three score years, burning every day I am out, never tanning any, and having onehellofa time generally. Margt and Jeff never burn, but take on a deep native Hawaiian color with the red showing through their cheeks; Collins never burns but takes on claret colored tan, Herb burns some then has a canary yellow tan for the rest of the season. They are a colorful lot.

Four years ago, I installed air conditioning. I did it because the man at the head of the company who sold it to us was an old friend and utterly dependable. He died a month after they started on our installation. For four long years this damned plant has not worked, and it is not working now. The up stairs plant is out, and has been for three days. There has been a procession of engineers, mechanics and what have you, parading through this house for four years. If Charley Stuart had lived the first year he would have torn the whole thing out and put in a new plant. But he died.

We have a swimming pool just south of the house. It aint the first cost, it's the up-keep. The vacume cleaner would not work this spring. A mystery! Finally found that the pipe going to the pump had not been drained, had cracked and the sucker was sucking air! Had to tear up sod and cement and a hellofa mess.

I sometimes think the Horse-and Buggy Days were the best. Why, I can remember if I had a pair of pliers and a yard of baling wire I could fix anything that happened to my T Model.

It makes me feel likehell to know that the Nazi have run all over Europe in such a short time. No one ever won a war, but it seems to me this louse Mussolini stands to really profit by Hitler's efforts.

I did not write the enclosed editorial, nor did I draw the cartoon, but if I were gifted enough I might have done both.

I do not like anything about FDR. I distrust him every turn of the road. It looks as tho we were going to have four more years of the impractical New Deal Gangsters running this part of the world and I am very fearful of the result. Hitler has made the world over by his success in Europe. At best we are going to have hard years to meet this world change, and we have a tough chance to meet with much success headed a man who has proven himself to be an impractical failure in the past 7 1/2 years.

Your first letter told of rain and rain and then more rain. Your second letter of sun and more sun. I asked a man who lived in Alberta what kind of a climate it was. He said it was very fine, ofcourse, he added we have only two seasons, the 4th of July and winter.

Margt and I will be leaving for Bemidji in about two weeks where we will stay until well into September. I doubt if any of the Weston boys can visit us, as they are all working and cant leave their jobs long especially at this time of year.

Our best to you and Florence and when weary of too much sun, or rain, tell me how things look to you from our western frontier.

Yours,

[HTW]

After the 4th, address:

RFD #5,

Bemidji, Minneaota.

Lanikai, Oahu, T.H.

June 27 1940

Dear Bert:

I liked the editorial in the WORLD-HERALD. If we only knew what is the best course. History, especially recent history, should have taught us that those who fight a purely defensive war lose that war. France, with the "best army in the world" commanded by the "world's greatest soldier" sat on her fanny until Hitler was ready to blizkrieg her; then she folded. I am afraid that England, now forced to fight a defensive war, may also fold.

What should we do? We don't want to fight an offensive war, but we should prepare ourselves to do so. We should prepare as though we intended to conquer the world, but we should confine our operations to the Western Hemisphere. If anyone says "Boo!" to us over here, we should land on him with both feet and conquer him. I mean Mexico, Equador, Bolivia, or any other Western Hemisphere country that gets out of line. If we discover that fifth column infiltration has made any country a menace to us, we shouldn't stand on ceremony or international law or ethics—we should just wipe that country off the face of the earth. That is what Hitler does; that is what Stalin does; that is what the hod-carrier in Rome does. That is the order of the international day; the only difference being that they don't have any legitimate excuse for what they do.

But first we should liquidate the Communists, Fascists, and Nazis in this country. Charity should begin at home. Unfortunately that is difficult to do. It is one of the weaknesses of Democracy, which gives aid and comfort to its enemies. The answer to that lies in an unselfish, patriotic Executive and Congress, or—a Dictator.

An unselfish, patriotic Executive and Congress are, like the dodo and the three toed Sloth, extinct animals; which brings us right to the crux of the matter—the cause of the failure of Democracy on the continent of Europe and the cause of the eventual failure of Democracy in the United States of America—the goddam politicians.

The best and sanest form of government I can imagine would be one run by General Motors or Standard Oil, and so I am praying that Wendel Wilkie will be nominated by the Republican Party and elected in November.

I am sick of politicians. I am fed up on politicians. I vomit at baby kissing, back slapping, and <u>my friends</u>. I am ashamed that I am compelled to feel that every pronouncement and every act of our Chief Executive is dictated by its vote getting effect upon the electorate. I may be doing him a wrong. I hope that I am, but I am afraid that I am not.

All of which brings us back in a vicious circle to the question, "What should we do?"

The answer will probably be: "Nothing."

Who said anyone paid $900 a month for my house? There ain't that much money. I'm netting a paltry $250, out of which I have to pay $125 for this house. Florence will not admit that it is a house, but it shelters us.

If Featherstone was only 52, he must have gone to Orchard Lake when he was six.

I know how you feel about your air conditioning plant. It reminds me of my $5000 steam heating plant at Tarzana. The damn thing never did work; and though the good friend from whom I purchased it lived for several years, he did nothing about it.

You're goddam right, the horse-and-buggy days were the best! What we didn't know about, we didn't miss. We didn't have Brain Trusters, New Deals, Hitlers, Stalins, Mussolinis, Jim Farley, or FDR.[97] We didn't know when we were well off. We got along very well with one horse open sleighs, Annie Rooney, Anna Held, E. H. Sothern, Lillian Russell, Charles Dana Gibson, Graustark, and Jerome K. Jerome.[98] Twenty-five miles an hour was too fast and Western Union was fast enough.

The weather here is delightful. Today I went to the weekly luncheon of the Junior Chamber of Commerce and made a speech. I have spoken before the Hawiian Civic Association, and made two radio appearances. I know of two more civic organizations who are just dying to hear me; and I am, absolutely, the world's lousiest public speaker. I'll say this much for Hawaiians: they are gluttons for punishment.

They had the police band there today — all full blood Hawaiians in full police regalia with guns. One chap did a couple of hulas, and he was a wow. He would go great in New York. He is a traffic cop, and to see him wiggle his hips with that big six-gun wobbling around was sump'n.

Well, give my best to Margaret, the boys, their wives, and all the little Westons to the ninth and tenth generations.

Yours,

Ed

Dear Ed:

This place is very demoralizing. We have been in a rut here for 15 years. When we return here in any July, we promptly go back in the same ole rut, wearing it deeper each year.

Since we have had this place, we have done practically the same thing every day for seven years from early in July until about the middle of September. I believe that is <u>bad</u>.

The only reason in gawdsworld I have not written to you is on account of the Rut and because I am just too damned lazy.

Yours of the 27th of June, nearly two months ago! was forwarded here. I got a great kick out of it, and especially because you wrote much how you feel about the present state of the world. I wonder what you are now feeling about politics of the USA?

Well, you got your wish, Wendel Willkie was nominated and in a very fine way, against the wishes of all the oldsters, and especially the Old Guard. That shows that at least part of the country is sane. It was a good deal like the Town Meetings I sometimes attended when a boy in the State of Maine.[99] Now, it is up to us non-politicians to see that he is elected.

Hull seemed to make some progress in his Pan*American Congress, but knowing the working of the Latin American mind as I do through Dayton Hedges, who has lived amongst them for 17 years, I am sure they detest the USA and just sop along to see what they can get out of it, and would turn over night to the Nazi, Japs, or any powerful nation, if they thought they could get as much and also see the USA get hell.[100]

I feel that the forced nomination of Wallace will not help the 3d Term Ticket. No one thinks that FDR will live through another term; gawd knows no one but FDR wanted Wallace ever nominated for any office, and I feel that the USA does not want him to be President, getting in through the back-door. The ruthless gaul of FDR forcing him down even his hand-picked convention's throat!

I am for Willkie, because I would be for a crippled bull head before I would be for any of the New Dealers, but even more than that I am for him because he is a young man with a fine record of accomplishment, and during <u>modern times</u>.

Conditions have so changed since the War I that old dobbers cant realize that these changes are really hear. Old Dobers want to go back to Old Times. That can never happen. So what the country needs is a man who has grown up and made a success under these New conditions.

So far as I and my gang go, we know of no better man for this job than Willkie.

Herb writes that the farmers he meets up with are quitting the Farm Program fast. I have talked to four natives up here. One is for the New Deal: three said they had voted for FDR twice, but never again. I hope that indicates the way the vote will go this Fall.

And, then, recently along comes along your Chain Letter, and my face was really red when I found I had not written you for several weeks.

In re to this Chain. Personally, I would be glad to enter into the spirit of this interesting experiement, but honestly, Ed, I do not know of four men who answer the description in the 3d paragraph of your letter. I do not know four "100% good hombres" who would not just toss any chain letter in the waste basket. And the chain would break there, or I'd have to try four more, with like result. So I am returning the works to you. I'm sorry.

We have had very little company this year. Jeff and family for 10 days and another couple for a week. Ofcourse, we have our Airedale, Zipper, who is a lot of company.

We are supposed to irrigate around here with artesian wells. There is something wrong on North Gate, for we have put down four, and they all pooh out after a year or two. When we got here in July it was dry as hell and the growings not doing so well. No more artesians for us! So I went into a dither to hook up with the Lake with an electric pump. We had one break, before I ordered, it commenced to rain, and has rained two or three times per week ever since, and the place looks better than it ever has under heavy irrigation.

Will doubtless be in Beatrice not later than September 15th. Depends upon the weather at both places.

If England has held the Nazi pretty well in the air since Dunkirk, what will the Nazi be able to do when Englad has an equal number of planes? Whatinhell would Hitler do with England if he got it?

From your Chain letter I suspect you are back in California, at least it was postmarked Tarzana, so I am sending this there and am glad you are back in this country and that the Japs did not git you!

We have played some contract while up here. Have lost twice! This country is under laid with heavy magnetic iron ore; it runs mostly north and south. Margt and I try to always set the N–S way!

Margaret joins me in best to you and Florence,

Yours,

[HTW]

2623 Halelena street, Honolulu T H

September 12 1940

Dear Bert:

Your very welcome letter of August 25th came yesterday. I was much intrigued by the vignette in the upper left hand corner, which I suppose is a portrait of your Bemidji hide-out; but wot-in-hell are the figures in the foreground? I have developed a definite eye strain trying to determine. Can they be a group of the Westons doing a Spring dance?

We are still in the Sandwich Islands; but, as you will note from the new address, we have moved over the Pali into town. We like it much better, and are quite comfortable and happy.

I have taken an office on Kapiolani Boulevard, over looking Diamond Head and the ocean. All the ships go by my front window. If they would cut down a lot of trees and wreck a few buildings, I could see them.

Having received a standing order for a 20,000 word novelette each week, I need an office. I am knocking them out on my Underwood now; but have sent for my dictaphone outfit, and expect that it will be much easier. I can talk at least twice as fast as I can write. I was 65 on the first. I expect to retire at 75, start playing golf, and have a heart attack; but I'll probably have croup. Believe it or not, I am just recovering from whooping cough!

You mention being in a rut. That, to my mind, is definitely the most soul satisfying place to be in all the world. I love a rut. If I were alone in the world, I would dig one so god damned deep that people would have to use binoculars to find me at the bottom.

Yes, I got my wish about Wilkie; but I'm afraid the GOP Old Guard is going to sink him—the first really great American they've had since I can remember.

Forgive the chain letter. It is the first time I ever did anything like that, but the doggone thing was so worded that I couldn't turn it down. My dollars have not started rolling in yet. If I get one, I'll break even.

Now I've got to stop and write a novel. Florence joins me in sending Alohas to Margaret and your own sweet self.

Yours,

Ed

Beatrice, Nebr.

October 22d, 1940.

Dear Ed:

Have been back to the home ranch for about a month.

When you refer to North Gate, Bemidji, Minnesota, as a hide out, you have said something: that is just what it is, and a damned good one! A much safer place that LA County or TH.

I do not believe that any one, not even you, or FDR can write 20,000 words per week for publication. You will have to tell me what "is wrong with that statement" you made, or else tell me where I can get hold of the magazine that is publishing this unheard of out put. I suppose you could write an African "Come with the Wind", if given 30 days time?

I hate watching foot ball games in my shirt sleeves. I know LA County takes this sort of thing for granted, but I do not like it, and that is what we have had this Fall. Today, as per example, Margt and the Jeff Weston tribe froliced in the pool from noon till 1 pm. That is going too far, even under the Fourth New Deal.

You brag about having whooping cough. Hell, anyone can have that, irrespective of age or sex. I, Bert, had croup steadily up until I was 25. Nearly died of it in Wallace, Idaho, in 1902.

Early this month we had the holy hell scared out of us here. Eight cases of polio broke out in this town in less than 48 hours. With so many little girls around here, it had us frightened plenty.

All the Weston boys signed up for conscription. Herb is an active

RO, Jeff is on the inactive RO list, Col was taken off this list only three months ago. There have been so many enlistments from this district that it is unlikely they will conscript any on the first two calls. Col of course wants to get into the Air. Perhaps he will, he has had over 100 hours.

In regard to Mr. Wendel Willkie. Do you recall before the convention, every professional politician in the US was against him? Do you recall that at one time the professional betting was 20–1 that he would not be nominated? That guy is going to be elected. He is coming right now and coming fast. As it was at the convention, it is going to be at the election.

Stalin nominated Stalin.

El Duce	"	El Duce.
Hitler	"	Hitler.
FDR	"	FDR.

THE PEOPLE NOMINATED WILLKE!! And these same people are going to elect Willkie.

See if I'm right.

Yours,

[HTW]

1298 Kapiolani Boulevard, Honolulu T H

November 7 1940

Dear Bert:

Your prophesy re Wendell came the day that your prophesy proved false. This is the people's country; if the people wish Mr. Roosevelt as President who am I to oppose their will?

As to no guy being able to write 20,000 wds a week for publication: From Oct 24 to Nov 5 I wrote two novelettes, one of 21,574 words and the other of 21,415 words; that's in eleven days with two Saturdays and Sundays in. Up to this evening, I have written 9,240 words on a new one. The strange part of it is that they are all selling.

If you don't like watching football other than in a white tie and tails, don't go to one here. I not only don't wear a coat, a collar, or a tie, but I don't wear any socks; the children don't wear any shoes; they don't wear any to school, and they go to the 100 year old, swank Punahou School, where the little kids are requested not to wear shoes or stockings.

I gotta quit, Bert; I'm so goddam tired I can't see; and it's after five; so I gotta go home.

Best to you all,

Ed

Beatrice, Nebr.

November 26th, 1940

Dear Ed:

All right, All Right! You can do this 20,000 word stunt per week with your hands tied, and your feet in the mud. And it is not strange to me it sells, I have always felt that you could not say: "Good Morning", without making it interesting.

In re the recent election: I, Bert, still think that Wendel Willkie is a great guy, and very much our kind of a guy. I have a very high regard for him and this remarkable effort to get the USA somewhat back on the Right Track. In my feeble way I am now, entirely loyal to the USA, and back of the USA, but am very critical of how the business of the USA is being handled by those recently put into control for the 3d time. But you and I are too old to go into all this no matter hotly we may feel about it.

You have remained in TH longer than I had thought you would, from what you told us in Pasadena. And I thought you were going there for a rest. Your idea of rest seems strange; why gawddam it, I could not ever count

21,574	words
21,415	"
42,989	"

in eleven days, let alone write them! Wonder what your idea of just a nice long rest is?

One by one our local lights are entering the army and navy. It is interesting to note that Reserve Officers are leaving town. I know one lt. col.

and three majors who have been in the Reserve since the last World War, who have volunteered and all of them are now drawing down salaries from twice to three times greater than they ever drew in civil life. So many volunteered in this district that no body was conscripted as yet.

If I were a youngish man and had no specially good job or future, I would get into the Army right now and make it my life work. The present set-up of the USA Army offers the best chance of a job and security there is. Also, the way things are going in England, the safest place is in the Army.

Several oldsters (like us) have been hounding me to show Movies I Have Made, dating from 1926. Yesterday I spent much of the day digging these dusty old films up, splicing them, etc. Half through the first reel the light on the projector burned out. Finally waded through the slush and borrowrd Col's projector, then spent $1/2$ an hour learning how to work the dmnd thing. A fine large evening!

We have had a good deal of winter todate. The moisture is good for our farms, so we take the bad cheerfully. I know you hate middle western winters.

We attended a dinner party recently, given by W?H.Kilpatrick at which were his son, his grandson, and his great grandson, all Middle Western products. Can you match that in Hawaii?

Yours
[HTW]

1298 Kapiolani Boulevard, Honolulu T H
January 27 1941

Dear Bert:

Florence's four generations were together at dinner in our home in Beverly Hills in 1935; so we beat the Kilpatricks to it by five years.

The Baldwins are one of the Big Shot families of the Islands. I think that I have been introduced to some of them, but I do not know any of them well. They live on the Island of Maui, and are not too popular over here, I understand. There is almost a blood feud between the Oahu Dillinghams and the Maui Baldwins. They meet every year on the polo field, and once there was some dirty work that started the feud. I don't know anything about the details. I understand that the Baldwins are extremely arrogant and overbearing; but, again, I know nothing about it; and, of course, I get the Dillingham angle on this island. I shall be very glad now to meet Mr. Baldwin, since he was an old buddy of yours.

Glad to hear that you got something back from the the Infernal Revenue Collector. More power to you. It is too bad that they have made us feel so bitter about taxes. I think every one is glad to pay fair taxes decently computed and collected, but the way it has been handled often comes damn near making a fellow hate his government. Al Capone was a tender philanthropist compared with the New Deal government.

Speaking of Willkie: I think he has pulled a very bright rabbit out of his hat by going to England. England's fear of him helped defeat him, I am sure. They are bound to like him, especially Churchill; and in 1940 that may help him a lot. And "There will always be an England".

What do you think of your old friend Mussolini now? He has been the one bright spot in my life during the past several weeks. Every morning I grab the paper to see what the Greeks or the English did to him the day before, and wait hopefully for what the Italians are going to do to him tomorrow. Do you read Westbrook Pegler? If you don't, you should. How he has escaped assassination, I don't know. He certainly has guts.[101]

Glad you all had such a swell time in Pasadena. I listened to the game and rooted for Nebraska. I really thought that they would win. Stanford must have played inspired foot ball.

Best to you all!!!

Ed

March 8th, 1941

Dear Ed:

I was interested in what you wrote me about the present generation Maui Baldwins. The last Baldwin I took a drink with was in '19, which is some time ago. But we can agree that the Ole Original Sin Missionary can rest peacefully in his grave, knowing that he left a long line of fighting, scraping fueding Baldwins to keep things from getting too dull.

You have been gone nearly a year. When you left I did not think you would stay away that long. How come? Margt and I may motor to Coronado the last of this month and we thought we might have some fun with you.

You asked me if I read Pegler. I used to read him when no one else did, and have continued the habit. I think he is a sour puss, but he and ole man Glass and the senior senator from Montana, seem to be the only ones with enough guts to stand up in meeting and tell the dumb voters the truth.

A number of the Old Guard lunch frequently together. Our favorite pastime is to give the New Deal hell and praise Mr. Pegler. A harmless occupation for oldsters. Last month the editor of our paper (who is younger and not entirely with us) said: "We had a wire to kill Pegler's column for today." I got a copy of the "killed" column, and am sending it to you. It was printed in a much modified form, but you will be interested in the origonal. Does he tell 'em, and it is all the truth, or they would have had him in a concentration camp long ago.

And in re this same man, Pegler. For two years a bright young man, named Al Dowling, worked on our local news paper. Everyone admitted his ability. In a spurt he showed up our ex-governor, who was running for the nomination for US senator, and striped him clean. Al was admired by all here, but mostly disliked personally, so he moved on, and has done very well, and is rating very well with the United Press. He well knows how the Back Bone of Gage County feels about Pegler, so he took time off, and wrote a letter to the paper here, which it printed. I am sending you this clipping. Read it, and if we were on the same side Mr. Allen Dowling is, would n't we think it a pretty damned good screed?

From the mis-information we get, I think all the Weston boys will be in the Army before Christmas. That is fine and all right. If this happens, I will have to go back into daily office work. That is ok too, but it is going to be a change for ole man Weston to stop merely super-vising, and get into an 8 hour per day active job, of details, et al, etc.

This seems to be my day to enclose things in my letter to you. On February 8th, Margt was 63 years old. Friends of ours gave her a very fine dinner that night. Herb, who is a candid camera adict, took the picture of the rest of us as we left 910 N 7th. From left to right: Marian, Herb's wife, Jeff, mammy, pappy and Jean, Jeff's wife.

I am going to be sorry if I do not see you in California in April.

Yours,

[HTW]

1298 Kapiolani Boulevard, Honolulu T H
March 20 1941

Dear Bert:

Thanks a lot for your letter of the 8th with enclosures. That picture of the Westons looks like the Idle Rich inviting the Revolution, but I will say that the male Westons are certainly all good pickers.

I enjoyed the Pegler article and also that by Allen Dowling: I agree with both of them, which is in a way of saying that I think the whole human race has done nothing much throughout its existence but make egregious blunders. It should go back into the jungle and hang by its tail and be happy. I'd like to see an answer to Dowling by Pegler: I'll bet that old boy could still mow 'im down. I'd rather go on Information Please than get into an altercation with Westbrook.

I am returning the articles to you, as you may wish them; and I am also sending you some enclosures: my file of correspondence with the professional wrestler, Prince Ilaki Ali Hassan. I am sending them for no good reason other than that I found them very amusing (his letters) and there is so little to add to the gaiety of nations these days.

The Prince is a Burroughs fan of many years standing, and when he found that I was in Honolulu, he phoned and asked if he might come and see me. As you will note from his letters, he is not one to stand on ceremony; nor has he any respect for gray hairs or obesity. I was "Ed" in five minutes after he called on me. Please return the file to me. He told me that he was a "Prince" because his father had owned 3000 goats in Arabia. Incidentally, he is a successful pulp writer: versatile, what!

Florence and the children returned to the mainland on last Friday's boat: they arrive home tomorrow. It is so difficult to get reservations and the possibility of war with Japan so definite that we thought it best to get them off while we could. I shall finish up my business here and follow in about a month. Perhaps when you next write you had better address me at Tarzana: if I haven't returned by that time, Ralph will forward the letter.

   With best to you all,

Yours,

Ed

Honolulu T H, 1298 Kapiolani Boulevard

April 24 1941

Dear Bert:

So the doggone idle rich are still idling! Hotel del Coronado, Hotel Arroyo Seco, touring in a magnificent Buick; and then back to the old family manor to really take up idling in a big way.

   I don't envy you, but I suppose that when I get to be your age I'll take up golf and start idling: I'll have Social Security security by that time, and how a guy can idle on $26.32 a month! He just couldn't afford to do anything else but.

   Somehow Social Security reminds me of the New Dealers, and I thought it might interest you to know that I believe that I have unearthed the original New Dealer. He was Nero, that mental giant who was Emperor of Rome. He said, "Money is of no use except to squander," or words to that general effect; and if that isn't the key stone of New Deal philosophy, I am one of the Quints.[102]

   I am, as your giant intellect may have deduced, still here. I sailed for here just a year ago today. I now more or less know my way around, though I still can pronounce less than $1/2$ of 1% of the street names. Here are a couple which you might practice on your ukelele: Kaneka-polei Place and Waikahalulu Lane.

   About the Buick: you hurt me. I love my Buick. It has never failed me. Even after a five ton truck with ten tons of crushed rock telescoped it, it still ran to the repair garage under its own power, after we had picked a fender out of the rear wheel, port. You must not have treated yours right: maybe you spoke to it harshly, causing it to weep oil from its hydraulic brakes. You should be more understanding with a sensitive car like the Buick.

THIS WAR! I think we have got our ass in a sling, as Henry Ward Beecher was wont to say.[103] We have the New Dealers, Baldwin, Chamberlin, and others of the Clivedon Set to thank for it. For seven or eight years they piddled around making Democracy safe for nobody and actually watched Germany rearm. I wonder what in Hell they thought that neurotic house painter was rearming for. I suppose they thought he was building the most powerful army the world has ever known so that they could march in Fourth of July parades. Now, the bastard has all the war equipment of all the countries he has conquered; and that's practically all of Europe; and he has all their resouces and man-power. So now is the psycological moment for us to leap into the breach and get the pants licked off of us; and that's just what we'll get, with Germany on one side and Japan on the other and our "good neighbors" south of us taking a crack at us every chance they get. If we had started rearming when we should have, we could lick Germany and Japan both on the seas; perhaps we can right now if the British navy escapes and joins us; but if England falls, what makes anyone think Hitler will let that navy get away? He would hold every man, woman, and child in England as hostages; and every gob on every British ship would know that surrender of the fleet would be the only way in which they could save their loved ones from slavery or death. Now, if there is anything more you would like to know about World affairs, just call on me.

AND THOSE DAMNED ITALIANS! I suppose they will go around bragging forever about how they licked the British and the Greeks, ignoring the fact that they were licked forty ways from Sunday until Handsome Adolph came to their rescue.

It is a very good thing that I haven't high blood pressure, or I should have long since blown up like a cigarette ravished balloon at the Captain's Dinner.

I hope that you and Margaret had a wonderful time on your trip and that you arrived home without any further misadventures and found all the 57 little Westons in the pink.

I still don't know when I am going home. Do you recall that song the boys used to sing just before vacation at Orchard Lake?

I'm going home; I'm going home; I'm going home tomorrow.
I'm going home; I'm going home, no more to sin or sorrow.

But instead of singing that, I'm going to run along up to the Chinese cemetery this afternoon and pick out a nice, quiet lot.

Yours,

Ed

May 16th, 1941

Dear Ed:

Just got your letter of the 24th ULTIMO. It was forwarded around some.

You put me on the floor with stitches in my sides when you talk about us as the "idle rich"! We are not "rich", we are running six businesses, and we work like hell to try to keep the well known tribal nose above the water.

Starting tomorrow we go into a 1941 session with our auditors, attorneys, and what-not, to try to keep something out of what we think we have. "Idle"!! Nuts!!!

I who am too damned old to chauf, tooled that family scow Buick to the west coast and back home, and did not dent a fender. We were gone just six weeks. We played golf 21 days, which Margt says was d——d good for us, and I was sort of pleased to note that I could still totter around a course in 100.

We do not like SoCal with too many so-called defense workers cluttering up the hi-ways. I doubt if we go to SoCal again. I think we will stay right here in the Middle West, where we really belong.

I am going to break down and confess that I was mighty disappointed when you did not return to the USA so that I could have seen you before we left California. I got onehellofa kick out of seeing you last year, and hoped to repeat. You will, ofcourse, never come to the Middle West, and I doubt if I will ever again be in SoCal. Sort of too bad.

You, who are a tax-payer will be pleased to know that I have had my S-A War pension raised from 35 to 60 bucks per month, which is a sure 6% on $12,000, and is the best investment I own. The occasion for this raise is that I happened to be 65 years old April 15th. As I always say, there is a lot of hard common sense to the way a democracy runs it's business!

I am so fed up on The News of The Day that I have followed Collins' advice. I do not listen to the radio nor read the scare war news in the papers, But I do read Time from cover to cover each week. Late news but I think the most reliable news.

I will slop over, however, to 40 ways endorse everything you said in your letter, in the paragraph headed "THIS WAR!" Also even more what you said about "Those Damned Italians".

It is all so useless, destructive, and just damned silly.

It is just too damned bad you did not return to LA County. We would have had a lot to talk over, and we would have, for once, agreed upon most things.

I suppose you recall Margt bought a couple of hi priced lots in the Mirimar Addition back in the very Gay 20s. She still has title to said lots. Last month may two SoCal nephews tried to show me this property of hers, I being her commercial manager, and checking up on her holdings.

The unheard-of rains had so soaked those mountains, that acres of the surface had just slid off! Road, sewer, water pipe and everything wrecked. It is a wreck and a sorry mess. I would not believe it if I had not seen it. Do you know, that I someway perfer the Middle West, with drouths, hot-winds, dust-storms, grass-hoppers, and what have you. At least our real estate does not just slide off.

Being remote as you are, you have not heard the news that Nebraska is also becoming an oil producing state. They have a real he-oil-and-gas-well 7 miles east of Beatrice, and this is only the beginning! I fear we are going to be run out of our tribal hometown since 1857, as we do not choose to live in a boom oil town. If this happens to us, I suppose we will dig in at Bemidji. That is certainly a very remote place.

I am sending this to Honolulu. I hope you have had a sane moment, and returned to the US. It is bad enough here, but this is the most decent place to be.

Yours,

[HTW]

TO WHOMEVER GIVES A DAMN:

As our experiences during and immediately after the Jap blitz may interest several of our friends and relatives, I'll record what I recall, send the ms to Tarzana with a request to Mildred to mimeograph several copies and mail them around. This will save me the trouble of writing the whole thing over a number of times. With the principal facts you are all acquainted, so I'll just set down our personal experiences and reactions, together with some of the wild rumors which circulated. You will be fully as capable as I to judge of the truth of such rumors.

When we awoke Sunday morning, December 7th, we heard a great deal of firing, some of it very loud; but we hear a great deal of firing here and had been informed by the newspapers the day before that heavy guns would be fired from various parts of the island during the ensuing several days; so we thought nothing of it and went to breakfast.

After breakfast we dressed for tennis and went out to the court which is on a point that projects out into the lagoon, giving an unobstructed view of the coast from Diamond Head in one direction far beyond Pearl Harbor to Barbers Point, with the Waianae Mountain Range looming up in the background.

There is an area of sand for sun bathers beyond the ocean end of the tennis court, and soon a great many of the hotel guests were congregated there watching the show. Bombs were falling on Pearl Harbor. We could hear the detonations and see the bursts quite plainly. Antiaircraft shells were bursting, fighting ships at sea were firing. We could see them plainly. Bombs were falling in the ocean not far from us. One nearly hit a large freighter or supply ship lying off coast perhaps a mile or so from us. It got out of there in a hurry. Black smoke was billowing up from Pearl Harbor. One among us, brighter than the others, said that it was a practice smoke screen. It was either an oil tank or a tanker or our burning fighting ships. We don't know yet. For several hours we alternated tennis with watching the show they were putting on before we learned definitely that it was the real McCoy. Even the truth did not interfere with our tennis, and I should like to say right here that all the people were calm and unafraid. There were several Navy women whose husbands were probably in it somewhere. Mrs. A's husband is attached to an old light cruiser then lying in the harbor. She knew that he was down there where all the bombing was going on. Cecile's husband commands a submarine which was at Manila the last she heard. Both these girls carried on quite normally, although Mrs. A. told me the next day that she had eaten scarcely anything since the beginning of the attack.

Cecile plays tennis with Hulbert and me every day, and she played with us all during the battle. There are many army and navy wives here, but there was no sign of hysteria. Every report that we have had concerning the civilians on the island has been the same. There has been no panic, but a great deal of co-operation with the military on the part of civilians, a very small percentage of whom are 100% white. But white, black, brown, or yellow they have all been splendid.

Bombs fell in the city not far from us. Smoke was rising from several fires. Ambulance, police, and fire sirens were screaming almost continuously. Anti-aircraft shells were bursting all over the place. I think that many of our civilian casualties, and there were a great many of them, were caused by our own fire. But of course that cannot be helped.

There seems to be more praise than bitterness expressed for the Japs. As one of the navy wives expressed it: "They caught us with our pants down." If anyone tells you that they can't shoot straight, you can give him the laugh. They flew in over Pearl Harbor at about fifty feet and sunk three cruisers with arial torpedoes. They bombed hell out of Hickam Field, Wheeler Field, Bellows Field, and the brand new navy flying field at Kaneohe Bay. They flew low over Rogers Airport (civilian) and machine gunned the place. I am told that we lost two hundred planes that never had a chance to get off the ground. Our fliers were not there! We take the week ends off from war. It was a long time before we saw one of our planes in the air. The navy also takes week ends off and most of our ships were undermanned. The Japs had been well informed as to the best day and hour to strike. The attack was brilliantly conceived and executed. It smelled of German efficiency.

We understand that six enemy planes were shot down. Something like fifty-four came over in the first wave. A navy man told me that every gun on every ship in Pearl Harbor was firing at one lone Jap who was flying low while bombing, and every shot missed him. One soldier is credited with bringing down one Jap with an automatic rifle. The Jap was flying low straight toward him, machine running as he came. The soldier said that he was scared stiff, but he kept firing and had the thrill of seeing the Jap crash just beyond him.

During all this, we continued to play tennis at the hotel. There was nothing else that we could do, as orders were constantly being broadcast to civilians to keep off the streets, to stay home, and not to use the telephone; also to remain calm.

I think our tennis is worthy of a few remarks. It is paddle tennis. We play it on a court that is not even quite a singles court, but we play both doubles and singles on it. The hotel had to remove some palm trees to build it, but they did not remove enough. There are several practically in the court. According to our ground rules if a serve bounces into a palm tree it is considered a net shot and may be taken over. Very often we have to run around a palm tree to return a shot. The end aprons are very short and there are no aprons along the sides, just a drop of a couple of inches to the ground among the palm trees. When an angling shot comes over, we have to look down first to see where we are stepping before we can get into position to return it. It is all very exciting. I can't understand why there are not a lot of sprained ankles. Close on one side of the court is the lagoon, which is also close to the ocean end of the court. When a ball goes into the ocean, someone has to wade in and get it—usually Hulbert. We play with regular tennis balls instead of the sponge rubber paddle tennis balls; so the game is rather fast for a too small court; but we get exercise and have a lot of fun dodging palm trees.

Shortly after lunch Sunday a radio call came in for all ablebodied men at the hotel to report to Pier 2; so Hulbert, a Mr. Rost, and I drove down in my car. They didn't want us at Pier 2 and told us to try the wharf at Kewalo Basin. This is where the Japanese fishing sampans are tied up. There, they took our names and told us to report back at 4:30. We had signed up for guard duty.

We came back at 4:30 and signed up again in another company. Nothing happened; so we found someone else with shoulder bars and signed up again in his company. We were now definitely signed up. There was much confusion. No one seemed to know anything. Sand bag machine gun emplacements had been erected pointing both inland and toward the beach. We never knew from which direction the enemy was supposed to come. Parachute troops were reported having landed in the mountains and three Japanese transports were reported off Barbers Point about five miles. There was still anti-aircraft fire, if I recall correctly. Dense smoke was arising from Pearl Harbor.

We were finally ordered to the Honolulu Tuna Packers Ltd. warehouse on the wharf, where Springfield rifles and ten rounds of ammunition were issued to each of us. Hulbert, Rost, and I were in Patrol 2, Company A, 1st Battalion. We stuck together — The Three Musketeers. We were then told that we would be on sentry duty from 10 P.M. until 2 A.M.

Just after dark we were sent over to the Kewalo Inn, a night spot, where we were given soup, sandwiches, and coffee. A few dim lights were burning in the back room where we ate. Volunteer girls waited on the tables, or rather cleared them. We waited on ourselves. One of the girls who came to our table is a photographer for Beers, whose studio is next to our office. She photographs patrons of the Kewalo Inn. But there was no photographing nor floor show Sunday night.

Later (after lunch): From a "usually reliable source" we learned this noon that three enemy submarines entered Pearl Harbor Sunday morning and torpedoed our ships. All three were sunk. Our informant said that he asked the officer who told him this how three enemy submarines could get into Pearl Harbor. The reply was that they gave the correct signal. Another report is that we have sunk eighteen Japanese fighting ships, that we have lost two carriers and the Japs one.

Back to Sunday: After we had eaten, Hulbert and I were detailed to guard twenty-two enemy aliens in a wire enclosure on the wharf. Hulbert was at the back end; I was at the front where the gate was. There was no lock on the gate. I also had to challenge everybody who passed my post entering the wharf and examine their passes. Inasmuch as I had no flashlight, my identification of passers-by was sketchy. The entire U.S. Army Engineering Department passed several times. My chief duty seemed to be to make the prisoners and others throw away lighted cigarettes and step on them.

Rost was posted at the door of the Packing Company's engine room with orders to let no one enter. Rost is a short, fat, middle-aged man. I believe he is a well known dog fancier and kennel show judge. He said that the first thing that happened was a Filipino who dropped down from the ceiling scaring Rost out of seven years' growth. Rost corralled him and called the sergeant of the guard. Then some men came and tried to get into the engine room. Rost wouldn't let them although they said they worked there. He said he had orders to let no one in, not even a general. So an officer came and tried to get in. Rost kept him out. Finally the officer of the guard, a regular, came and relieved Rost — he was too good.

I was told that the FBI would send a truck for my prisoners. A police car came for them and I wouldn't let them have them until an officer came and O.K'd it. We had our orders, by God, and we were going to obey them; and as we had Springfield rifles with a clip of five cartridges in them we were able to convince every one. We guarded the prisoners for over an hour, and then I thought we'd get some rest; but no. Every time our company commander saw me, he had something for me to do that required walking — and I hate walking. And then, at 10 P.M. we, Hulbert and I, were given a post a long block long on Ward Avenue, the street that runs into Fisherman's Wharf from inland. It was very dark, as the whole city was blacked out and it was raining much of the time. We had to stop and question every pedestrian and the driver of every car. I halted the United States Army in jeeps and trucks a dozen times or more and several police cars. I reminded myself of a funny little Shriner I once saw directing traffic in Los Vegas, Nevada, at midnight. Was he taking it big!

December 12th: Hulbert and I are now attached to G-1 at Iolani Palace. We are chauffeurs, because we each have a car. I have mine, and we borrowed one from Cecile Burnside for Hulbert. Mrs. Burnside is the girl with two little tots, whose husband commands a sub at Manila. She hasn't heard a word from him and does not expect to for God knows when.

I work from 8 A.M. to 4 P.M. Dinner at hotel at 4:30 on account of Blackout — then Blackout; so I have no opportunity to write much. Damn the Blackout! It is, for most of us, the worst part of this war. Damn Hitler! Damn the Japs! Damn everybody!!!

I'll send along what I have written, and maybe some day I can add to it.

In closing this I want to repeat that the spirit of the people here is marvellous. Regardless of what you may hear, there is practically no sabotage here—absolutely <u>none</u> that I have heard of from official sources. White, black, brown, yellow—every one is working willingly and with a broad grin. There has never been any panic, and what fear there is is well camouflaged. We are more afraid of the little boys with Springfields than we are of the Japs.

Aloha!

Ed.

[ERB Collection]

910 North Seventh Street, Beatrice, Nebr.

1/8/45

Dear Ed:

This Jo Jack has been in town. I asked her about you and she said you looked fine and were so charming. Ah, the ole charm still working over time! I thought Jo looked pretty good herself.[104]

As I have told you often enough, we have never seen any of your UP reports in any news paper, which hurt our feelings. The other day Fred Nichols, who is sojourning in Tucson, for a cough and wheezing, sent me a clipping from the Tucson News. It was your account of the hospital in Honolulu, and ended by your quiping about you and your friend being older than God. Which same pleased us very much.

Fulton Jack, Joe's father was 75 a few months ago. His firm has been our attornys for 30 years. Fulton is an intellectual to the Nth degree. He reads German, Greek, Hebrew, Sanscrit and Swedish for diversion, yet is an interesting guy to be with.

Today it is 10 above with a 40 mile wind from the north, so you are missing that kind of weather anyway.

This is just a line to tell you how glad I am to have seen you in print again.

Yrs

Bert—

[ERB Collection]

1298 Kapiolani Boulevard, Honolulu 42 Hawaii

February 8 1945

Dear Bert:

Found your letter of January 8 on my return here last Saturday from the Mainland, where I have been since November 18.

The reason you have never seen anything I have written as a War Correspondent is possibly due to the fact that practically none of it was ever printed. I have had Army credentials since 1942, but as I didn't have Navy credentials until about three months ago, I understand that the so-and-so who was Navy public relations officer killed all my stuff. He is out now and a nice chap has the job.

If Miss Jack is still in town, please giver her my best. She is very nice.

Hulbert and I flew to California together, and for the first time in eleven years I was with my children and grandchildren on Christmas. We had a wonderful time, the adults of my family all being good judges of Bourbon or what have you.

Hulbert, who left Los Angeles a week ahead of me, is still at an airport in Northern California awaiting transportation. I was very fortunate, having to wait only four days, and that due to such bad weather that only one plane got off ahead of me.

It was good to get back here and get warmed up. It was cold all the time I was in Southern California and colder while I was in Northern California. Why people as lousy rich as you continue to live in your beastly climate is quite beyond me. Were I there and short of gas, I'd hitch hike to Palm Springs, even though I don't care much for Palm Springs. At least it doesn't snow there.

My best to the Weston family, long may they freeze!

Yours,

[ERB]

[ERB Collection]

Dear Ed:

Had yours of the 8th, the first in a good while and I thought you were off covering the Phillipine activities, and here you have been back in the USA! I am glad you had a fine Christmas with your kin folk.

I do not just like your dirty cracks about the climate of Gage County, and like even less your remarks in re of whoever it is you are referring to you when you talk about "the lousy rich". And then your little wise crack about hitch hiking to Palm Springs. You have a habit of being mostly wrong. Just to prove my points: my very good friend Wallace Robertson went to Palm Springs six weeks age mostly to bask in the sun. He got the hell out of there some time ago, as he wore his over coat most of the time (Slept in it, I believe) and had one (1) day of basking. He is beating it back to Gage where he knows we have an honest climate, tho somewhat rugged.

Then about this lousy rich stuff, you earned more money that we had even ever heard of long before the time when we were broke by the middle of the month: you lolled in dough when we were pinching dimes from month to month. Just because Margt bought those two d——d lots at Mirimar is no indication. And besides that we miss sort of travelling around as we used to do, but we are damned if we are going to be pushed around on trains and we will not go any place where we cannot have our own car.

And then, besides that we are a lot better off right here at the home ranch than we should be out seeking just a better climate, which we seldom got, and eating fish instead of good corn fed beef. Why, in the last week we have had twice as fine steaks as we have ever had. Think that over, you fish, fruit eating hombre!

Dont talk to me about climate and what you refer to as "the lousy rich"!

I sent you a clipping about our town gal Jo Jack a few days ago. Your trail will likely cross hers again is the Pacific War lasts long enough.

I heard the broad cast from Manilla tonight. It was not too clear but I liked what General Arthur said. It at least had the great virtue of being short and to the point.

I notice that fewer and fewer Nip prisoners are being taken. Many of us here in the Middle West think it would be fine if no Japs were taken prisoner. And more of us also feel that way too many Nazi prisoners are being taken. I am sure this feeling is becoming more strong as our mutilated fine youths return to us, and we hear more of what kind of a war this is. The feeling is that they started it, they carried it on for some time, and in their way, so why should we not just finish it also in their way, and once and for many years to come.

It is our fond hope that now you have passed the Navy hurdle, that we will see more of your articles in our news papers. You last letter came un-censored.

As the sergt son of my neice, when he writes, says, well enough is enough, and I guess he is right!

Yours,

Bert—

[ERB Collection]

1298 Kapiolani Boleverd, Honolulu 42 Hawaii

15 March 1945

Dear Bert:

Your letter of 26 February has given me an idea. If I want to get an unusually good, interesting letter from you all I need do is write something that annoys you. However, I should think that you would be perpetually annoyed by Gage County weather. And all I know about it is what you have written me over a period of some fifty years, during which you have never appeared to have enjoyed any pleasant weather.

And as to the lousy rich: I have photographic evidence. Among other cherished pictures in my two large photograph albums is one of the Weston tribe decked out in sable and mink. When my friends come to that picture, they stop, goggle-eyed. And am I proud! For there is evidence that at one time in my checkered past I have rubbed elbows with the lousy rich. I do not use that term in ridicule or disparagement, but in awe and envy.

I would speak of climate again. Your very good friend Wallace Robertson must have been in Sunny Southern California about the same time that I was, and I can agree with him that the weather was most unusual.

I was there nearly three months, and damn near froze to death most of the time. But the Chamber of Commerce will see that it does not happen again. There must be a lot of unusual weather everywhere. It has been unusual here. This can unquestionably be traced to the New Dealers.

Those damned lots at Mirimar! Does Margaret still own them? Those and the ride that Hulbert took us on in the trailer are among the high spots in my life.

I received the clipping about Joe Jack (a cute name), and passed it on to Eleanor Jenkins, Gray Lady friend of Jo. But I shall not see Miss Jack in the forward area, nor will you be enlightened by any more stories from this War Correspondent. The Lord giveth, and the Lord taketh away. The Navy has taken away my credentials. I don't know why, and I don't give a damn. If the Navy thinks it can win the war without me, let it go ahead and try.

One reason that few Nip prisoners are taken is almost entirely the fault of the Nips. Our boys discovered that you can't trust a Jap even when he is carrying a white flag. They are among the lowest forms of animal life and absolutely without honor or decency.

Lots of the best to you all, and my sincere hope that you don't freeze to death during the remainder of Gage County's salubrious winter.

Yours,

[ERB]

[ERB Collection]

1298 Kapiolani Boulevard, Honolulu 42 Hawaii

19 July 1945

Dear Bert:

Have been out again, and found your letter of 24 May awaiting me on my return Sunday.

I, too, like Truman so far. I think that he will make so much better President than Roosevelt that it won't even be funny. I am a life-long Republican, probably for the highly intelligent reason that my Father was a Republican; but I somehow have faith in Truman, and shall be for him 100% until he does something I don't like.

You wonder what we are going to do with the conquered people. My guess is that we will continue to appease, we will dandle them on our knees, and they will despise and double-cross us. We should send a hell-for-leather, profane, fire-eating so-and-so like Patton over to run our section of the occupied country—someone who will slap the bastards' ears down three times a day after meals. We will probably send college professors and Milquetoasts who will try to make the sons-of-bitches love us. We don't know how. Russia does, and will win them all over to Communism eventually, either by persuasion or purges. We don't want any part of them. We should just make them fear us so that the fear would last for a hundred generations. Then they would hesitate to war with us again. I thank you. (Continued applause.)

I was out with the Navy this time. Got into the Tung Hai (Look it up in your atlas, dope—I just did). Was ashore on Okinawa, on one of the Kerama Retto islands, Ulithi, Guam, Kaajalein, Johnston. Was in a small boat right under a Kamikase kid as he was circling to bomb an admiral's flag ship, after which he suicided into another ship. Shortly before that I had been shot at by a Jap sniper while ashore. Found a Marine Officers' Club that sold excellent Bourbon highballs for 10¢. Flew to Guam in a ship piloted by Lt. Tyronne Power on my way back here. Incidentally, he is a swell pilot and a swell guy. I had known him back in the States.[105] All in all, I had a marvellous time, cruising between ten and eleven thousand miles and flying about 5000.

Hoping you have plenty of corn likker and with love to Margaret
and you, I am,
[ERB]

[ERB Collection]

7 December 1945

Dear Bert:

Yours of 28 October must have gone by water wings to Honolulu and back here, for I only just received it today. The evening of the day you typed it I boarded a c-54 for Hamilton Field. I am now home for good, and I guess that I am lucky to be home or anywhere. In July I had an attack of angina pectoris while aboard a Navy tanker in the Philippine

Sea. I guess I ran up and down too many ships' ladders and crawled up and down the sides of too many ships for a doddering old septuagenarian. Then in mid-September I had another one in Honolulu which nearly finished me off. I was horizontal for six weeks, up to the day I took off for home. But I am afraid now that I am going to live.

Hulbert came back on terminal leave shortly before I was taken ill. He married as soon as he got to San Francisco, and we landed in Southern Cal about the same time. Neither of us had any place to live, nor was there a place we could rent. I went in with Joan and Hulbert and his wife finally found a single furnished room. Then we each bought a home in the Valley. We have had fun furnishing our homes, and still are. There is a shortage of almost everything. I can't buy any dining-room furniture. Fortunately, I had a Bendix washing machine and an old Electrolux gas refrigerator; and I was lucky to get the last six burner gas range that Barker Brothers had.

As I tire very easily, am not allowed to lift anything, and can't hire any help, the children have had to do all the work for me. And they have been wonderful. I have a cute little place not far from my office—a half acre with lots of fruit trees, grapes, shrubs, and ornamental trees. Also a chicken house where I am going to install some Rhode Island Reds. There was no servants' room, so I am building detached quarters for a couple. Until that is finished, I'll have no help other than a part time gardener and a woman who will come in a couple of times a week to clean. It takes forever to get things done now. The thing I am building consists of a bedroom and bath and a storeroom, and it will take three months to build. I hope that you are duly thrilled with all this, but I have nothing else to write about.

I hope that I have my couple before you and Margaret can buy tires and come down here; then I can at least feed you, even if I can't sleep you; unless you would care to move in with the hired help. There were only two small bedrooms in the house. I grabbed one and turned the other into a bar.

Hope that you are all well and that you have a wonderful Christmas and New Year.

Yours,
[ERB]

[ERB Collection]

Notes

Introduction

1   The correspondence reprinted here demonstrates vividly Roger Chartier's observation that "automatic association of letters with intimate outpourings and the view that correspondence is a relation between two individuals are both called into question. [. . .] Business and the expression of feelings could go together. Commercial letters often made room for family news or chitchat." Roger Chartier, Alain Boureau, and Cécile Dauphin, *Correspondence: Models of Letter-Writing from the Middle Ages to the Nineteenth Century* (Princeton: Princeton University Press, 1997), 17.

2   Bryan Garman, " 'Heroic Spiritual Grandfather': Whitman, Sexuality, and the American Left, 1890–1940," *American Quarterly* 52:1 (2000): 107.

3   "Beatrice" is pronounced with emphasis on the second syllable.

4   Mary Evaline Burroughs wrote a book about her war years called *Memoirs of a War Bride* that was privately published in a limited edition in 1914 — the year of the start of the Great War, of course, but also the year of Tarzan's emergence and popularity in book form. Edgar Rice Burroughs wrote the foreword to Mary Evaline's *Memoirs*.

5   Carlo Rotella, *October Cities: The Redevelopment of Urban Literature* (Berkeley: University of California Press, 1998), 45. The tensions produced by this process found expression in, among other events, the Haymarket Riots of 1886, which took place when Burroughs was eleven years old. Rotella reminds us that three-fourths of the U.S. population "was listed in the 1890 census as foreign born or as children of foreign-born parents" (47). Burroughs's later paranoiac xenophobia and his discomfort with labor activism grew from white Chicago's reaction to the immigration brought on by its own labor needs. For a reading of Tarzan in this context, see Catherine Jurca, *White Diaspora: The Suburb and the Twentieth-Century American Novel* (Princeton: Princeton University Press, 2001).

6   Toward the end of her life Helen Towle Weston stayed in bed for ten straight years, though she was not ill. She was known among her chil-

dren, according to Herb Weston Jr., my grandfather, as "the great objector."

7 Bert's siblings, in order of oldest to youngest, were Elizabeth (Lizzie), Ralph, and Katharine (Kitty).

8 Weston Family Collection, Beatrice, Neb.; many of the family's books are now in the Beatrice Public Library. For information on J. B. Weston, see his obituaries, *Beatrice Daily Express*, 15 September 1905; *Beatrice Daily Sun*, 16 September 1905; *Daily Sun*, 19 September 1905.

9 Weston to Burroughs, 11 November 1927.

10 Weston to Burroughs, 15 January 1933. At J. B.'s funeral, one speaker would comment: "His religion was as broad as all mankind, as broad as the Universe. It was narrowed by no dogma. It was contracted by no creed. He believed, as did the great poet, 'In one stupendous whole, whose body nature is, and God the soul.'" *Beatrice Daily Sun*, 19 September 1905. The poet quoted is Alexander Pope, from *An Essay on Man* (1732–44).

11 Brian J. Bohnett, *Them Was the Days! Edgar Rice Burroughs and the History of the Michigan Military Academy* (Holt, Mich.: Mad Kings, 2001), 23. The school's maximum enrollment was 184 in 1889. The facility, now called "Orchard Lake Schools," is a national historic site and collection of schools.

12 Bohnett, *Them Was the Days*, 21; Burroughs's comment is from an autobiographical sketch for *Amazing Stories*, June 1941, quoted in Irwin Porges, *Edgar Rice Burroughs: The Man Who Created Tarzan* (Provo: Brigham Young University Press, 1975), 28.

13 Sherman's speech is reproduced in Bohnett, *Them Was the Days*, 127–36.

14 Bohnett, *Them Was the Days*, 73.

15 Edgar Rice Burroughs, "Autobiography," Edgar Rice Burroughs Memorial Collection, University of Louisville, 14–15, quotation 14. Maximillian Elser Jr., publisher of *Metropolitan*, asked Burroughs for the autobiography, which he sent in installments (intended as part of the promotion of *Tarzan and the Lost Empire*) between July and September 1929.

16 This photo is faded and has a paper loop attached to the back, suggesting that it hung in one of Burroughs's work spaces. Several images of Weston from the Burroughs collection also show evidence of long display. While I argue here particularly for the importance of correspondence in reconfiguring our understanding of the dynamics of male friendship, photographs are an equally important resource. The Burroughs-Weston correspondence offers insights into the middle-class adoption of home still and motion photography; it is clear that letters and photographs became collateral media during this time. See Laura Wexler, *Tender Violence: Domestic Visions in an Age of U.S. Imperialism* (Chapel Hill: University of North Carolina Press, 2000); John Ibson, *Picturing Men: A Century of Male Relationships in Everyday American Photography* (Washington:

Smithsonian, 2002); David Deitcher, *Dear Friends: American Photographs of Men Together, 1840–1918* (New York: Abrams, 2001); and Russell Bush, *Affectionate Men: A Photographic History of a Century of Male Couples, 1850's to 1950's* (New York: St. Martin's, 1998).

17 See Bohnett, *Them Was the Days!* 87–89.

18 *[18]98s Class Book* (New Haven, Conn.: n.d. [ca. 1898]), 122–23. The initial quotation adapts the first two lines of Sir Walter Scott's poem "Lochinvar," from *Marmion, a Tale of Flodden Field* (1808), canto 5. Weston and hometown friend Lin Sherwood are sitting beside each other in the Yale freshman class photo. The final sentence refers to the fact that Weston was a redhead.

19 Weston and others were graduated early so they could fight in the Spanish-American War; the date "1/97" appears on the pan in the bottom center of figure 8, Weston Family Collection. For one of several discussions of manhood at Yale, see Robert J. Higgs, "Yale and the Heroic Ideal, Gotterdammerung and Palingenesis, 1865–1914," in *Manliness and Morality: Middle-Class Masculinity in Britain and America 1800–1940*, ed. J. A. Mangan and James Walvin (New York: St. Martin's, 1987), 160–75.

20 Weston to Burroughs, 13 December 1918.

21 Weston to Collins, 2 March 1896, Weston Family Collection.

22 A daughter, Jane, was born in 1908 but survived only a few months.

23 Burroughs, "Autobiography," 32–33.

24 Gail Bederman argues convincingly that the Rough Riders functioned predominantly as a public relations mechanism for Roosevelt's political career. Gail Bederman, *Manliness and Civilization: A Cultural History of Gender and Race in the United States, 1880–1917* (Chicago: University of Chicago Press, 1995). In a letter to Burroughs dated 12 December 1929, Weston claims also to have applied: "I had already applied to be numbered amongst the Ruff Riders, but was silly enough to wire my withdrawal."

25 Burroughs's drawing and his drafting of short, humorous pieces seem to have been among his few consistent habits during the years leading up to the composition of *A Princess of Mars*, his first novel-length work. He enrolled briefly at the Chicago Art Institute in 1897. The sheer volume of sketches and cartoons in the Burroughs collection — and Burroughs's obvious talent for capturing the visual idiom of virtually any popular style — suggests that *Tarzan of the Apes* might never have been written.

26 Burroughs to Weston, 22 March 1906.

27 John F. Kasson, *Houdini, Tarzan, and the Perfect Man: The White Male Body and the Challenge of Modernity in America* (New York: Hill and Wang, 2001), 170.

28 Burroughs, "Autobiography," 54.

29 Porges, *Edgar Rice Burroughs*, 106.

30 Porges, *Edgar Rice Burroughs*, 69; 192. Harry appears to have been the brother who helped Ed the most in his early years.

31 Burroughs's brothers also did well financially until their father died in 1913. At that point, when Ed had begun to make real money from writing, the family's fortunes on the whole turned downward. Still, Frank and Ed apparently supported themselves, and all three managed to maintain moderate, if not accumulative, financial prosperity.

32 Kasson, *Houdini, Tarzan, and the Perfect Man*, 178. See Kasson's excellent situating of Burroughs's career in relation to the ethos of masculine professionalism and self-improvement.

33 Burroughs to Weston, 4 September 1918.

34 Weston to Seth Thomas, 17 July 1918.

35 Burroughs to Weston, 9 July 1928.

36 Culver, now called the Culver Academies and embracing the Culver Military Academy and the Culver Girls Academy, was founded in 1894.

37 Harvey Green, *The Uncertainty of Everyday Life: 1915–1945* (New York: HarperCollins, 1992), 125–27. Green points out that the "expansion of college enrollment that occurred in the 1920s—from 341,000 in 1920 to 754,000 in 1930—was predominantly a middle-class phenomenon at nonelite universities" (125).

38 Weston to Burroughs, 15 January 1933. Weston refers to Burroughs's "spark" in the same letter.

39 *The Eternal Lover* (1925) and *The Efficiency Expert* (1921) both mention Beatrice as well; Burroughs refers to the "Beatrice Corn Mills," which are presumably modeled on Nebraska Corn Mills.

40 Weston's letter of 15 January 1933 testifies eloquently to the penetration of anxiety into families that had been to that point buffered from the Depression's effects. Weston alternately justifies their staying at home as a way of protecting themselves financially and of being true to the community of Beatrice while confessing that he lacks "the courage to go to SoCalif., where we both like to go, and face our actually hungry friends."

41 Roosevelt quoted in Edmund Morris, *The Rise of Theodore Roosevelt* (New York: Coward, McCann and Geoghegan, 1979), 294.

42 Burroughs to Weston, 6 November 1933; quoted in Porges, *Edgar Rice Burroughs*, 436.

43 Barbara Ehrenreich, *Fear of Falling: The Inner Life of the Middle Class* (New York: HarperPerennial, 1990), 83.

44 Porges, *Edgar Rice Burroughs*, 342. Edgar Rice Burroughs, Inc., so powerfully structured Burroughs's life and finances that after their divorce, Emma remained an employee of the corporation; she was listed as a copy editor. The entire immediate family was in the employ of Edgar Rice Burroughs, Inc. See Porges, *Edgar Rice Burroughs*, 575.

45 Porges, *Edgar Rice Burroughs*, 404.

46 A provocative treatment of Twain and the publishing world is Richard S.

Lowry, *"Littery Man": Mark Twain and Modern Authorship* (New York: Oxford University Press, 1996).

47 Porges, *Edgar Rice Burroughs*, 178–80.

48 Porges, *Edgar Rice Burroughs*, 223–24. Later he would propose a similar organization to protect the rights of authors against movie producers; see Porges, *Edgar Rice Burroughs*, 331.

49 Burroughs to Weston, 14 March 1934.

50 Marianna Torgovnick notes that Jane disappears from the Tarzan books for about ten years, a period "correspond[ing] to his [Burroughs's] own marital troubles." She returns in 1935–36 in *Tarzan's Quest*. Marianna Torgovnick, *Gone Primitive: Savage Intellects, Modern Lives* (Chicago: University of Chicago Press, 1990), 63.

51 Weston to Burroughs, 20 May 1939.

52 Burroughs to Weston, 25 May 1939.

53 Weston to Burroughs, 25 June 1939.

54 Burroughs to Weston, 20 March 1941.

55 Weston to Burroughs, 5 May 1947; quoted in Porges, *Edgar Rice Burroughs*, 694.

56 Emma died of a stroke, in California, on 5 November 1944. Margaret Weston lived until 1956.

57 Lauren Berlant, *The Queen of America Goes to Washington City: Essays on Sex and Citizenship* (Durham: Duke University Press, 1997); Dana Nelson, *National Manhood: Capitalist Citizenship and the Imagined Fraternity of White Men* (Durham: Duke University Press, 1998); Joel Pfister and Nancy Schnog, eds., *Inventing the Psychological: Toward a Cultural History of Emotional Life in America* (New Haven: Yale University Press, 1997); Priscilla Wald, *Constituting Americans: Cultural Anxiety and Narrative Form* (Durham: Duke University Press, 1995); Chris Castiglia, "Abolition's Racial Interiors and the Making of White Civic Depth," *American Literary History* 14:1 (Spring 2002): 32–59. On imperialism in particular, see Amy Kaplan, *The Anarchy of Empire in the Making of U.S. Culture* (Cambridge: Harvard University Press, 2003); and Bederman, *Manliness and Civilization*. Other studies offering complex theories of masculine self-formation include Kaja Silverman, *Male Subjectivity at the Margins* (New York: Routledge, 1992); and Jay Mechling, *On My Honor: Boy Scouts and the Making of American Youth* (Chicago: University of Chicago Press, 2001).

58 Kasson, *Houdini, Tarzan, and the Perfect Man*; Eric Cheyfitz, *The Poetics of Imperialism: Translation and Colonization from* The Tempest *to* Tarzan (Philadelphia: University of Pennsylvania Press, 1997 [1991]); Torgovnick, *Gone Primitive*; Bill Brown, "Science Fiction, the World's Fair, and the Prosthetics of Empire, 1910–1915," in *Cultures of United States Imperialism*, ed. Amy Kaplan and Donald E. Pease (Durham: Duke University Press, 1993), 129–63.

59 E. Anthony Rotundo's *American Manhood: Transformations in Masculinity from the Revolution to the Modern Era* (New York: Basic Books, 1993), based heavily on epistolary evidence and secondary arguments, has been criticized on this account.

60 Erving Goffman, *The Presentation of Self in Everyday Life* (Garden City, N.Y.: Doubleday, 1959), 252.

61 Joan Wallach Scott, *Gender and the Politics of History* (New York: Columbia University Press, 1988), 38–39.

62 Theodore Roosevelt, *The Winning of the West*, 4 vols. (Lincoln: University of Nebraska Press, 1995 [1889–96]), 2:373–75; 3:44–46. Bederman points out that "Burroughs began writing *Tarzan of the Apes* in late 1911, about a year after Theodore Roosevelt returned from his highly publicized African safari. Burroughs's fictionalized Africa echoes hack journalists' sensationalized versions of TR's trip." Bederman, *Manliness and Civilization*, 220.

63 Burroughs's racism is customarily discussed by critics in terms of his black characters, but his approach to Native Americans has not been thoroughly explored. The distinction is significant for many reasons, not least because Burroughs took a great many photographs of Great Plains tribes, drew real or imagined Indians obsessively while at Fort Grant, and wrote two novels based (loosely) on the Apaches.

64 Bederman, *Manliness and Civilization*, 187.

65 "The Black Man's Burden (a Parody)," *Pocatello Tribune*, 1899; reprinted in Porges, *Edgar Rice Burroughs*.

66 This poem's authorship has not been definitely proven, though most experts agree that Burroughs wrote it; at the least, he clipped and saved it his whole life. The poem could also be read as a projection from the position of the white young man who is failing—as Burroughs was at the time—in a business world controlled by impersonal forces. See Willard Gatewood, *Black Americans and the White Man's Burden* (Urbana: University of Illinois Press, 1975), for a discussion of black parodies and fiercely critical reactions to the poem.

67 Weston to Burroughs, 24 October 1918.

68 As Michael Kimmel points out, a "resurgent Ku Klux Klan flourished in the 1920s, especially in Midwestern border states like Indiana. Lynchings and other forms of racist violence increased dramatically during the decade." Michael Kimmel, *Manhood in America: A Cultural History* (New York: Free Press, 1996), 195. See also Laura Wexler, *Fire in a Canebrake: The Last Mass Lynching in America* (New York: Scribner, 2003).

69 Weston to Burroughs, 22 October 1939.

70 Kasson, *Houdini, Tarzan, and the Perfect Man*, 179.

71 The term *extracolonial* might be more precise, since the United States had since at least the days of Andrew Jackson made a policy of internally colonizing Native Americans.

72 "Albert J. Beveridge's Salute to Imperialism, 1900," in *Major Problems in American Foreign Policy*, vol. 1, ed. Thomas G. Paterson (Lexington, Mass.: Heath, 1989), 391.

73 Amy Kaplan, "Romancing the Empire: The Embodiment of American Masculinity in the Popular Historical Novel of the 1890s," in *Postcolonial Theory and the United States*, ed. Amritjit Singh and Peter Schmidt (Jackson: University Press of Mississippi, 2000), 220.

74 Torgovnick, *Gone Primitive*, 60.

75 Green, *Uncertainty of Everyday Life*, 142.

76 Burroughs appears less emotional in the middle-period letters, particularly the ones written through his secretaries. But I would argue that the affective side of his correspondence is conveyed through irony and thorniness. He began during this time to worry about his "posterity"—about the very kind of project I am undertaking here, for example. On 30 July 1927 he wrote to Weston: "Every once in a while we destroy a bunch of photographs that were taken several years ago and which now make us appear ridiculous. What's the use of leaving something to posterity that will make them ashamed of our poor taste and sorry for our lack of intelligence? Caesar, Napoleon and George Washington would be no great heroes if we had 16 mm movies of them." But Burroughs was nonetheless willing to make aggressive jokes about, for example, their comparative finances and to argue about politics or sport in an edgy tone that relies on having a good friend on the receiving end.

77 Weston to Burroughs, 25 August 1940.

78 Burroughs to Weston, 30 September 1939.

79 This warning is inspired by one Martha Banta gives in reference to Henry Adams's writings. Martha Banta, "Being a 'Begonia' in a Man's World," in *New Essays on* The Education of Henry Adams, ed. John Carlos Rowe (New York: Cambridge University Press, 1996). On Metcalf and Davis, see Porges, *Edgar Rice Burroughs*, 206.

80 Kasson, *Houdini, Tarzan, and the Perfect Man*, 11. See Burton Bledstein, *The Culture of Professionalism: The Middle Class and the Development of Higher Education in America* (New York: W. W. Norton, 1978).

81 Kasson, *Houdini, Tarzan, and the Perfect Man*, 72. The pyramid in figure 8 appears to be simultaneously a parody of and homage to one of Sandow's popular feats of strength.

82 Kasson, *Houdini, Tarzan, and the Perfect Man*, 211.

83 See Katheryn Grover, ed., *Fitness in American Culture: Images of Health, Sport, and the Body, 1830–1940* (Amherst: University of Massachusetts Press, 1989); and Kasson, *Houdini, Tarzan, and the Perfect Man*. Weston and most of his friends were athletes, and many of them had been to military school as well.

84 See Katherine V. Snyder, "A Paradise of Bachelors: Remodelling Domesticity and Masculinity in the Turn-of-the-Century New York Bachelor

Apartment," *Prospects: An Annual Review of American Cultural Studies* 23 (1998): 247–84.

85 *Decennial Record of the Class of 1898, Sheffield Scientific School*, comp. Joseph W. Alsop (New Haven: Tuttle, Morehouse and Taylor, 1908).

86 *Decennial Record*, 89–90.

87 Nelson, *National Manhood*, 11, 22.

88 Burroughs to Weston, 9 December 1918.

89 Kevin White, *The First Sexual Revolution: The Emergence of Male Heterosexuality in Modern America* (New York: New York University Press, 1993), 17. Both men also participated in fraternal organizations — Weston in his golf club and local fraternal groups, and Burroughs in several literary social clubs, both in Chicago and in Los Angeles.

90 On fraternal organizations in the late nineteenth century, see Mark C. Carnes, *Secret Ritual and Manhood in Victorian America* (New Haven: Yale University Press, 1989); and Mary Ann Clawson, *Constructing Brotherhood: Class, Gender, and Fraternalism* (Princeton: Princeton University Press, 1989).

91 Weston to Burroughs, 15 January 1933.

92 Burroughs to Weston, 30 December 1903.

93 Burroughs, "Autobiography," 55.

94 See Alan Trachtenberg, *The Incorporation of America: Culture and Society in the Gilded Age* (New York: Hill and Wang, 1982), for an interpretation of a range of incorporative tropes in the United States.

95 One of the reasons Burroughs never completed his draft "Autobiography" may have been precisely that an author biography was not the kind of promotional material — the kind of advertising — that made the most of the genre in which Burroughs was working. It propagated a formula of authorship and celebrity that Burroughs explicitly rejected and on some occasions parodied.

Correspondence

1 Edgar Rice and Emma Burroughs briefly joined Ed's brothers George and Henry (who are listed in the letterhead) in a mining venture in Idaho.

2 Margaret Collins Weston and Emma Burroughs (née Hulbert). The gift "bug" may have been a stuffed or ceramic Gila monster.

3 Weston had probably announced Margaret's pregnancy with Collins, who would be born in October, in an earlier communication; hence Burroughs's ironic projection of the name and the cartoon predicting that the baby would follow in Weston's footsteps. The Burroughs's first child, Joan, would be born 12 January 1908; she lived until 1972.

4 Announcing the birth of Jane on 12 March 1908; she died on 30 September 1908.

5 Rajah was the Burroughs's collie.

6 This sentence and later ones suggest that the Westons had seen a recent photo of Burroughs.

7 Burroughs had published a number of stories by this time, most with Frank A. Munsey in the *All-Story*. *Tarzan of the Apes* appeared in book form in 1914 with A. C. McClurg. Jefferson B. Weston was born in 1911; Herbert T. Weston Jr. in 1914.

8 Charles Bird King, a popular novelist, was briefly the commandant at MMA.

9 Robert Davis was Burroughs's second editor, after Thomas Metcalfe, at Munsey's.

10 Hulbert Burroughs was born on 10 August 1910; he lived until 1991.

11 Porges notes that Burroughs had had pain in his left shoulder for some time. Porges, *Edgar Rice Burroughs*, 197.

12 Plutocrats.

13 Tarzan was the Burroughses' new dog.

14 The United States entered World War I on 7 April 1917.

15 Burroughs joined the Illinois Reserve Militia and was made the captain of Company A, 2nd Infantry.

16 The Westons and their friends referred to Margaret as "Margaret Medora," using her maiden middle name.

17 MMA was at Orchard Lake, near Detroit, Michigan.

18 John Coleman Burroughs, known to family and friends as Jack, was born in 1913; he died in February 1979.

19 Burroughs's brother Harry's wife, Ella (Nell), and daughter Evelyn.

20 The Burroughs and Weston families were fortunate; 28 percent of U.S. citizens were infected during the influenza pandemic of 1918, and almost 750,000 died. See Alfred Crosby, *America's Forgotten Pandemic: The Influenza of 1918* (Cambridge: Cambridge University Press, 1989).

21 Margaret's parents, Chester Worthington Collins and Margaret Medora Collins, of Brooklyn, New York.

22 G-1 was a wartime home guard rank, the equivalent of a "desk job."

23 This letter more likely dates from 24 October 1918; thus its placement here.

24 On 23 October President Woodrow Wilson insisted that the United States and the Allies should not negotiate with the military dictatorship then ruling Germany. Wilhelm Solf, former governor of Western Samoa, was by this time serving as Kaiser Wilhelm's imperial foreign minister, and he negotiated the armistice that went into effect 11 November 1918.

25 Lynching was still common in the United States in 1918. Weston's comment here unwittingly characterizes his own anti-German hatred as of a type with southern racism, despite the implied critique of lynching as an inappropriately parochial form of "justice."

26 Nebraska Corn Mills would be dissolved in 1923.

27 Sherwood Holbert, Seth Thomas (millionaire New York clock manufacturer), Colonel Charles Lloyd, and Murry Sanders.

28 Mack Sennett's Bathing Beauties. Sennett was a motion picture actor, producer, director, and discoverer of many stars; his Keystone Studios produced the famous Keystone Kops shorts.

29 Theodore Roosevelt died 6 January 1919 in Oyster Bay, New York.

30 Emma's father had died the week after she and Burroughs married, in 1900.

31 Elizabeth Weston also lived in Beatrice, next door to Bert and Margaret.

32 Chester Collins was invested in railroads, and as a partner in Kilpatrick and Collins coordinated the contracting for western railroad building; as Weston suggests here, it was a lucrative concern.

33 Nebraska Corn Mills would, however, be audited and asked to pay back taxes. A young tax accountant, Dana F. Cole, successfully defended the company and enabled it to remain in the black when the shareholders agreed to dissolve it, though not, as Weston predicts in the next paragraph, at the profit the original investors had expected.

34 Presumably *Tarzan and the Jewels of Opar* and *Tarzan the Untamed*.

35 Fred Onthank was one of Burroughs's employees at the ranch; his wife, Grace, was one of Burroughs's secretaries. They had come from Oak Park with the Burroughses, and both quit within a year of the move, claiming that they were not being paid the salaries Burroughs had promised them. See Porges, *Edgar Rice Burroughs*, 306.

36 Weston refers here to the beginning of Prohibition. Bootlegged alcohol could be obtained considerably more cheaply where Burroughs lived; it is curious that he does not mention this among the attractions of Los Angeles.

37 Weston here refers again to the last day before Prohibition went into effect.

38 This secretary might be John Shea, given the initials, but he reportedly quit in 1922.

39 The house on the hill had been given over to Burroughs's golf course project. The subdivision mentioned here was on part of the Tarzana acreage that had been sold in residential lots.

40 Roy Alberts; Carter is unidentified. Both were probably MMA alumni.

41 William Waterhouse, Burroughs's secretary for a year in 1926–27.

42 Away from home; see 1 Kings 4.25, "And Judah and Israel dwelt safely, every man under his vine and under his fig tree, from Dan even to Beersheba, all the days of Solomon."

43 Chester Collins had died in 1925, and Margaret Collins suffered from illness intermittently before she died in 1931.

44 The Weston boys all attended Culver Military Academy in Culver, Indiana; Collins, who struggled academically more than the other boys, spent time at the University of Nebraska as well.

45 Burroughs and Weston had been football teammates at MMA.

46 James H. Pierce, whom Joan would marry the following year.

47 This probably means Collins; they dined at the Cornhusker Hotel.

48 "Blew" here refers to the Blue River. Beatrice is still occasionally called "Beatrice on the Blue."

49 Gene Tunney was the reigning heavyweight champion of the world. He was probably on his way to exhibition matches with Eddie Eagan and Frank Muskie held 11 April.

50 4d here probably stands for "Ford."

51 Secretary unidentified.

52 This transcription was taken from a carbon copy; the position of the comment "defunct!!" indicates that Weston used Nebraska Corn Mills stationery for this letter.

53 Sally was Weston's brother Ralph's daughter.

54 Charles Lindbergh had completed his famous solo transatlantic flight on 21 May of that year.

55 In the seventh round of the Tunney-Dempsey fight held at Soldier Field in Chicago, on 25 September of that year, Dempsey knocked Tunney down for a count of nine that has been considered a "long count" by many ever since. Illinois State Athletic Commission rules required that a knockdown count not begin until the opponent moved to the farthest neutral corner; Dempsey may have lingered over Tunney too long.

56 Joe Stecher from Dodge, Nebraska, held the wrestling world championship in 1927. His opponent in this case was probably former world champion Stanislaus Zbyszko, from whom he had won the title in 1925.

57 Joe Dundee and Ace Hudkins were both popular boxers in the 1920s; the match mentioned here was probably an exhibition.

58 The St. Francis dam, in the San Francisquito Canyon, collapsed on 12 March of that year, killing five hundred people; damage was estimated around $20 million.

59 The Westons owned or were partners in several small businesses in Beatrice during the 1920s; one of them, the Owl Pharmacy, sold camera equipment—hence the discount to which Weston refers.

60 Burroughs often dictated his fiction and correspondence using a Dictaphone or Ediphone.

61 Alfred Smith ran against Herbert Hoover in the 1928 presidential election.

62 Murad was a popular brand of cigarettes.

63 The University of California, Los Angeles, was founded in 1919 and known as the "Southern Branch," hence Weston's abbreviation (which may also, of course, be a pun).

64 In the Rose Bowl game that year, University of California center Roy Riegels ran a Georgia Tech fumble back to his own one-yard line before

he was stopped by a teammate. Georgia Tech went on to win 8–7 after blocking the ensuing California punt for a safety.

65 Burroughs and the Westons invested together in the Los Angeles Metropolitan Airport—unfortunately, as the following letters show, on the eve of the stock market crash.

66 This comment likely refers to the practice of buying stock that was oscillating wildly in value.

67 Gumbo is a loose, silty soil that turns into sticky, difficult-to-negotiate mud in rain; the Dakotas were famous for it, and it is a favorite substrate for mud racing today.

68 Burroughs, too, had applied to be a member of Theodore Roosevelt's Rough Riders, but had been rejected. Weston served with Battery A of the First Connecticut Light Artillery in the Spanish-American War, without, as he implies here, seeing combat.

69 Joan Burroughs Pierce was born to Joan and Jim on 24 December 1929.

70 Burroughs would take up flying, in fact, in January 1934.

71 Cecil B. DeMille (1881–1959), Hollywood producer and director.

72 A "shypoke" is a Great Blue Heron.

73 Unfortunately the hot epistle is not extant. St. John is presumably Lloyd L. St. John of the Los Angeles Metropolitan Airport, Ltd.

74 Burroughs had written accounts of several of the family's previous overland trips; Weston no doubt had read some of these.

75 The Corn Husker is still the mascot of the University of Nebraska, Lincoln, where Collins and Jeff Weston were during this time.

76 This program included Joan and Jim in the parts of Tarzan and Jane; Hulbert helped market the show.

77 The Scotts were, and still are, Weston family friends from Beatrice.

78 Collins's and Mabel's baby would be named Margaret.

79 The Long Beach earthquake, one of the most severe in the state's history, happened at 5:55 P.M. on 10 March 1933 and claimed 120 lives.

80 Presumably "somewhat touchy."

81 Arlington Spangler Brugh (1911–1969), film actor; his screen name was Robert Taylor.

82 KM probably stands for kitchen maid.

83 Numa and Kala were animal characters from Burroughs's Tarzan books; Numa was a generic term for "lion" throughout the series, and Kala was Tarzan's ape foster mother.

84 This letter more likely dates from 25 December 1933.

85 Burroughs had, in fact, moved out in February 1934. Porges blames the split on Emma's excessive drinking, but the reason for the breakup has never been established. ERB had begun a relationship with Florence Gilbert Dearholt at the time he left. He married her in April 1935; they were divorced after Florence left him in March 1941.

86 QM here stands for Quarter Master.

87 Herb married Marian Sherwood (see letter of 10 June 1929) on 14 June 1937.

88 The granddaughters were Margaret, Patricia, Ann, and Sue.

89 Jack married Jane Ralston on 12 December 1936. Their first child, John, was born in June 1942; their second, Danton, was born in June 1944.

90 These were likely Lee and Caryl Lee, Florence's children from her first marriage.

91 Germany invaded Poland on 1 September, probably the day Burroughs received this letter.

92 In 1925 Stefan Sorel published *Tarzan der Deutschenfresser* (Tarzan the German-eater), which criticized the recent publications in Germany of translations of Burroughs's books on the grounds that they were anti-German. The controversy rendered Burroughs's works unmarketable in Germany until the 1950s. See Porges, *Edgar Rice Burroughs*, 390–94.

93 Burroughs had by this date been an avid tennis player for several years; the "we" here includes presumably at least Florence, also a tennis player.

94 Sue (now O'Neill) is the daughter of Jeff and Jean Weston, born 19 January 1938.

95 This text is now missing from the Weston Family Collection, which contains many inscribed editions of Burroughs's work. The inscription in a copy of *The Return of Tarzan* (1915 edition), evidently a birthday gift to Herb when he was still very young, reads: "To Herbert Towle Weston, Jr. from his father's bad influence & his mother's pet aversion, with best wishes/Edgar Rice Burroughs/Oak Park/Jan. 13, 1918."

96 Katharine Weston was born on 6 May 1940.

97 James A. Farley (1888–1973) was the postmaster general and campaign manager, adviser, and confidante for Franklin Delano Roosevelt. In 1940 he had left his post and was running for president.

98 Gibson was a famous illustrator; Jerome was a well-known writer; Annie Rooney was a film character (*Little Annie Rooney*, ironically, would be remade just two years after this letter, with Shirley Temple as the lead); E. H. Sothern and Anna Held were early film stars (Sothern was a renowned Shakespearian, while Held earned fame working with Florenz Ziegfield Jr.); Lillian Russell was a famous soprano. Graustark may refer to the novel of that title by George Barr McCutcheon, or to the 1925 film version, starring Norma Talmadge.

99 Weston's father, J. B., was from Maine; Weston visited relatives there periodically from an early age.

100 Cordell Hull (1871–1955) served as FDR's secretary of state. A key player in the formation of the United Nations, he won the Nobel Peace Prize in 1945.

101 James Westbrook Pegler (1894–1969) was a controversial columnist of the day.

102 Probably Burroughs refers here to the Canadian Dionne quintuplets, who were much in the news at the time.

103 Henry Ward Beecher (1813–1887) was a well-known minister and abolitionist orator.

104 Fulton and Angie Jack and their daughters Jo (Josephine) and Elizabeth were Weston family friends; they lived on Fifth Street in Beatrice.

105 Tyrone Power (1914–1958) was a well-known movie star before and after World War II.

Index

A. C. McClurg & Co. *See* McClurg's
Aging, 9, 18, 27–28, 36, 44, 67, 69,
  79, 97–98, 100, 146, 149, 161,
  164, 168, 175, 182, 200, 210, 222,
  234, 251, 257, 260, 262–63, 271,
  273, 280, 286; and friendship,
  236; and masculinity, 30, 62, 78
Agua Caliente, 171–74
Air conditioning, 257, 259
Air mail, 187, 189, 197
Airplane crash, 231
Alberts, Roy, 94, 97
Alcohol, 168, 172
Ali, Muhammad, 38
Amazing Stories, 107
American Battery Company, 5
American Legion, 179, 240
Angina, 27, 285
Anselmo, Joanne, 28
Anti-Semitism, 33
Apache Motors, 24, 152, 160, 164–
  66, 180, 183, 186–87
Army, U.S., 26; book donations to,
  60–67; Camp Kearney, 65; Camp
  Steever, 60–61; Camp Taylor, 69,
  77; Fort Grant, 15, 17, 292 n.63;
  reserve, 243, 267
Arthur, General. *See* MacArthur,
  Douglas
Austin, Ed, 213
Australia, 26
Authors' League of America, 23

Autobiography, 10, 16, 17, 46
Automobiles, 19; accidents in, 61,
  93, 105, 213, 225; Aerocars, 187–
  88; Air-Flow, 241; Auburn, 213;
  Big 6 Touring, 104; Buick, 108,
  150, 271, 273; Cadillac, 71; Cole-8,
  71, 82; Cord, 193; Ford, 1, 71, 93,
  99–100, 102, 104, 113, 139, 149,
  152, 187; Franklin, 4, 71; Lincoln, 99–103, 107–8, 130, 149,
  213; Marmon, 71; Packard, 130,
  187; Plymouth, 213, 222, 225;
  Studebaker, 107

Babies. *See* children
Bacardi rum. *See* alcohol
Baldwin family, 267–68
Baldwin, Stanley, 272
Ball, Sue, 84, 97, 199, 215, 219
Ball, Woodruff, 98, 113, 171, 212
Bank holiday, 224
Bank robbery, 188
Beach house, 210, 212, 215, 218–19
Beach, Rex, 114
Bear Creek, Nebraska, 75
Beasts of Tarzan, The, 23, 65
Beatrice National Bank, 6, 14, 20,
  224
Beatrice, 2, 4, 7, 13–14, 21, 75, 77,
  85, 125, 127; founding of, 6, 100
Bederman, Gail, 29, 32
Beecher, Henry Ward, 272

Beers (photographer), 278
Bell & Howell, 118–19
Bemidji, 103–6, 125, 182–85, 215,
    228, 229, 239–42, 258, 263–64
Berlant, Lauren, 29
Bernard, Mildred, 275
Beveridge, Albert Jeremiah (sena-
    tor), 35
"Black Man's Burden (A Parody),
    The," 32
Blue Book, 112, 164
Boats, 228–29, 256; yachting, 153,
    167–68, 174
Boeing, 148; airfield, 181, 184
Boulder Dam, 123, 225
Boxing, 111, 174, 176
Bray, Joe, 253
Brewster, Charles, 89
Bridge. See Contract bridge
Brown, Bill, 29
Brugh, Arlington Spangler (Robert
    Taylor), 227, 239
Brummel, Beau, 135
Buffalo Bill's Wild West Show, 156
Bulletin, The, 23
Burnside, Cecile, 276, 279
Burroughs, Edgar Rice: childhood
    of, 5; education of, 6–12; fiction
    by, 12, 21, 23, 31–32, 35–36, 47, 58,
    60, 63, 65, 67, 71, 87, 89, 101–2,
    108, 112, 120, 130, 133, 136, 164,
    221, 237, 240, 248, 253; incorpo-
    ration of, 22–23, 27, 46; letters
    of, 2–4; theatricality of, 9, 10
Burroughs, Ella (Nellie), 62
Burroughs, Emma, 5, 16–17, 21–25,
    63, 68, 71, 141, 230–38
Burroughs, Evelyn, 62
Burroughs, Florence Gilbert Dear-
    holt, 24–26, 237, 249–55, 270
Burroughs, Frank, 5
Burroughs, George Tyler, 5
Burroughs, George, 5
Burroughs, Harry, 5, 62, 253

Burroughs, Hulbert, 16, 22, 26, 63–
    65, 69, 104, 150, 171–72, 179, 185,
    210, 222, 231, 239, 276–81, 286
Burroughs, Joan, 16, 22, 28, 55, 63,
    67, 69, 98, 103, 110–17, 121–27,
    161, 215, 286
Burroughs, John Coleman (Jack), 16,
    22, 63, 69, 139, 141–42, 176–77
Burroughs, Marion T., 28
Burroughs, Mary Evaline, 5

California: development of, 167;
    investments in, 220; move to, 21,
    57, 68–82, 87, 93, 121, 210, 215
Capone, Al, 268
Carter, John, 94
Carter, John (fictional character), 18,
    21
Chain letters, 169–70, 262, 264
Chamberlain, Neville, 272
Cheyfitz, Eric, 29
Chicago, 4–5, 15, 33, 97, 124–25,
    127–28, 152
Children: babies, 55, 226; chang-
    ing diapers of, 56–57; education
    of, 19–22, 70, 72, 94, 172; and
    friendship, 210; raising of, 75,
    100, 112, 130, 188, 190, 209, 214,
    221
Christmas, 230–31, 238
Civil War, 5–6
Class, 42, 51; and education, 20, 22;
    expectations of, 5–6
Claws of the Hun, The, 35
Clayton, Jane, 89
Clemens, Samuel Langhorne. See
    Twain, Mark
Coldwater, Michigan, 58–60, 79,
    127–28, 179, 184
Collins, Chester Worthington, 7, 14,
    19–21, 74, 77–80, 85; estate of,
    220, 238
Collins, Margaret Butler. See
    Weston, Margaret Collins

Collins, Margaret, 10, 20–21, 74, 77–80, 85, 96, 101, 192
Colorado Springs, 78, 101
Columbian Exposition of 1893, 37; White Palace at, 12
Commencements, 176–77, 211
Communism, 36, 86, 244–45, 259, 285; fifth column, 259
Conscription, 264–67
Contract bridge, 45, 192, 213, 222–23, 251, 253, 263
Cook, Margaret, 197
Corn, 106; Argentine, 79; feed, 72–73; meal, 86; milling of, 21, 69, 78, 90; Nebraska, 73
Corn Belt, 33–34, 74, 85, 246
Corwin, Bill, 154, 166–68
Croup, 263–64
Cuba, 19, 35, 115–17, 157–58, 162–64, 167, 172, 188
Culver Military Academy, 19–20, 97, 107, 112, 115, 131, 133, 138, 141, 143, 152, 161, 176, 179, 191, 195, 209, 211, 213, 222, 227, 250
Curtiss Aeroplane and Motor Company, 148

Davidson, Frank, 54, 62
Davis, Robert H., 23, 36, 58
Dearholt, Caryl Lee, 26
Dearholt, Florence Gilbert. See Burroughs, Florence Gilbert Dearholt
Dearholt, Lee, 26, 190
Debt. See Great Depression; Poverty
Democratic Party. See Politics
Dempsey, Jack, 101, 103, 110
Dempster family, 205
Detroit, 6
Dieting, 137, 146, 149
Dillingham family, 267–68
Dionne quintuplets, 271
Divorce, 24–26, 232–38, 250
Doane College, 222

Dogs, 86; collie, 57; Don, 92; Jack, 92; Jet, 102; Lobo, 92, 102; Morning View Julliete, 225; Morning View Sergeant, 89–90, 92; Rajah, 57; Tarzan, 59, 91, 130, 210; Zipper, 262
Dowling, Allen, 269–70
Driving, 193. See also Automobiles
Drought, 159, 161, 166
Drury, Morley, 113
Dundee, Joe, 111

E. S. Winslow Company, 54
Earthquakes, 149, 223–24
Eastman (Kodak), 118–19, 129, 176. See also Home movies; Motion pictures
Edgar Rice Burroughs, Inc., 22–23, 27, 46
Education. See Children: education of
Elections. See Politics
Embargo, 247
Empire State Building, 34, 246
Eulalie, Infanta, 12

Fairbanks, Douglas, 35, 138
Farley, James A., 260
Farm Relief Program, 123, 191, 262
Farming, 70, 83, 84, 86, 91; goat, 88–93; hog, 68, 72–74, 85, 88, 90
Fascism, 36, 244, 259
Featherstone, Ed, 132, 256–57, 260
Fidelity Finance Company, 238
Film Booking Office Studio (FBO), 123
First Connecticut Light Artillery, Battery A, 14, 93, 157
First editions, 240, 248, 253
Football, 7, 10, 12, 38, 98, 112, 152, 191, 193, 197, 246, 265; Army-Navy game, 97; Nebraska-Army game, 134; Nebraska-Stanford game, 268; at Pasadena, 139–40;

Football (continued)
  Pomona-University of Arizona
  game, 193; Stanford-Alabama
  game, 98; USC-Notre Dame
  game, 98, 113; USC-UC game,
  111; USC-Washington game, 113;
  Yale-Princeton game, 132
Fort Grant, 15, 17
Fort Meade, 213
Fred Thompson Motion Picture
  Company, 121
Friendship, 9, 76, 102, 233, 236; and
  correspondence, 199, 227, 238;
  and money, 221–22; and sports,
  7, 112; threats to, 23–26, 182–87,
  236–38, 273

Gambling, 24, 181–22, 217–18
Gause, Frederick Taylor, 42
Gay, Charles, 208; Gay's Lion Farm,
  103
Gender, 29–31. See also Masculinity
General Motors Corporation, 148,
  259
Geneva Lake, 60–61
Gibson, Charles Dana, 260
Gilbert Islands, 27
Glass, Carter, 269
Glendale, California, 110, 117. See
  also Stock theater
Goat farming, 88, 93
Goffman, Erving, 30
Golf, 146, 182, 184–85, 207, 210,
  271, 273; and Caballero Club, 132,
  135
Goodrich Rubber Company, 167
Grand Canyon, 101, 103, 107, 174,
  202, 206
Grant, Dick, 85
Grant's Pass, Oregon, 187
Graustark, 260
Great Depression, 2–3, 20–21, 181,
  183, 186, 192, 199, 221

Greene, Hiram M., 80
Guard duty, 277–79

Halliday, John, 256
Hapsburgs. See Hohenzollerns
Hassan, Prince Ilaki Ali, 270
Hawaii, territory of, 26, 254, 266
Hedges, Dayton, 261
Hedges, Jimmie, 183
Heffron, McCray and St. John: and
  Los Angeles Metropolitan Airport
  investment, 145, 151, 160
Held, Anna, 260
Herr, Herb, 93
Hitler, Adolf, 241–43, 257–65, 272,
  279; Danzig speech of, 243
Hog farming, 68, 72–74, 85, 88, 90
Hohenzollerns, 33, 66
Holbert, Sherwood, 75–76, 155
Home Guard, 63
Home movies, 104–5, 118–41, 164,
  176, 267; in color, 133, 137, 139,
  211
Homosociality, 44. See also Mascu-
  linity
Hoover, Herbert, 87, 123, 134–35,
  218
Hoover Dam, 191
Horses, 68, 132; horse show, 98–
  99; ponies, 63, 84, 86; riding, 10,
  63
Hot Springs, 7, 150–52
Hudkins, Ace, 111
Hughes, Howard, 135
Hulbert, Alvin, 5
Hulbert, Emma Centennia. See
  Burroughs, Emma
Hulbert, Emma Theresa, 79
Hull, Cordell, 261
Hunter family, 220

Illinois Reserve Militia, 18, 60–61
Illness, 175–79, 199, 203–4, 252–

53, 263; and masculinity, 209; of
parents, 78–79
Incorporation. *See* Edgar Rice Bur-
roughs, Inc.
Indian Creek, 75
Ingwersen, Burt, 190
Investment: in construction, 214,
219; in real estate, 88, 153–54, 158
Iolani Palace, 279

Jack, Fulton, 280
Jack, Jo, 280–84
Jenkins, Eleanor, 284
Jerome, Jerome K., 260
J. H. Bell and Company, 54
Johnson, Hiram, 27
Jones, Mary L., 60–64
Julian, California, 171
Jungle Tales of Tarzan, 221
Just So Stories, 136

Kahanamoku, Duke, 254
Kamehameha I (king), 255
Kaneohe Bay, 256
Kaplan, Amy, 29, 35
Kasson, John, 16, 29, 34, 37–38
Kewalo: Basin, 277; Inn, 278
Kilpatrick Brothers and Collins
(contractors), 7, 14
Kilpatrick, W. H., 267
King, Charles Bird, 9, 58
Kipling, Rudyard, 31–32, 136
Knights of Columbus, 62
KSTP radio station, 215

Lanikai, Oahu, 255
Lay, Robert, 9–10, 171, 229, 235,
237, 249, 250–51
Liberty Magazine, 114
Life, 237
Lincoln, Abraham, 135
Lincoln, Nebraska, 4, 81–82, 104,
112, 226

Lindbergh, Charles, 108
Literary Digest, 67
Lloyd, Charles (colonel), 13, 75, 93,
97
Los Angeles, 21, 76, 83, 112, 115; city
golf tournament of, 184–85
Los Angeles Athletic Club, 44, 72,
77
Los Angeles Investment Company,
167
Los Angeles Metropolitan Airport,
24, 146–51, 159–66, 172–73,
177–87
Los Angeles Soap Company, 167
Lowe's State Theatre, 206

MacArthur, Douglas (general), 282
Madison Square Garden, 156
Mad King, The, 21
Mark Anthony, 180
Marriage, 138; of Collins Weston
and Mabel, 201; divorce of Edgar
Rice Burroughs and Emma, 24–
25; and economics, 16; of Edgar
Rice Burroughs and Emma Hul-
bert, 5, 16, 24–25; of Herbert
Weston and Margaret Collins, 7,
14; of Hulbert Burroughs and
Marion, 286; of Jeff Weston and
Jean Wilhelmy, 229–31; of Joan
Burroughs and James Pierce,
122–36, 230
Marshall Islands, 27
Martian stories, 67, 101
Masculinity: corporate, 37–38, 45;
construction of, 3, 13, 17–18, 29,
46–47, 89; and creativity, 46;
and fitness, 39–40; and football,
190; and ideology, 27, 30–31;
and imperialism, 12, 18, 29, 35;
and individuality, 12, 27, 38, 42,
47; local, 42; and nostalgia, 9;
and performance, 30–31, 39, 44;

Masculinity (*continued*)
and politics, 135; taming of, 38;
theories and histories of, 29
Mastermind of Mars, The, 108
Mattison (MMA alumnus), 110, 112
May Have Seen Better Days Club,
17
McClurg's, 60, 63, 136, 253
McCook, 13, 73
McSweeny, Jack, 97
Medorah, Margaret. *See* Weston,
Margaret Collins
Mellon, Andrew, 135
Metcalf, Thomas, 36
Metro-Goldwyn-Mayer, 208, 242
Michigan Military Academy (MMA),
6–15, 19, 38, 105, 112, 191, 200;
alumni, 62, 64, 94, 110, 112
Military service: by Burroughs, 15–
18, 27, 61–64; and individuality,
19; and masculinity, 9, 67; in
Spanish-American War, 12, 14–16,
18; by Weston, 14, 18, 64, 69; in
World War I, 18, 35, 89; in World
War II, 266–67, 269
Miramar, lots at, 129, 155–59, 163,
165, 167, 170, 178–79, 180, 189,
194–98, 228, 252, 274, 282, 284
Missouri River, 6
Mitchell family, 256
Monroe Doctrine, 244
Motion pictures, 18. *See also* Home
movies
Mumps, 114, 133
Munsey, Frank A., publishing, 23,
36, 58
Murad, 132
Mussolini, Benito, 198, 257, 259–
60, 265, 268. *See also* World
War II

Naylor, Frank, 62, 64
Nazis, 36, 241–44, 257, 259, 261–
62, 283. *See also* World War II

Nebraska Corn Mills, 14, 19–21, 27,
86–87
Nebraska, 6, 142, 274
Needles, The, 59
Nelson, Dana, 1, 2, 29, 42
Neuritis, 58–59, 81–82
New Deal, 228, 238, 251, 258, 260–
62, 268–72, 284
New Haven, 12, 43, 92, 157, 229
Newspapers: *Chicago Tribune,* 75,
126; *Daily News,* 67; *Free Press*
(Detroit), 103–4; *Los Angeles Ex-
aminer,* 180; *Los Angeles Times,*
167; *Saturday Evening Post,* 241–
42, 252; *Tucson News,* 280; *The
World,* 58; *World-Herald,* 258
New York City, 7, 14, 33–34, 75,
78–80, 93, 97, 115, 134, 246–47
Nichols, Fred, 280
Nickell, Bob, 86
Norman of Torn, 101
North Gate, 239, 262, 264. *See also*
Bemidji

Oahu, 255
Oak Park, Illinois, 16, 61, 75
Oil, 274
Okinawa, 285
Onthank, Fred, 88
Orchard Lake, Michigan, 6–11, 14,
61–62, 104–5, 112, 235, 256–57,
260
Orr, Jack, 97
O'Sullivan, Maureen, 206, 208, 212
Otis, Harrison Grey (general), 83,
90
Owl Pharmacy, 125–26, 149

Pacific Southwest Tennis Tourna-
ment, 244
Palm Springs Raquet Club, 253
Pan American Congress, 261
Parades, 63, 66, 68
Parkinson's disease, 27

Parma, Idaho, 51

Patent medicines, 59

Pearl Harbor, bombing of, 26, 36, 275–80

Pegler, James Westbrook, 268–70

Pension. *See* Spanish-American War: pension

Phi Psi fraternity, 188, 191

Philippines, 35

Phillips, Charlie, 252

Phillips Academy, 6–7

Photography, 11–12, 38–44, 107–9, 114, 116, 128, 141, 154, 176, 200, 219, 230, 248, 270, 283; and friendship, 11, 19; and masculinity, 38; of the White Palace, 12, 39

Pickford, Mary, 35

Pierce, James H., 22, 98, 121, 123, 126–32, 161, 215

Pierce, Joan Burroughs, 161

Pitkin, Walter B., 36, 245

Pocatello, Idaho, 31

Polio, 264

Politics, 68–71, 122–23, 134–35, 191, 214, 218, 248, 259, 261–66, 284; and marriage, 135

Porges, Irwin, 17, 25

Porter, Henry, 229

Porter, Jane, 71

Poverty, 16–17, 87, 94, 106–7, 116–17, 120, 220–21, 242, 270–73, 281–83

Power, Tyrone, 285

Prisoners of war, 282–84

Proctor and Gamble Company, 167

Prohibition, 90, 122–23, 172, 218

Punahou School, 266

Quarantine, 75

Quirk, James, 80–81

Race: Burroughs and, 31–32; and class, 31, 33; in Hawaii, 276; and imperialism, 34–35; and irony, 36–37; and masculinity, 31; Weston and, 33–34; and xenophobia, 34, 66

Radio, 245; Burroughs interviewed on, 246–48

Randall, George, 161

Reconstruction, 37

Red Book, 87

Red Cross, 62

Religion, 7–8

Reserve Officers' Training Corps (ROTC), 211–13

Return of Tarzan, The, 65

Reunion: of Burroughs and Weston, 28; of Michigan Military Academy class, 9; of Yale class of 1898, 41–43, 92

Riegels, Roy, 139–40

Robertson, Wallace, 229, 282–83

Rooney, Annie, 260

Roosevelt, Franklin Delano, 224, 244, 247, 258–62, 265, 284

Roosevelt, Theodore, 3–4, 15, 21, 31, 38, 78, 108

Rosenberger, Charles, 25–26, 30, 122, 129, 131, 171, 233–35, 240

Rosenow influenza treatment, 69–70

Rotella, Carlo, 5

Rothmund, C. Ralph, 24, 27, 122, 128, 145, 165, 172–73, 175, 178–79, 195–96, 198–99

Rough Riders, 15, 18, 21, 157

Russell, Lillian, 260

Sabotage, 279

Sanders, Murry, 75, 93

Sand Island, 256–57

Sandow, Eugen, 37

Sandwich Islands, 263

San Fernando Valley, 21, 83, 140

Santa Monica Mountains, 21

Santa Monica Yacht Club, 131–32

Scott, Joan Wallach, 31
Scott, Ralph, 119, 125, 155, 222
Scribner's, 240, 249
Sears, Roebuck and Company, 16
Sennett, Mack, 197; and Triangle
    Girls, 76, 84
Sherman, William T., 9
Sherman House, 128
Sherwood, Lin, 13–14, 142, 174
Sherwood, Marian. *See* Weston,
    Marian
*Short Introduction to the History of
    Human Stupidity, A,* 36, 245
Sigma Q fraternity, 94
Simmons, Helen Jane, 107–8
Simmons, Sally Weston, 107, 152, 155
Simmons, Windsor (Simmy), 152,
    155, 158, 163
Sinclair, Upton, 23
Smith, Alfred, 122–23, 134–35, 247
Social Security, 271
Soldier Field, 191
Solf, Wilhelm, 66
Son of Tarzan, The, 65
Sothern, E. H., 260
Sousa, John Philip, 12
Southern Pacific Railway, 168
Spanish-American War, 12, 14–15,
    18, 27, 35, 142, 157; pension, 192,
    194–95, 224, 273
Spanish influenza, 63–72, 78, 86,
    101, 133, 135, 137–38, 222
Sports. *See under individual sports*
Stace-Burroughs Company, 16, 46
Stalin, Joseph, 259–60, 265
Standard Oil Company, 259
Stecher, Joe, 111
St. Francis Dam catastrophe, 117
Stock, 145, 153, 174–75; assessment
    on, 172–73, 177–78, 181–83; and
    market crash, 23, 161. *See also*
    Apache Motors; Los Angeles
    Metropolitan Airport
Stock theater, 110–11, 115–16

Strong, Fred, 103
Stuart, Charley, 257
Submarines, 247
Sunburn, 256–57
Swimming, 61
System, 16–17

Tarzan, 3, 18, 21, 29, 38, 45, 47, 71,
    89, 91, 143, 208, 237; in films, 91,
    206–8, 212, 215, 242; in news-
    paper strip, 151; in novels and
    stories, 31, 35, 71, 87, 101, 112, 120,
    130, 133; in radio broadcast, 215,
    232; in serial, 143–44
Tarzana, California, 4, 21–24, 83–
    86, 91, 93, 96, 103, 108, 132, 135,
    195, 218, 232, 260
Tarzan and the Golden Lion, 102
Tarzan and the Jewels of Opar, 65, 87
Tarzan Finds a Son, 237
Tarzan of the Apes, 12, 47, 65, 221,
    237, 240, 248, 253
Tarzan the Untamed, 87, 89
Tarzan Twins, The, 136
Taxes, 87, 224, 238, 268; on Mira-
    mar lots, 155–59, 163, 165, 178–
    79, 194–98
Taylor, Robert. *See* Brugh, Arlington
    Spangler
Taylorization, 17
Tennis, 277
Thomas, Seth, 13, 18–19, 75, 93, 97,
    134, 213–14
Thomason, Hugh, 155–59
Time, 274
Tinee, May, 75
Torgovnick, Marianna, 29, 35
Travel, 19, 27, 96, 111, 113, 116, 271;
    frequency of, 122, 207, 218
Triangle Girls, 76, 84
Truman, Harry S., 284
Tuba, Arizona, 121
Tunney, Gene, 101, 103, 110
Turner, Frederick Jackson, 38

Twain, Mark (Samuel Langhorne Clemens), 23, 77
Tyner (MMA alumnus), 64

Union College, 6
Union Pacific Railroad, 14
United Press, 26, 28, 280
University of California, 135
University of Nebraska, 7, 107, 190, 246; law college of, 190
U.S. Military Academy (West Point), 9, 12, 97, 161

Vacations, 60, 82, 85, 89, 106–8, 122, 152–53, 161, 163, 166, 187, 193; in California, 58, 95–97, 100, 110, 115, 162–64, 168, 171–75, 200–203, 230, 232, 249, 254–55; in Nebraska, 100, 128–30, 142, 177, 179, 183, 230
Van Dyke, W. S., 206
Van Nuys, California, 151
Visiting. See Vacations

Wallace, Henry A., 261
War correspondence, 280–81, 284
Warfield, Jeanne, 184
Weather: in California, 59, 61, 68, 72, 78, 95, 131, 159, 197, 201, 243, 244, 254, 284; in Hawaii, 255, 258, 260; in Nebraska, 69, 74, 88, 94, 104, 106, 112, 125, 143, 146, 152, 158, 161, 166, 179, 190, 225, 227, 241, 246, 251–52, 264, 281–83
Weddings. See Marriage
Weight. See Dieting
Wertz, Fred, 174
West Point, United States Military Academy at, 9, 12, 97, 161
Weston, Collins, 15, 19–20, 28, 54, 69–71, 78, 86, 89, 106, 112, 115, 158, 174, 182, 184, 190, 201, 209, 214, 216, 222

Weston, Helen Towle, 6, 7
Weston, Herbert Towle: business of, 19–21; childhood of, 4; education of, 6–13; letters of, 2–4; nicknames of, 13
Weston, Herbert Towle Jr., 13, 15, 19–20, 115, 130–31, 138, 140, 191, 199, 211, 213, 222
Weston, Jane, 55
Weston, Jean, 224, 229, 230, 251, 252
Weston, Jefferson, 15, 19–20, 87, 104, 107, 112, 114, 133, 143, 152, 161, 179, 191, 208, 210, 213, 222, 224, 229–31
Weston, Jefferson Burns, 6, 7, 13, 20; as auditor of the state of Nebraska, 6
Weston, Mabel, 28, 209, 215, 226
Weston, Margaret Collins, 7, 13–15, 19, 21, 24–25, 27–28, 33, 45–46, 61, 71, 74–75, 81, 85, 91, 134–35, 149, 197, 198, 225, 228, 269
Weston, Margaret-Collins, 226
Weston, Marian, 13, 142–44, 252
Weston, Sue, 246, 248
Weston Real Estate Company, 238
West Point. See U.S. Military Academy
Wheat, Canadian, 86, 90
White City. See Columbian Exposition of 1893
"White Man's Burden, The," 31–32
White Paper Club, 80–81
Whooping cough, 263–64
Wilhelmy, Jean. See Weston, Jean
Wilhelmy family, 230–31, 238
William II (Kaiser Wilhelm), 33, 66, 79, 89
Willkie, Wendell, 259, 261–68
Wilson, Woodrow, 70, 86; letter to the Kaiser, 66, 68
Wister, Owen, 38
Wood, Tom, 53

Woolworth, Frank W., 252
Word-counts, 263–66; graphed, 17
World War I, 9, 18–21, 29, 44, 64–67, 71, 87
World War II, 26, 36, 244, 255, 258–59, 270, 274, 283, 285; Pacific theater of, 28
Wrestling, 111

Xenophobia, 35, 36, 244–47, 259, 284–85

Yale battery. *See* First Connecticut Light Artillery, Battery A

Yale University, 12, 20, 27, 38–39, 92, 112; class of 1898, 38, 41–44; Sheffield Scientific School at, 5, 12–13. *See also* New Haven
Yates, "Irish," 305
Yates, Jack, 205
Yosemite National Park, 206, 249–51
Youll family, 207
Young Men's Christian Association (YMCA), 62, 184

Zbyszko, Stanislaus, 111
Zelzah, California, 148

MATT COHEN

is an assistant professor of English at Duke University
and an editor with the Walt Whitman Archive.

Library of Congress Cataloging-in-Publication Data
Burroughs, Edgar Rice, 1875–1950.
Brother men : the correspondence of Edgar Rice
Burroughs and Herbert T. Weston / edited and with
an introduction by Matt Cohen.
p. cm.
Includes bibliographical references and index.
ISBN 0-8223-3529-8 (cloth   )
ISBN 0-8223-3541-7 (pbk.   )
1. Burroughs, Edgar Rice, 1875–1950 — Correspondence.
2. Novelists, American — 20th century — Correspondence. 3. Burroughs, Edgar Rice, 1875–1950 — Friends
and associates. 4. Weston, Herbert T. — Correspondence.
I. Weston, Herbert T. II. Cohen, Matt, 1970– III. Title.
PS3503.U687Z486 2005
813'.52 — dc22
2004022943